Scandal
The Sexual Politics of Late Victorian Britain

Scandal
The Sexual Politics of
Late Victorian Britain

TREVOR FISHER

ALAN SUTTON PUBLISHING LIMITED

First published in the United Kingdom in 1995
Alan Sutton Publishing Ltd · Phoenix Mill · Far Thrupp
Stroud · Gloucestershire

British Library Cataloguing in Publication Data

Fisher, Trevor
Scandal: Sexual Politics of Late Victorian Britain
I. Title
941.081

ISBN 0–7509–0435–6

Typeset in 11/12pt Erhardt.
Typesetting and origination by
Alan Sutton Publishing Limited.
Printed in Great Britain by
Hartnolls, Bodmin, Cornwall.

Dedicated to the memory of
Edward Palmer Thompson, 1924–93, Historian Nonpareil

Contents

Illustrations

Thanks are due to the following for permission to reproduce illustrations: Birmingham Museum and Art Gallery for 1; the Fawcett Library for 5 and 6; the Mary Evans Picture Library for 3, 9, 11, 15, 17, 19 and 24.

Acknowledgements

I should like to thank Dr John Stephenson for invaluable advice; Professor John Callaghan for valued comments on the early work; Robert and Susan Howard and Ruth Raymond for unravelling the mysteries of the computer world; and Sarah for tolerating prolonged visits to the nineteenth century.

Trevor Fisher
April 1995

INTRODUCTION

The Mythology of 'Victorian Values'

The mythology of 'Victorian values' has been repeatedly invoked in recent years. When Prime Minister Margaret Thatcher sought to define her political creed, she chose the phrase as convenient shorthand. It was a shrewd choice. For substantial numbers of people, 'Victorian values' suggest a lost paradise of self-reliance and upward mobility – a golden age when the virtues of hard work, thrift, abstinence, honesty, sobriety, self-help and strict morality were venerated.

The image created by the phrase 'Victorian values' is of a world dominated by the work ethic and material advancement. It is thought of as a world dominated by self-denial and deferred gratification, in which pleasure was subordinated to serious pursuits; and sexual pleasure most of all. Sex is believed to have become unmentionable, and sexual activity confined within the family unit and limited to procreation. For many observers of Victorian society, indeed, it is precisely the ability of the Victorians to subordinate sexuality to the work ethic which explains the economic success of Victorian Britain. Victorian puritanism, it is argued, sublimated sexuality into a drive for material accumulation. The channelling of sexual energy into family and work was a decisive factor in making Britain the 'Workshop of the World'.

This perspective on nineteenth-century Britain remains influential. It was most clearly stated by Sir Robert Ensor in his volume of the authoritative *Oxford History of England*. Discussing sexuality in late Victorian England, Ensor argued 'The religion-ruled Englishmen then dominant in the governing, directing, professional and business classes spent, there can be little doubt, far less of their time and thought on sex interests than either their continental contemporaries or their twentieth century successors; and to this saving their extraordinary surplus of energy in other spheres must reasonably in part be ascribed.'[1]

This stereotype has remained one influential pole of debate about Victorian morality, but is deeply questionable. The argument that upper- and middle-class Englishmen sublimated their sexuality is difficult to sustain. The apparent solidity and respectability of the Victorian family certainly coexisted with widespread prostitution. And for informed observers, England was not notably different from the decadent Continent in making available sex for sale.

Ensor wrote the passage quoted above to rebut the view of W.T. Stead, at his famous Old Bailey trial in 1885, that there were 50,000 to 60,000 prostitutes in London in the early 1880s.[2] Ensor thought this a wild exaggeration, arguing that if middle-class men did give way to immorality, they visited the fleshpots of the Continent where, unlike Britain, vice was freely available. Informed observers of Victorian morality took a different view. 'I am afraid', Gladstone told the House of Commons in 1857, 'as respects the gross evils of prostitution, that there is hardly any country in the world where they prevail to a greater extent than in our own.' [3]

Twenty-four years later, a well-informed observer of London life, Howard Vincent, held a similar view. Appearing before a committee of peers in 1881, Vincent said, 'I should think that prostitution in England is considerably in excess of the prostitution in other countries . . . '.[4] Vincent was in a position to make an informed estimate, as he was director of the Criminal Investigation Department at Scotland Yard.

Both Gladstone and Vincent had firsthand experience to support their views. Gladstone, after a day in Parliament, was prone to seek distraction by walking the streets of London attempting to reclaim fallen women. Vincent was a professional whose duty was to track the low life of the capital. As we will see, neither had far to go to discover evidence of substantial immorality. Yet despite considerable discussion of the role widespread prostitution played in Victorian society, the myth of a society dominated by an inviolable respectable ethic of family and work persists.

The myth certainly has a basis in reality. The existence of Victorian respectability and its hold on the dominant middle classes is certainly unquestionable. Compared with the eighteenth and twentieth centuries, both moral codes and actual behaviour were stricter in the nineteenth century. The prevalence of respectability within the middle classes, and its spread to elements of the aristocracy and the aspiring elements of the working class, is undeniable. The prudery epitomized by Dr Bowdler's emasculation of Shakespeare was widespread, the work of puritanical groups such as the Society for the Suppression of Vice (established in 1799) made a significant impact, and decorous behaviour became essential for those aspiring to respectability. By the time Victoria came to the throne in 1837, respectable status demanded strict adherence to holy matrimony, and the relationship of Victoria and Albert provided a model of what was expected.

Yet while the influence of puritanism was considerable, the stereotype of an all-powerful repressive morality channelling sexual drives into economic activity will not do. Respectable morality was not an unchallenged framework into which Victorians fitted their lives. Indeed, the failure of respectability to impose itself totally on the society has led to an alternative stereotype which holds that it was a hollow code to which little more than lip-service was paid. The myth of Victorian hypocrisy, of a society maintaining a standard which was widely evaded, has developed as a counter to the image of Victorian respectability. It is not a helpful view. Hypocrisy, cant and the evasion of conventional morality undoubtedly existed, but it cannot be assumed that the codes of respectability were mere formalities. Respectable morality provided a more complex pattern of attraction and repulsion than either stereotype allows. And it is the ebb and flow of puritan influence which has led to the best of recent historical debate.

One pole of this debate has been provided by Lawrence Stone. Writing in his enormously authoritative *The Family, Sex and Marriage in England* Stone argues that the puritanism of the Evangelical Revival dominated the nineteenth century; by the 1860s, however, evangelical puritanism was on the wane. Assessing the broad sweep of English history from 1500 onwards, Stone talks of a

> Second phase of repression . . . which was at its peak from about 1800 into the 1860s or later. The tide turned slowly again. Since then there has developed a second phase of permissiveness, beginning slowly among the middle classes in the 1870s, and spreading to the social elite in the 1890s. Then, in the 1920s and more dramatically in the 1960s and 1970s, spreading for the first time to all sectors of the population.[5]

Lawrence Stone's analysis contrasts sharply with that of Jeffrey Weeks. Weeks sees little evidence that puritanism was at its strongest in the mid-nineteenth century, and even less of an ebb and flow of morality. In his influential *Sex, Politics and Society*,[6] he argues that the nineteenth century witnesses a long and complex battle between puritanism and libertinism. The forces of puritanism, he contends, gain the upper hand in the latter decades of the century, and it is only in the twilight years of Victoria's reign that puritanism becomes sufficiently dominant for its opponents to be forced to contest 'Victorian values'. In a seminal passage, he suggests

> What seems to be happening in the nineteenth century . . . is a continuous battle over the definition of acceptable sexual behaviour within the context of changing class and power relations . . . there was no blanket imposition of 'repression'. Not till the 1880s did 'social purity' have any major legislative purchase. And it is significant that it is from this period that the earliest critiques of 'Victorianism' stem.

I agree with Weeks. Far from the puritan ethic being at its most influential in the middle years of the century, its influence was far from supreme. In the crucial area of prostitution, official attitudes were markedly ambiguous. The historically ancient double standard of morality was deeply embedded in political attitudes, and came close to being officially sanctioned at the height of Victoria's reign. It is a telling paradox of Victorian morality that at a time when Victorian respectability appeared most assured, the government was moving in the direction of legalizing prostitution and establishing continental-style state-run brothels.

The mid-Victorian period saw a substantial state move towards regulating prostitution. In major garrison and naval towns, three Contagious Diseases (CD) Acts (1864, 1866 and 1869) registered prostitutes and enforced their rigorous medical inspection. These acts were the result of the growing influence of the public health lobby. Having secured growing acceptance for government action over other infectious diseases, public health activists in the middle years of Victoria's reign began treating venereal disease as if it were little different from cholera or smallpox. Their confidence grew from a sense that despite the enormous influence of *laissez-faire* ideology, the government was moving towards state-regulated prostitution to tackle venereal disease.

The Rubicon of state-regulated prostitution, however, was never crossed. Venereal disease was not comparable to other infectious diseases, and the early feminist movement was outraged by legislation which treated women as mere sexual vessels for men. More significantly, the legal sanction for vice infuriated puritan Christians, provoking them to campaign for the strict enforcement of respectable morality with unprecedented vigour. A remarkable alliance of feminists and puritans developed, led

Drawing for Found, *by Dante Gabriel Rossetti, c. 1855. Mid–Victorian moralism is shown here. A drover taking a calf to market finds his former sweetheart walking the streets. She cannot face him*

by the proto-feminist Josephine Butler and the Liberal MP James Stansfeld. The campaign met strong resistance from a libertine male contingent in Parliament which set up sustained resistance. That resistance was only broken by an extraordinary press campaign in the summer of l885, organized by the editor of the *Pall Mall Gazette*, W.T. Stead. But once the libertines had been overcome, the puritans came to dominate sexual politics in Britain. The 'purity lobby' forged itself into a most formidable political organization. By the mid-l890s, the power of this lobby had forced fundamental changes in the legal framework governing sexual behaviour in Britain, driven out the double standard as an element in the value system of the British state, and placed evangelical puritanism in a position to hold the commanding heights of the moral economy for over half a century. By heightening awareness of deviations from sexual respectability in Victorian society, the purity lobby paved the way for a rigorous enforcement of respectable standards which led directly to the downfall of Sir Charles Dilke, Charles Stewart Parnell and Oscar Wilde.

Puritanism in Britain thus gained in strength, rather than weakened, in the last three decades of the nineteenth century. Weeks, rather than Stone, seems to be correct. The triumph of puritanical respectability was far from complete in the middle of the century. It was not until the 1890s that the 'official' values of British society are recognizably 'Victorian'. And it is precisely at that point, in the work of George Bernard Shaw and others, that the serious battle against 'Victorian values' begins.

This book traces the development of the purity lobby in its campaign to repeal the CD laws and establish rigorous moral standards in public life. It focuses at key points on major sexual scandals. It is through these traumatic incidents that we can lift the veil of secrecy draped over Victorian sexuality and examine what contemporaries were actually doing. Respectable Victorians disliked talking about sexuality; but they took an enormous interest in the deviations from their code which were reported in newspapers and official investigations. Scandal was the mechanism by which the boundaries of respectable behaviour were established.

The struggle to establish puritanical codes is essential to an understanding of the sexual politics of late Victorian Britain. The starting point of this struggle, however, lies in an earlier period – the l850s and '60s, when a fierce debate over prostitution led by the public health lobby seemed likely to lead to the legalization and regulation of prostitution on the continental model. The moves in this direction taken by the governments of the 1860s triggered a fierce struggle which lasted for a quarter of a century. By studying this struggle and its outcomes, we can assess Lawrence Stone's contention that this was a period of growing moral permissiveness, and come to an understanding of the sexual politics of late Victorian Britain.

ONE

Women for Sale – the Underbelly of Victorian Respectability

THE DEBATE ON PROSTITUTION

To many self-satisfied contemporaries, mid-Victorian Britain appeared to be a tightly ordered society in which respectability was firmly in control. Vice in its many forms might be available on the Continent, but in Britain, sexuality was firmly channelled into marriage, family and the domestic world of 'Home Sweet Home'. Yet from the 1850s onward, a fierce debate raged in the highest political circles in the land about an unpleasant reality behind the respectable image – the existence of widespread female prostitution.

Female prostitution was a national issue, affecting all the large and most of the small towns of the country. Its impact was particularly marked in London, where the close proximity of open prostitution to Parliament provoked sharp debate about the failure of respectable society to enforce its codes. The West End, particularly the area around Piccadilly, was notorious. Howard Vincent told peers in 1881: 'from 4 o'clock, or one may say 3 o'clock in the afternoon, it is impossible for any respectable woman to walk from the top of the Haymarket to Wellington Street, Strand . . . Villiers Street and Charing Cross station, are crowded with prostitutes openly soliciting in broad daylight'.[7] The throng spilled into Lower Regent Street north of Piccadilly Circus. A police survey suggested as many as five hundred prostitutes crowded the pavements at midnight.

For those who could not wait for darkness to seek pleasure, the Burlington Arcade, a glass-roofed parade of little shops off Piccadilly, was a convenient venue. The *Saturday Review* wrote that 'at late afternoon when the garish gas casts appropriate light on tawdry surroundings [the scene is] . . . the western counterpart of an eastern slave market'.[8] The shops used their upper rooms as bedrooms in which street women entertained their clients. More worryingly for

THE GREAT SOCIAL EVIL.

TIME :—Midnight.   A Sketch not a Hundred Miles from the Haymarket.

Bella. "AH ! FANNY ! HOW LONG HAVE YOU BEEN *GAY* ?"

A comment from Punch *contemporary with the Acton debate, 12 September 1857*

the evangelicals, when they applied pressure to the police to clear the streets of prostitution, it simply reappeared elsewhere. Arthur Munby, the remarkable observer of London street women, noted of the police purge of 1859, ' . . . The clearance, so called, of the Haymarket and Casinos produced a large and still flourishing crop of secret dens and night haunts all about . . . '.[9] Police knowledge of this fact led to apathy in the face of what appeared to be an intractable problem. The police had no power to prohibit solicitation unless it caused a threat to public order, or unless a citizen lodged a formal complaint. These conditions were so rarely met that police action was virtually non-existent.

The *Saturday Review* was well informed about the existence of prostitution in the West End. It was also shrewdly aware of the inconsistencies displayed by the authorities in handling a phenomenon which respectable opinion regarded as a social cancer. The *Review* commented sharply on the policies adopted by the magistrates towards the Argyll rooms in Great Windmill Street. These had been opened by a wine merchant, Robert Bignell, between 1849 and 1851, soon becoming notorious as a haunt for prostitutes and their clients. The rooms were closed down in 1852, but reopened in 1853. The *Saturday Review* of 16 October 1853 commented, 'Last year, in a transport of moral and popular indignation, we closed the Argyll rooms because they were the focus and complex of all metropolitan vice. This year, we open them because, on the whole, it is better that the vicious population should be brought together than that it should be let loose on society . . . '.[10]

The *Review* took up the classic utilitarian position on the regulation of prostitution, arguing, 'What can't be cured must be alleviated . . . Whatever thins the loose population of the Haymarket and Regent Street is so far a social gain . . . it will not do to attempt a system of prosecuting these vicious places by instalments . . . All immoral houses can be suppressed by the parochial authorities . . . But to carry out the law is simply impossible. What is cut down in one street grows up in the next . . . '.[11] These words were quoted approvingly by William Acton, the leading writer on prostitution of the mid-nineteenth century, who used them as ammunition in a campaign to legalize and regulate prostitution.

Acton was part of a powerful public health lobby, including many in the medical profession, for whom the magazine *The Lancet* spoke. This body of opinion regarded prostitution and its frequent accomplice, venereal disease, as social problems, not moral issues. Their view was that these problems could only be dealt with by state regulation of prostitutes, as happened in the state-run brothels of countries like Belgium and France. This position was fiercely opposed by the churches and the moral lobby, who upheld the law rendering brothels illegal. But the *Saturday Review* was right when it said that the law could not be enforced. Female prostitution was endemic in mid-Victorian society, at every level of society from the aristocracy to the lumpenproletariat of London's East End.

If there were any illusions about the vices of London's male élite, they were dispelled by the controversy, in 1862, over the activities of courtesans in Hyde Park. After the success of the Great Exhibition, which was held in Hyde Park in 1851, the park had become fashionable among the rich inhabitants of Belgravia. Riding in the park, particularly along Rotten Row and the Ladies' Mile, became a feature of the Season. Rich young men with a talent for horsemanship took to displaying it in the park, alongside young women of their own class who sought a handsome marriage.

But other women also saw possibilities. Young women of easy virtue who could ride realized that while a prostitute soliciting on foot was anathema in Belgravia, a handsome young woman poised on horseback was socially acceptable. The convention was soon exploited by a group of courtesans, or demi-monde, who became known as 'pretty horse breakers' because in theory they were breaking in horses for rich stable owners (who were little better than pimps). The situation was increasingly unacceptable to respectable opinion. The storm broke in 1862 when Lord Hartington met Catherine Walters.

Catherine Walters, known as 'Skittles', was a Liverpool prostitute of exceptional good looks, vivacity and riding skills. She had come to London to make her fortune, and after a period patronizing the Argyll rooms, she was hired by a prosperous livery stable owner near Berkeley Square to ride his mounts in Hyde Park, ostensibly to display his horses for sale. She was then in her prime, aged twenty-two. It was while she was playing this role during the spring of 1862 that she met Lord Hartington. Hartington was at that time twenty-eight years old, and the most eligible bachelor in London. He was not particularly handsome or dynamic, but he was outstandingly wealthy. He was the eldest son of the 7th Duke of Devonshire, and in due course would become duke and inherit the Devonshire estates, including the great houses at Chatsworth and Hardwick in Derbyshire.

'A Social Contrast'. The harlot's progress in mid-Victorian England, from riding in Rotten Row to walking the streets

Such a man was endlessly pursued by ambitious women of his own class, and it may have been the lack of such ambition in Catherine Walters which first attracted him to her. How they met is not known, but she quickly became his mistress. This was not particularly unusual; St John's Wood housed many women discreetly kept by rich men. However, Hartington behaved with extraordinary indiscretion. He installed her in a house in the heart of Mayfair, allegedly bestowed an annual income of £2,000 on her for life, and was seen with her at the Derby that June.[12]

The relationship had become sensational, and became publicly so when, in July 1862,[13] *The Times* carried an anonymous letter openly wondering who the beautiful young woman (dubbed Anonyma) was who was causing such a sensation in Hyde Park? Ostensibly the author was concerned with traffic congestion.

If this was an attempt at a joke, it quickly backfired. The next day the *Daily Telegraph* responded with a broadside on behalf of respectability with a leader attacking the situation whereby Hyde Park was 'infested with a number of lewd women . . . well paid by wealthy profligates for selling their miserable bodies' and accusing Anonyma of having 'plenty of fine clothes and sparkling jewels, and a pretty body which she sells to the highest bidder . . . '.[14]

Under this pressure, the relationship between Hartington and his mistress collapsed. Hartington may have been besotted, but he was not stupid. He was a man already tipped for high office, well regarded by the queen, and a Liberal MP for a Lancashire constituency. Such a man could not afford to be involved in a public controversy over the activities of courtesans. Hartington fled to the USA, to observe the Civil War. Skittles fled to Ems in Germany. Hartington later returned to resume his political career and rose to cabinet rank. It is a testimony both to the power of the aristocracy in the 1860s and the relative weakness of the puritan current at the time, that society was prepared to overlook his blatant fall from grace. It is unlikely that society would have been so tolerant thirty years later.

Hartington abandoned his mistress. Other men of his class continued to consort with the demi-monde. In the 1870 edition of his book on prostitution, Acton quoted the *Pall Mall Gazette* of 16 April 1869 as complaining that

> Until very recently there was no such thing as a demi-monde in London (i.e.) . . . systematised sufficiently to form a regular set . . . But within a very brief period . . . there has been a change amongst us. Previous to that time, indeed, moralists in the press complained of the frank terms which young men of fashion held with such women in places of public resort. This familiarity is now so much on the increase (as anyone who watches what is going on in the Ladies' Mile can perceive) that it calls for some remonstrance.[15]

While the activities of the courtesans were deeply scandalous to respectable upper class opinion, the demi-monde was the wholly untypical élite of the profession in the mid-century. Most prostitutes operated in far less selective locations than Rotten Row and Ladies' Mile, and served a much less exalted clientele. Much prostitution took place in working class areas, though Engels' comment that 'Next to intemperance in the enjoyment of intoxicating liquors, one of the principal faults of the English Working Man is sexual license'[16] has to be treated with some caution. Judith Walkowitz has argued that the clientele for the Victorian prostitute was concentrated disproportionately among the unskilled, middle and professional classes, with significantly less immorality among the stable semi-skilled and skilled labouring populations of mining, textile and agricultural areas.[17] Walkowitz bases this judgement on the statistical police returns on known prostitutes in different geographical areas, 1857–69, and the statistics of venereal disease in the early twentieth century.

There is little doubt that prostitution was endemic in the capital. In 1861, Henry Mayhew[18] published an extensive account by Bracebridge Hemyngs of London prostitution, which explicitly referred to the prevalence of brothels across the city. He commented: 'In order to find these houses [low lodging houses – cheap brothels, TF] it is necessary to journey eastwards, and leave the artificial glamour of the West End, where vice is pampered and caressed. Whitechapel, Wapping, Ratcliff Highway, and analogous districts, are prolific in the production of these infamies.'[19] Hemyngs, however, argued that brothels were not just an East End phenomenon. 'We may', he argued, 'find many low lodging houses without penetrating so far into the labyrinth of east London. There are numbers in Lambeth; in the Waterloo Road and contiguous streets; in small streets between Covent Garden and the Strand, some in one or two streets running out of Oxford Street.' In short, the brothel was a well-rooted and widespread phenomenon. Sex was for sale across mid-Victorian London, not merely in the plutocratic West End or the shiftless, lumpenproletarian East End, but across the city as a whole.

London was certainly not typical of the Victorian city, but prostitution was rife in most Victorian towns. In York, for example, a small and comparatively respectable town, the authorities recorded 1,400 prostitutes and brothel keepers operating in the city between Victoria's accession in 1837 and her jubilee in 1887. York was a minnow compared with London. Between 1831 and 1881 the population of York expanded from 26,260 to 49,530, while over four million lived in the capital at the jubilee. Yet prostitution was both rife and visible. Drunken prostitutes made themselves a public nuisance in the town, and the *York Gazette* reported in 1860: 'Almost every day some of these poor outcasts were . . . charged with disorderly conduct during the previous night. From 11 o'clock until 1 or 2 o'clock in the morning these unhappy females prowled about the streets and being affected with liquor they conducted themselves in a riotous and disorderly manner.'[20]

Female prostitution was so obviously widespread that from the earliest years of Victoria's reign there was public debate about prostitution and its effects. In the early years of the reign evangelicals associated with the anti-vice campaign held the stage, but their influence was consistently limited by their one-sided approach. Statistics emanating from the Society for the Suppression of Vice or the London Society for the Protection of Young Females and Prevention of Prostitution (founded in 1835) were inevitably suspect. The most extensive survey of London prostitution in the early Victorian period, for example, Michael Ryan's *Prostitution in London* (1839), came to the conclusion that one in five women in London between the ages of 15 and 50 was a prostitute. It was easy for critics to dismiss this as ludicrous.

More objective studies came from sources outside London. In 1840 the Edinburgh surgeon William Tait published a study of prostitution in that town, *Magdalenism*. In 1842 Ralph Wardlaw produced *Lectures on Female Prostitution*, and two years later J.B. Talbot produced *The Miseries of Prostitution*. However well informed the study, however, the government was deeply reluctant openly to debate a subject so repugnant to Victorian opinion, and still more reluctant to admit that the phenomenon could not be suppressed. But the survival of extensive female prostitution was so manifest that by the middle of the century, the focus of debate among the informed had shifted from suppression to regulation.

In 1850 the *Westminster Review* printed a well-informed article on prostitution which was reprinted as a pamphlet entitled *The Great Sin of Great Cities* by W.R.G. in 1853. The author was William Rathbone Greg,[21] a conservative writer on religious and social matters. Greg did not share the puritan desire to suppress prostitution, and was among the first to argue that the phenomenon could not be abolished. Greg steered the debate in a new direction by calling for state regulation of prostitution in terms of more Lock Hospitals (closed hospitals for treating venereal disease), periodical medical inspections, compulsory detention of the diseased, and the imprisonment of uncertificated prostitutes.

Greg did not follow up his article. Far more influential, because part of a life-long crusade, was William Acton's *Prostitution*. William John Acton (1813 or 1814–75) was the most noted writer on venereal disease of the mid-Victorian period, whose book *Functions and Disorders of the Reproductive Organs* went through six editions between 1857 and 1875. Acton was an important pioneering sexologist, whose reputation today is not high. *Functions and Disorders* was the prisoner of its age, giving credence to the view that male masturbation led to insanity, semen was a rare commodity which had to be hoarded, and most notoriously, that women 'are not very much troubled by sexual feeling of any kind'.[22] Acton clearly agreed with the male sexual biases of his age.

Nevertheless, he was an important polemicist who had considerable influence precisely because, unlike Greg, he attempted to found his polemics on hard fact. Acton's interest in prostitution was founded on the classic utilitarian view that prostitution was inevitable and should be regulated, as on the Continent. Believing this, but being well aware that the strength of puritan feeling was a formidable barrier, he set himself to win support in the (all-male) political élite by outlining the major features of prostitution as it existed in his society. Acton was careful not to offend the moral sensibilities of his audience, but equally insistent on securing accurate information. His work is still valuable today, despite criticism, as a source of information on mid-Victorian prostitution in London.

Acton relied heavily on the police returns, which, he notes, do 'not include the vast numbers who regularly or occasionally abandon themselves, but in a less open manner'.[23] According to the official figures, 6,371 women had become known to the police as prostitutes in 1839. In 1841 the figure was 9,409, and on 20 May 1857 the police were officially aware of 8,600 prostitutes in the metropolitan police area.[24] Acton commented that:

> these returns give but a faint idea of the grand total of prostitution by which we are oppressed, as the police include in them only those women and houses whose nature is well and accurately known to them. There can be little doubt that numbers of women who live by prostitution lead apparently respectable lives in the lodgings or houses which they occupy; but all such are necessarily excluded from the returns. Were there any possibility of reckoning all those in London who would come within the definition of prostitutes, I am inclined to think that the estimates of the boldest who have preceded me would be thrown into the shade.[25]

Acton was, however, too wise to attempt an estimate of this 'dark figure' himself.

The greatest importance of Acton's work was, however, his open advocacy of state-regulated prostitution, and his willingness to pursue his views where others – notably Greg – had been reluctant to crusade. He made no secret of his views.

He argued: 'I regard prostitution as an inevitable attendant upon civilised, and especially close packed, population. When all is said and done, it is, and I believe ever will be, ineradicable.'[26] And from this baseline he developed a sophisticated argument for state regulation.

Acton was gratified by the response to his work. In January 1858, shortly after it had appeared, he published a letter in the *British Medical Journal* (Vol. 99), observing with satisfaction that 'but a few weeks ago . . . prostitution . . . did not admit of discussion; and yet to-day no less than two leading articles and several letters, have appeared in the public journals'. Acton was claiming too much. Greg's article of 1850 had lifted the veil, allowing the emerging public health lobby, led by a powerful group of doctors, to campaign for a full discussion of the issue. *The Lancet* had already carried an editorial in 1852 calling for more Lock Hospitals to deal with venereal disease cases, and followed this up three years later by calling for the regulation of prostitution (20 January 1855).

Nevertheless, Acton was right to argue that the pace was quickening. *The Times* had carried an editorial on 6 May 1857 discussing how best to deal with what it called 'a great social evil'. The paper regarded prevention as better than cure, by teaching girls household skills with a view to careers in domestic service. *The Lancet* weighed in on 7 November 1857 with a campaigning editorial on 'Prostitution – the need for its reform', in which it supported Acton's views on the state regulation of prostitution, though it was far from careful in examining the evidence. Its editorial argued ' . . . on good authority, that one house in sixty in London is a brothel, and one in every sixteen females (of all ages) is, *de facto*, a prostitute'. The editorial moved wholly into the realm of fantasy by suggesting 'The typical pater-familias, living in a grand house near the park, sees his sons lured into debauchery, dares not walk with his daughters through the streets after nightfall, and is disturbed from his slumbers by the drunken screams and foul oaths of the prostitutes reeling home with daylight'. These comments testify more to the fears and frustrations of the writer than to reality. Had the debate remained at this level, the campaign for state-regulated prostitution might have foundered. But at this point the debate shifted to a narrower focus closer to the concerns of Whitehall – the impact of venereal disease on the military.

THE GENESIS OF THE CONTAGIOUS DISEASES ACTS

Early in 1858, *The Lancet* changed tack. Abandoning sweeping assaults on prostitution, it took aim on a smaller but more manageable target – the issue of venereal disease in the army. On 20 February 1858 it carried a very important editorial discussing the extent of disease among the military. It argued that treating the men was proving a wholly inadequate policy for a problem so serious that about one-fifth of the effective force of the country was in hospital with venereal disease for an average of twenty-two days per year. The solution proposed by *The Lancet* was to treat the prostitutes instead.

This line of argument struck a chord in Whitehall. The authorities had become seriously alarmed by the increase in venereal disease, ascribed to prostitution, in the lower ranks of the military. From 1823 onward, military returns had been recording a steady increase in VD. The problem had become the focus of acute attention in government circles in the late 1850s because of the disastrous record of the British Army in the Crimean War.

The impact of the Crimean War in triggering what became known as the Contagious Diseases Acts is not always fully appreciated. Judith Walkowitz, approaching from the perspective of 'cultural' history, wonders 'Why were they [the CD acts] introduced in the 1860s, and why, from a European standpoint, so late? However blatant the sex prejudice, the acts were not simply a sign of the relative strength of the double standard in the mid-Victorian period . . . . What may have changed was the increased official concern over prostitution as a dangerous form of sexual activity, whose boundaries had to be controlled and defined by the state.'[27] This hardly answers the question, why the 1860s? The key factor is the impact of British military failures in the Crimea.

The Crimean conflict had mercilessly exposed the inadequacies of the British military. The army sent to fight the Russians alongside the French landed on the Crimean peninsula in late 1854 without the clothing and supplies needed to face a Russian winter. Privation and freezing weather brought on cholera, dysentery and malaria. During the months of January and February 1855 the sickness toll rose to such heights that the *Oxford History of England* records bleakly that 'If there had been no reinforcements from home, the British force would soon have ceased to exist'.[28] On one day in January the total number of troops defending the British lines was a mere 290 – facing a force twenty times that number.

As the catastrophe unfolded, the government decided to send Florence Nightingale and her nurses to tend the sick. To send women into a war zone was a sign of sheer desperation. The decision did not save Lord Aberdeen's administration, for press reports from the front reported massive incompetence, of which the Charge of the Light Brigade was only the best-known example. Though the heroism of the troops helped save face, it was widely known, in Tennyson's famous words, that 'someone had blundered'. The Charge was not the only blunder, and despite eventual victory, informed opinion knew that the victory had been secured by the French and not the small, badly led British force. Official post-mortems exonerated the bone-headed incompetence of the officer class, postponing serious changes till the Cardwell reforms of Gladstone's first ministry (1868–74).

But within Whitehall the scale of the disaster was fully appreciated, and the professionals sought excuses. One channel which was explored was the abysmal health of the army, which all agreed was cause for concern. A Royal Commission into the Health of the Army was set up in 1857. The physical and moral condition of both sailors and soldiers was indeed so poor that it provided a plausible excuse for those in authority. The military authorities formed a *de facto* alliance with the powerful medical sanitary lobby whose voice was *The Lancet*. The lobby had, in 1848, forced the government to pass the first Public Health Act. For many public health reformers, regulation of prostitution to protect the public from venereal disease was a logical step forward after regulating sewage and water supplies to protect the nation from cholera.

Greg's *Westminster Review* article had called for the newly created Board of Health to establish legally enforceable medical inspection of prostitutes. The débâcles of the Crimean War turned government attention to this argument. Acton published *Prostitution* in the same year as the publication of the Royal Commission Report into the health of the army. He provided fuel for an increasingly important debate taking place almost unnoticed in Whitehall.

Acton pointed out that one of the most important causes of prostitution was the virtual prohibition of marriage to soldiers. The married establishments of non-commissioned officers and rank and file soldiers were not permitted to exceed 7 per cent of the total. A soldier had to have completed seven years' service, and be in possession of at least one good conduct badge, in order to have his name placed on the role of married men. Acton concluded: 'Considering that the men subject to the above restrictions are for the most part in the prime of life, in vigorous health, and exposed to circumstances particularly calculated to develop animal instincts, we may reasonably expect to find a large demand for prostitutes in all garrison towns, and may feel sure that there is always a supply in proportion to the demand. Our principal seaport towns are, of course, exposed to the same evil, from a similar cause.'[29]

One possible conclusion that could be drawn from Acton's analysis was that the men should be allowed to marry. This was not a conclusion favoured by the authorities, who feared that an army of married men would lack the will to fight. Within the War Office, especially the Army Medical Department, the argument for regulation was being pressed with increasing urgency. In 1859 the compulsory medical inspection of soldiers for venereal disease had been abandoned because officers feared the hostility of the men to such intimate investigation. The focus had shifted to treating prostitutes rather than the men. The hostility of prostitutes could be ignored. Those who opposed state regulation of prostitutes fought a rearguard action aimed at raising the moral standards of the men. In 1860 Lord Herbert, secretary of state for war, set up an inquiry into the state of the army and instituted reforms designed to improve soldiers' conditions by providing day rooms, institutes and clubs. According to an ardent propagandist against the CD laws, these cut the incidence of venereal disease from 146 to 87 per thousand in six years.[30]

Such arguments cut little ice. The pro-regulationists were in the ascendancy and the morality lobby was losing ground. In 1861, Florence Nightingale, the leading proponent of improved conditions for the ordinary soldier to combat disease, wrote despairingly to her friend and co-worker Harriet Martineau that 'The disease of vice is daily increasing in the Army . . . it is to be feared that the present War Secretary, who is totally ignorant of his business, considers that there is no remedy for this but the French plan . . . a plan invented expressly to degrade the national character'.[31] This was an accurate assessment of the direction of political thinking. The following year, Palmerston's government set up a committee to inquire into the prevalence of venereal disease in the army and navy.

Sir John Liddle, director-general of the navy medical department, justified the hygienic control of diseased prostitutes to this committee on grounds of public health. The committee, however, under Samuel Whitbread MP, reported against the regulation of prostitution, finding that it only worked in Malta, a small island which was a special case. It recommended more facilities for recreation, and was

Florence Nightingale, drawn in 1857 by G. Scharf

ignored by the authorities. In April 1863 a new secretary of state for war was appointed, Earl de Grey, who was immune to the nagging used by Florence Nightingale to influence previous ministers. He was increasingly swayed by the arguments of the regulationists, particularly as a campaign of letters and leaders in *The Times* urged the regulation of prostitution. Florence Nightingale briefed Harriet Martineau with the arguments against regulation, and Martineau published a notable series of articles in the Liberal *Daily News*.

The morality lobby, however, was in retreat. The authorities refused to concede the argument for raising the moral level of the armed forces. Recreational facilities would be expensive. Marriage was ruled out both because of the expense of married quarters, and a widespread belief that marriage would sap the fighting spirit. Instead, the authorities decided to provide the men with women they could use with impunity. A committee of ministers and ex-ministers met to take action, and drafted what was to become the first of the Contagious Diseases Acts.

Florence Nightingale found herself powerless to influence developments, despite her enormous prestige. When she was shown a draft of the bill, she was startled by the draconian powers it gave the police. She wrote to Harriet Martineau on 31 May 1864 that 'I don't believe any Ho of C [sic] will pass this bill. Any honest girl might be locked up all night by mistake by it.'[32] Despite considerable political experience, Florence Nightingale underestimated the determination and deviousness of the government. Notwithstanding the presence of the notoriously evangelical Gladstone as chancellor of the exchequer in Palmerston's cabinet, the government was determined to institute the inspection and forcible treatment of prostitutes in garrison towns.

It was not, however, prepared to argue its case openly. The bill 'for the prevention of Contagious Diseases at certain Naval and Military stations' was introduced into the Commons by Lord Clarence Paget, secretary to the admiralty, in a badly attended House on 20 June 1864. The bill was reached shortly after 1 a.m., as the last item of business, and was read without debate. It received its second reading on 15 July, was referred to select committee, was amended in committee and passed its third reading on 21 July. It was moved in the Lords the following day, received its second Lords' reading on 23 July, went to committee, and passed through its third reading on 26 July. Royal assent was given on 29 July, and the principle of state regulation of prostitution had become law in little over five weeks. During the whole passage, not one word of debate had been uttered on the floor of either the Commons or the Lords.

The speed and silence of this process shocked moralists like Martineau and Nightingale. They were even more shocked to find that while they were well aware of what was being proposed, their knowledge was not widely shared. Indeed, they discovered that as the short title of the bill was simply 'Contagious Diseases Bill', it was widely assumed that this was merely one of a series of acts being introduced to control disease among cattle. Indeed, in one sense, this was exactly what it was.

The central thrust of the 1864 act was to subject women in eleven stated garrison and naval towns (Portsmouth, Plymouth, Woolwich, Chatham, Sheerness, Aldershot, Colchester, and Shorncliffe in England, Cork, Queenstown and the Curragh in Ireland) to compulsory medical examination. If found to be diseased, they were to be forcibly treated. It is surprising that such legislation should have been passed in mid-Victorian England, in a society sternly committed to the moral high ground and the liberty of the individual. Benjamin Scott, in his highly moralistic account of the repeal campaign, noted caustically the fact that 'It was reserved for a Liberal Government in the reign of a virtuous Queen to launch in England the Pagan system of organising, licensing and protecting prostitution with the added iniquity of enforced surgical examinations of the bodies of women.'[33]

The 1864 act went into operation without any sign of opposition, and the government was emboldened to go further. Florence Nightingale, Harriet Martineau and their supporters watched in horror as the government proceeded to extend and consolidate the system of police-regulated prostitution with further acts in 1866 and 1869. They were incensed by the open canvassing, by Acton and the medical-sanitary lobby, of plans to extend the scheme from the garrison towns to the whole nation. They attempted to oppose these plans with the discreet, behind-the-scenes lobbying traditionally employed by respectable middle-class women to influence politicians, and found themselves wholly ineffective.

After the passing of the 1869 act, Nightingale, Martineau and their supporters faced the unpalatable conclusion that if trends continued, they would witness the ultimate triumph of the public health lobby. Despite the apparent dominance of evangelical puritanism in Britain – and indeed partly because the triumph of prudery had rendered prostitution an unmentionable subject – the law was being changed to legalize vice. Both the moralists who abominated sex outside marriage, and the embryonic feminist movement which objected to women being forcibly treated while their male patrons went free, were scandalized. However, the moralists came to realize that if they continued to remain discreet, prudish and respectable, their objections would continue to be ignored. Their only chance of stopping the advance of state-regulated prostitution was to break the taboo of silence around prostitution, expose the moves towards regulation, and fight the public health lobby with an organized lobby of their own.

In the aftermath of the passing of the 1869 act, the opponents of the Contagious Diseases Acts decided to launch a public campaign to repeal them. It was a decision which would transform the sexual politics of Victorian Britain.

TWO

The Making of a Great Crusade

REGULATION AND OPPOSITION

With the advantage of hindsight, an implacable campaign against the Contagious Diseases Acts seems an inevitable development. In the context of mid-Victorian society, it was anything but inevitable. Only after five years of discreet but fruitless lobbying, three acts of parliament steadily extending the boundaries of regulation, and a growing clamour for a nationwide system of state-approved prostitution, did the opposition raise the flag of rebellion. The reluctance to oppose the developing campaign for legalized prostitution was not due to any lack of awareness by the opposition of the threats to conventional moral and liberal notions of civil rights contained within the acts. The threat to conventional morality was manifest, and it took little effort to perceive the threats to the liberties of women. As we have seen, when Florence Nightingale saw the draft of the first CD act, she wrote to Harriet Martineau that 'any honest girl might be locked up all night by mistake'. She was only wrong in thinking that the police might merely be guilty of mistakes.

Yet the opposition, particularly the women, could not easily break the respectable taboos against speaking out on sexual matters, among which prostitution was probably the most unmentionable. For women of Florence Nightingale's generation, it was almost wholly impossible to break so fundamental a taboo. Only under the most extreme pressure could they do this, and it was a matter of years before pressure reached breaking point. It is therefore less than surprising that opposition to the acts in their early years was virtually non-existent. Apart from Florence Nightingale and her circle, most informed opinion was strongly in favour of the acts, while the wider public was largely unaware they existed. The supporters of regulation were well organized and influential, and could count on strong support from powerful elements within parliament, and from equally well-organized groups within the military and the medical establishment. These pushed hard for extensions to the system.

The 1864 act had been passed as a limited experiment to last for three years. The pro-regulation lobby campaigned successfully for it to be made permanent.

An official committee set up in 1866 to investigate the working of the act (the Skey committee) had no difficulty in finding a majority of witnesses were in favour and in recommending that the system should cease to be an experiment. Parliament complied the same year. It was noteworthy that it was the staunchly evangelical chancellor of the exchequer, Gladstone, who wound up the very short Commons debate on the second reading of the 1866 bill. He promised that a select committee would look into 'the numerous difficulties with which this matter was surrounded'. But in the meantime he 'hoped there would be no objection to having the bill read a second time' because it 'merely proposed the continuation of a system which had already received the sanction of parliament'.[34]

By 1883 Gladstone had forgotten his role in this debate. In the repeal debate of that year, he said that although he had been a member of the government that had passed the acts, he had no idea how or by whom they had been carried through the House of Commons. They had been passed 'almost without the knowledge of anyone'.[35] By 1883, however, the opposition to the Contagious Diseases Acts had become so formidable that Gladstone could be forgiven for his lapse of memory. In 1866, opposition was minimal. In the decade following the Crimean War the campaign to provide disease-free prostitution for the armed forces was sailing with the wind. The ideas of the regulationists matched the unspoken assumptions of the all-male political élites.

This was partly because the regulationists had focused initially on the problems of the military following the Crimea. The army and naval establishments saw no objection to regulation at all. They saw their men as little more than animals, and treated them accordingly. Wellington at the time of Waterloo had commented 'I do not know if my men scare the enemy, but by God they scare me', and this attitude was still held by the officer class in the 1860s. The public acquiesced. The British expected the common soldier to perform heroics while being treated with neglect and brutality. Pay was kept low – the Napoleonic scale of a shilling a day was still the rate in the 1860s[36] – and barracks were appallingly overcrowded. They were built on the principle that each soldier was allowed 300–400 cu. ft, in sharp contrast to prison convicts who were allowed 1,000 cu. ft each. In 1857 the death rate in barracks was higher than in the worst slums.[37]

In consequence, an army career attracted few but the unemployed, the unemployable, or those on the run. Until 1847, they signed on for life, and even after 1847 for twenty-one years – a life sentence. Draconian discipline was inevitable. Public flogging was an intrinsic part of army life, and a hundred lashes was considered light punishment. Recruits could receive 1,000 lashes before the regiment, which took four hours to administer and was a sentence of death. Service life was savage, and the quality of the men poor. To military minds used to dealing with this situation, the provision of sanitized women to service the men was the obvious solution to the problem of venereal disease.

Parliament was indifferent, believing that what one outcast group (soldiers) did with another outcast group (working-class prostitutes) did not involve any general principles of importance. Those supporters of the CD acts who bothered to consider issues of principle argued that this was a special case. The CD acts involved a peculiar condition of men – the debased sort who enlisted in the services – and a peculiar condition of women, prostitutes. And had this remained the case, then the repeal of the Contagious Diseases Acts might have proved impossible. But the regulation enthusiasts saw their successes as merely the first step to a general process of licensing vice and regulating women.

The provisions of the 1864 act, however, applied only to eleven towns. On police suspicion of being prostitutes suffering from VD, women were brought before magistrates empowered to order their medical examination and if necessary their compulsory detention in the Lock Wards of a hospital. This system appeared to be hermetically sealed from the wider world. The 1866 act introduced two new principles: periodical examination for a year on police suspicion of being a 'common prostitute', and the compulsory detention of infected women for up to six months on the authority of a surgeon's certificate, without benefit of a magistrates' hearing. The 1866 act added Windsor to the schedule, with the further act of 1869 extending the schedule further to Canterbury, Dover, Maidstone, Gravesend, Winchester and Southampton. The period of detention was increased to nine months.

The system was growing with an internal logic of its own, and without thorough discussion of the principles involved. This apparently effortless growth encouraged regulationists to work to extend the system to the civilian population as a whole. In 1867 the Harveian Medical Society of London resolved to set up a campaign for the purpose of extending the 1866 act to the civil population of London and other large towns. The resulting grouping was known as the Extensionist Association. Under the direction of two active secretaries, Drs Berkeley Hill and Brendon Curgenven, the campaign recruited 400 members, including thirty MPs, a number of clergy and the vice-chancellors of Oxford and Cambridge universities. In May 1868 a memorial was presented in the House of Lords, leading to a select committee. The select committee was packed with supporters of extension, a tactic which was to backfire on the regulationists. The blatant bias produced the first signs of open opposition.

The dissenting note was first sounded by the 1868 report of the Rescue Society, an evangelical body engaged in the reclamation of 'fallen women'. The secretary, Daniel Cooper, denounced the 1866 act under the heading 'a dear remedy'. This led the society to summon a conference of similar bodies to protest against extension when the Lords committee's report was published (2 July 1868). A strongly worded protest was sent to all members of both Houses of Parliament. Silent opposition to the acts had now ceased.

The Home Office referred the issue of extension to Sir John Simon, medical officer to the privy council, who rejected the idea. Simon was willing to defend the existing system as exceptional legislation designed to remedy a problem related to the maintenance of the armed forces, but not an extension to the civilian population. The government, now headed by Gladstone, took the hint, and referred the proposal to a Commons select committee. The select committee met in the late spring of 1869, interviewing thirteen witnesses, all of whom were sympathetic to the CD acts. This committee not surprisingly recommended continuing the acts and extending them to further military bases, but cautiously advised a further select committee to consider the specific question of applying the acts to the civilian population. The government accepted the recommendations of the committee, and on 23 July Lord Northbrook, under-secretary for war, introduced a bill which went through all its stages in Lords and Commons without debate, receiving the royal assent on ll August.[38]

Supporters of regulation could not know this, but the 1869 act was to be the last of the Contagious Diseases Bills. The opponents of the acts had taken note of the success of organized pressure from the regulationists in obtaining legislation. They concluded that despite the apparent success of evangelical puritanism in setting the moral tone of respectable Victorianism, that success had been shown to be partial. Vice not only continued to exist, but under pressure from the well-organized public health lobby was on the way to being officially condoned and organized. This prospect finally broke the hold of respectable taboos over the opponents of the CD acts. Prudishness and the code of discreet silence ceased to operate. The opponents of state-regulated prostitution found their voices.

THE BIRTH OF THE REPEAL MOVEMENT

As the third Contagious Diseases Act slipped easily through Parliament in the summer of 1869, the opponents of legalized prostitution were finally spurred into open rebellion. The formation of the repeal campaign began with the efforts of a relatively unknown northern doctor, one Dr Hoopell, based in South Shields. Dr Hoopell had successfully challenged the arguments of the extensionists at a meeting in Newcastle, and managed to get his views into print. The report was seen by a Nottingham doctor, Charles Bell Taylor, who decided to organize a meeting at Bristol in October, during the Social Science Congress which was being held there. The two abolitionists saw this as an ideal platform for their views.

A meeting of abolitionists was held at the congress and attracted seventy people, including Professor F.W. Newman, Dr Thomas Worth of Nottingham, and most importantly Miss Elizabeth Wolstenholme, an advocate of higher education for women who was friendly with the charismatic Josephine Butler. The meeting concluded with the passing of a motion denouncing the CD acts. After the meeting Miss Wolstenholme sent an urgent telegram to Josephine Butler asking her to 'haste to the rescue' of the campaign against the acts. Wolstenholme rightly saw Josephine Butler as having the qualities needed to lead the fight for repeal.

At the congress itself, Bell Taylor read a paper criticizing the Contagious Diseases Acts. At a session on 4 October with about a hundred people present the acts were debated and condemned by a two to one majority. The following day at a meeting in the Victoria Hall it was decided to form a National Anti-Contagious Diseases Acts Association (hereafter National Association or NA). Drs Hoopell and Worth were honorary secretaries and F.C. Banks, a Nottingham bookseller, provided an office. Although this was not intended to be an all-male organization, women decided to form their own grouping and the Ladies' National Association (LNA) was the result.

As Banks began to issue pamphlets and handbills from his Nottingham publishing house, the campaign received powerful support from Dr John

Chapman, the editor of the *Westminster Review*. The *Review* had in 1851 published the Greg article which brought prostitution into public debate. But later the same year, the *Review* had been bought by Chapman, who determined to rescue the magazine from Greg's conservatism and return it to the philosophical liberal utilitarianism of its founders, James Mill and Jeremy Bentham, and its most famous editor, John Stuart Mill. The campaign against the CD acts was entirely in line with this emphasis on individual rights and hostility to state power. Late in 1869 and early in 1870 Chapman published four powerful articles against the CD acts, including Simon's report opposing their extension. Josephine Butler told the Royal Commission of 1871[39] 'I have been instructed by the *Westminster Review*'.

The campaign was launched on New Year's Day 1870, when the *Daily News* published a protest against the CD acts drawn up by Harriet Martineau and signed by one hundred and forty women, including Florence Nightingale, Josephine Butler, penal reformer Mary Carpenter and suffragist Lydia Becker. This was a foundation document of the feminist movement in Britain. It made eight charges against the acts, three specifically feminist in nature, focusing on the ill-treatment of women while men benefited from the acts, two moral in nature stressing the iniquity of state approval of vice, two focusing on the dangers to civil liberty arising from the powers given to police, surgeons and magistrates punishing an ill-defined offence, and one attacking the nub of the regulationist case by disputing that regulation could diminish disease.[40]

The exclusively female manifesto caused deep consternation. Josephine Butler recalled in her memoirs that an unnamed leading Commons politician had said to her 'we know how to manage any other opposition in the House or in the country, but this is very awkward for us – this revolt of women. It is quite a new thing; what are we to do with such an opposition as this?'[41] The press reprinted and discussed it at length, and was generally critical of the women concerned for daring to intervene on such a delicate subject. Censure failed to check the movement. Within a few months all major provincial cities in England and Scotland had repeal societies and many had ladies' committees as well. On 7 March Hoopell began publishing a weekly journal, *The Shield*, a move made necessary by a wall of silence in the press. Both Liberal and Conservative parties frowned on the repeal campaign, and their respective supporting papers hoped to kill the campaign by ignoring it. This was to be a forlorn hope. Any prospect of the repeal campaign fading into obscurity was destroyed by the sensational Colchester by-election of 1870.

The repealers were nearly all Liberal supporters, but found Gladstone's ministry frustratingly uncooperative. The ministry thoroughly incensed the campaign when it attempted to find a seat for Sir Henry Storks, ex-governor of Malta and a military man whose support for Cardwell's controversial army reforms was urgently needed in Parliament. Storks, when in charge of Malta, had enforced the CD acts with severe efficiency. He was a noted extensionist, who had publicly stated that 'I am of the opinion that very little benefit will result from the best devised means of prevention, until prostitution is recognised as necessity'.[42]

Such a man was anathema to the repealers. They opposed his candidature when he first attempted to enter Parliament at the Newark by-election in the spring of 1870. The town was placarded and Storks withdrew on the day of the election, a candidate pledged to repeal being successful. Following this modest success, the Quaker MP William Fowler introduced a repeal bill in May 1870. The bill was defeated by 229 votes to 88 in July, but during the debate Gladstone promised a Royal Commission into the acts. The repealers were deeply suspicious, especially when the government put up Storks again at a by-election. Colchester had returned a Liberal MP at the 1868 general election, and was a garrison town which had received the full benefit of the CD acts. Liberal Party managers thought Storks would find a by-election in Colchester relatively easy, but repeal campaigners decided to run a third candidate and draw off enough Liberal votes to let in the Conservative. The Conservatives were not in favour of repeal, but the repealers wanted to shake the Liberal government into action. Dr Baxter Langley was chosen as candidate. He was a member of the National Association, which was organizing the campaign in Colchester.

The actual electioneering was led by the then obscure Josephine Butler and James Stuart (Fellow of Trinity College, Cambridge, later Professor of Applied Mathematics, still later Gladstonian Liberal MP) who went to Colchester for the duration.[43] Their arrival was the signal for astonishing events. After holding prayer meetings, the repealers went into the streets to distribute thousands of handbills proclaiming Storks' view that in addition to prostitutes, soldiers' wives should be compulsorily examined for disease. Liberal partisans attacked the hotel where Butler and the repealers were staying. Dr Langley and James Stuart held a meeting in the local theatre, but were driven from the platform by a mob. Langley had his clothes torn, was covered in dirt and flour, and had a bleeding face, while Stuart was wounded in the arm by a blow from a chair.

Gender was no protection. Correctly identifying Mrs Butler as their main opponent, the supporters of the CD acts placarded the town with posters which gave a description of her appearance and dress. Butler then had to risk mob violence whenever she went outdoors. Seeking to avoid the campaign of intimidation, she took a room in a hotel under the name of Grey. This proved little protection. In the middle of the night she was roused by the proprietor who informed her that 'the mob are round the house, breaking the windows. They threaten to set fire to it if you don't leave at once. They have found out you are here. Never mind your luggage, leave it here; dress quickly and I will show you out the back door.' Butler was then shepherded out at the back while the landlord parleyed with the mob at the front. After running down dark, unfamiliar streets in fear of attack, she was saved by an anonymous housewife who gave her shelter. The next morning it was seen that the doors of the hotel had been battered, and the windows shattered by stones.

The national press could ignore neither the astonishing levels of violence, nor the fact that the campaign was largely a women's initiative, led by a woman of courage. Women's prayer meetings were maintained throughout the campaign despite having to run a gauntlet of hooligans who threatened physical violence. During the meetings the mob kept up an intimidating howling and cursing outside, threatening to burn the hall down. Passions grew so intense that when a Wesleyan minister in the town wrote a letter against Storks, his pious congregation drove him from the church and out of Colchester. All issues other than the Contagious Diseases Acts had become irrelevant, and it became clear to Storks that the violence of his supporters was losing him support. As the campaign drew to a close, he sought terms with the repealers. They demanded a pledge that he would support the repeal of the CD acts, which he refused. Langley withdrew from the contest before the vote, but he had succeeded in damaging the Liberals. When the result was announced, Storks had lost heavily.

Result of the Colchester elections 1868 and 1870		
	1868 election	1870 election
Liberal	1467	869
Conservative	1284	1396
	Lib majority 183	Con majority 527

The repealers hailed this as a triumph, but it was a Pyrrhic victory. Gladstone's administration viewed the Colchester result as a mid-term aberration, and held to its policy of setting up a Royal Commission. The Colchester by-election achieved few tangible gains for repeal. It did, however, establish Josephine Butler as unquestionably the leading figure of the repeal campaign.

Josephine Butler (1828–1906) was a figure of outstanding ability and integrity. She was a veteran of the long-running campaign against slavery which came to a successful conclusion with the triumph of the North in the American Civil War. She was the most important of the group of women who, having learnt campaigning in the anti-slavery movement, found their energies released for campaigning on domestic issues.[44] After the Civil War, she found it natural to transfer her energies to campaigning on behalf of prostitutes, drawing on the woman–slave analogy and contending that scripture supported both women's equality and race equality. Looking back on the origins of the campaign to repeal the CD acts in her autobiography, she drew the analogy herself. Men, she argued,

> have had the opportunity for many years of looking at the question in its material phases, of appreciating its hygienic results . . . NOW, for the first time, . . . they are asked to look upon it as a question of human nature, of interest to both men and women . . . The cry of women crushed under legalised vice is not the cry of a statistician or a medical expert; it is simply a cry of pain, a cry for justice and for a return to God's laws . . . the slave now speaks. The enslaved women have found a voice in one of themselves . . . It is the voice of a woman who has suffered, a voice calling to holy rebellion and to war.[45]

The resonant evangelical fervour displayed here may be unattractive to later generations, but Josephine Butler's passionately felt evangelical Christian beliefs (she was, like Gladstone, an Anglican) were essential to her work. In the climate of mid-Victorian England, only a strong religious impulse, giving impeccable respectable credentials, could give a woman any chance of success in the teeth of a deeply hostile political environment.

In 1852 she married the Revd George Butler, MA, eldest son of Dr George Butler, dean of Peterborough and former headmaster of Harrow. After five years of teaching at Oxford, he became vice-principal of Cheltenham College where he remained from 1858 to 1866. During their period at Cheltenham in 1864 they suffered an appalling family tragedy when their youngest daughter Eva fell headlong downstairs as she rushed to greet her parents. She died in her father's arms.

The tragedy haunted Josephine Butler for the rest of her life and she suffered a prolonged trauma after Eva's death which was only overcome when she found a cause into which to sublimate her grief. This was the cause of prostitutes, usually referred to as 'fallen women'. The family moved to Liverpool in 1866, a town in which she later said 'it was not difficult to find misery', and became intensely involved in work aimed to rescue women from the streets. Josephine Butler sought them out in workhouses and night shelters and brought them into her own home for reclamation. She was also involved, with James Stuart, Frances Clough (headmistress of the North London Collegiate School) and Miss E.C. Wolstenholme, in the movement for higher local examinations, which led to the development of university extension lectures and eventually higher education for women. In the 1860s, Josephine Butler already took her conception of Christian duty well beyond the limits of conventional alms-giving. In the next decade and a half, she would go much further.

In the summer of 1869, the Butler family went on holiday in Switzerland with James Stuart. When the party returned, Mrs Butler found awaiting her Miss Wolstenholme's telegram requesting her participation in the anti-vice campaign. Josephine Butler hesitated for three months. She was acutely conscious that any woman involving herself actively in such a campaign would attract intense odium from respectable society. The prudery of Victorian Britain was intensely hypocritical. It was prepared to tolerate vice, as long as it was hidden away in areas which did not impinge on family life – a trait on which *The Lancet* had attempted to play in its heavy-handed editorial of November 1857. It was deeply unrespectable for a respectable woman to acknowledge the existence of the harlots. Nor was it in any way permissible for a woman to attempt to enter the political sphere; laws were made by men. Josphine Butler had already flouted convention by helping prostitutes; political campaigning was unprecedented. She came to the conclusion, however, that combating the CD acts was a God-given duty which she had no right to reject.

This was, however, mid-Victorian England, and before she could give her answer she had to ask her husband for permission. She did this, in classic Victorian style, by writing him a letter. George Butler took three days to ponder the issue before, pale-faced and serious, he gave his wife his blessing. Melodramatic though this episode appears today, it points to the seriousness of the choices facing Josephine Butler. Charitable work among fallen women was just within the pale of respectability. Political campaigning was not. Even the anti-slavery movement failed to provide formal equality of opportunity for women.

Josephine Butler addressing a crowd during the campaign for the repeal of the Contagious Diseases Acts

For a respectable woman, political campaigning on the issue of prostitution was fraught with difficulties.

But once she had made her decision, Josephine Butler threw herself unsparingly into the fray. She became the secretary to the Ladies' National Association and in the first year of the campaign travelled 3,700 miles and addressed ninety-nine meetings. Butler was a brilliant strategist and very quickly grasped the potential of support among working-class organizations. Respectable working men were particularly conscious of the dangers that prostitution posed to their families, and had no illusions about the sensitivity of the police when dealing with working-class women. However, Butler was not a good tactician, and the LNA was committed to frontal attack on the CD acts.

This led it into a fundamentalist position when Gladstone honoured his promise to set up a Royal Commission into the operation of the acts. The LNA was deeply suspicious of the 1871 Royal Commission, and boycotted it on the grounds that it was a 'foregone conclusion'. It dismissed the inquiry with the memorable statement that 'into this trap of a Royal Commission, so cunningly devised by the astute and unscrupulous clique who have succeeded in placing these laws on the statute book, the LNA is resolved not to walk'.[46]

Like many moralistic pressure groups, the repeal campaign was making its task more difficult by militant fundamentalism. The 1871 Royal Commission was the first inquiry into the subject which was not overwhelmingly biased towards regulation. The commissioners were chosen to represent both sides and though the number of witnesses called shows some bias towards the supporters of the acts, the bias was nowhere near as great as in previous commissions. McHugh argues that before the 1870-71 commission, 115 witnesses to commissions had been in favour, 35 against and 27 neutral; with the 1870–71 commission the balance was 49 in favour, 32 against and 2 neutral.[47] The anti–regulation case was at least given a reasonable airing.

The opportunity was not, however, well exploited. Josephine Butler, who was prevailed upon to appear, proved a particularly poor witness, haranguing the commission as if it were a street meeting. Her intransigence was notorious, notably in her reply to question 12,932, an invitation from the chair, Massey, to make a statement. Mrs Butler replied:

> I should not be doing my duty . . . if I left your presence without very clearly declaring to you that all of us who are seeking the repeal of these Acts are wholly indifferent to the decision of this commission. . . . those who I represent . . . consider it an absurdity, a mockery, that any tribunal . . . should be sent to inquire into a moral question like this. We have the Word of God in our hands – the Law of God in our consciences. We know that to protect vice in men is not according to the Word of God . . . You may be sure that our action in this matter will continue to be exactly the same, even if the Commission pronounce the Acts highly moral. We shall never rest until this system is banished from our shores . . . [48]

Other contributions proved more persuasive, particularly an authoritative liberal statement of the rights of the individual from John Stuart Mill. Yet the immediate outcome justified the cynicism of the LNA. The final report contained a breathtakingly open justification of the double standard, in a statement that

> We may at once dispose of [any recommendation] founded on the principle of putting both parties to the sin of fornication on the same footing by the obvious but no less conclusive reply that there is no comparison to be made between prostitutes and the men who consort with them. With the one sex the offence is committed as a matter of gain; with the other, it is an irregular indulgence of a natural impulse.[49]

Yet the apparent unanimity of the committee concealed deep divisions which rendered the report ridiculous. Although the final report was signed by all twenty-three members, several notes of dissent were appended which made a mockery of the exercise. The final report suggested repealing the 1869 act and reverting to the acts of 1864 and 1866. Six pro-repeal commissioners (W. Cowper-Temple, Anthony John Mundella, J.F.D. Maurice, Robert Applegarth, Holmes Coote and Peter Rylands) dissented from the proposal to revive the compulsory powers of surgical examination and committal to hospitals of the 1864 act, and Rylands, Mundella, Applegarth and Holmes Coote further dissented from nine of the twelve recommendations which they had just signed. They argued they only signed to support the main recommendation that 'the periodical examination of the public women be discontinued'. Josephine Butler commented that 'It is almost laughable, if it were not so terrible an exhibition of weakness – "a house divided against itself".'

The effect of the Royal Commission was to reveal the deep divisions between supporters and opponents of the acts. In early 1872 the Liberal home secretary, H.A. Bruce, made a very half-hearted attempt to introduce a compromise bill modifying the CD acts along the lines suggested by the Royal Commission report. The attempt at a compromise was doomed to failure. The LNA campaigned against the bill, while Bruce was confronted in May by 150 MPs urging maintenance of the acts in their existing form (eighty-seven Conservative and sixty-three Liberal – the repealers could not muster anything like this cross-party strength). Bruce concluded no compromise was possible and withdrew his bill in July 1872.

This outcome strengthened the militant current in the repeal lobby, which saw it as proof that Parliament was a lost cause unless the Liberal administration was put under extra-parliamentary pressure. Their views were strengthened by the Pontefract by-election of August 1872. The repealers realized they could not unseat the Liberal candidate, H.C.E. Childers, who was a popular local figure, but campaigned to reduce his majority. H.J. Wilson, a Sheffield manufacturer, provided money for the LNA's agent, Samuel Fothergill, to work full time in Pontefract, Josephine Butler and James Stuart again campaigned, Wilson and his wife joined them, and there was violence. In the most notorious incident, Josephine Butler and Mrs Wilson were trapped in a hayloft by roughs who tried to smoke them out.[50]

The result seemed to justify the campaign. Childers was returned, but his majority was cut from 233 to 80. He had been a relatively favourable Liberal, asserting in a letter to *The Times* that he supported Bruce's bill as a step to repeal, and apologizing for the excesses of his supporters. He even offered to prosecute any who could be identified. A reduced majority for a popular local candidate was a national sensation. The hostile London press denounced the repealers but gave them credit for the result. The *Northern Echo*, then edited by W.T. Stead, treated the whole thing as a triumph for morality.

The militants drew the lesson from these events that if they were better organized at elections, they could threaten supporters of the CD acts with electoral ruin, and reverse the level of support for the acts within the Commons. For the next two years, the priority of the repeal campaign was to forge an electoral machine which would, in Josephine Butler's words, 'make these fellows afraid of us'.[51] The repealers had completely misjudged the political situation. The rough handling they had received at the two by-elections had increased their own sense of self-righteousness – it was not for nothing that Josephine Butler thought in terms of a crusade – while the national coverage they received gave them a renewed sense of their self-importance. They were, however, a small and marginal pressure group, overwhelmingly reliant on the Liberals, with no purchase on the Conservatives. The repealers could induce Liberal voters to abstain and let in the Conservatives – but this only strengthened the supporters of the acts.

The parliamentary leadership was acutely aware of this, and was extremely circumspect in criticizing Gladstone's ministry. The most optimistic estimate of parliamentary strength gave the repealers the votes of 173 MPs, mostly Liberals, out of a total of 658. Even these were hard to mobilize. When William Fowler, Quaker, Liberal MP for Cambridge city and effectively the repealers' parliamentary leader, failed to produce a private member's bill, the NA persuaded another Quaker, Charles Gilpin, to introduce one. Gilpin brought his bill in on 9 July 1872. The bill was not even discussed, the house being six MPs short of the forty needed for a quorum.

It was clear that repeal of the Contagious Diseases Acts was not on the parliamentary agenda. The repeal campaigners, obsessed with their cause, refused to accept this when told by sympathetic MPs such as Mundella and Fowler, and insisted on believing that they could force the Liberals to undertake repeal by sustained pressure such as the Colchester and Pontefract by-elections. Prudent advice about the dangers of weakening the Liberal government and letting in the Tories was swept aside. From the summer of 1872 to the general election of 1874, strident militancy aimed at forcing a reluctant Liberal government was the order of the day. It was to prove a disastrous mistake.

MILITANCY CONFOUNDED

The repeal campaign from 1872 to 1874 was dominated by militants who assumed that the reasons for lack of success were rooted in a lack of spirit among the parliamentarians. They believed the gates to the New Jerusalem could be forced, if only sufficient spirit and energy were applied. This delusion fed upon a latent anti-metropolitan feeling. As with many pressure groups, the provincial supporters were deeply suspicious of the fleshpots of London, assuming that the attractions of the capital diluted the campaigning spirit. It was therefore not surprising that militancy emerged most strongly in the north of England, with a less powerful offshoot in the Midlands.

Initially, the moving spirit in the more militant current was Henry J. Wilson of Sheffield, Josephine Butler's aide-de-camp at the Pontefract by-election. Wilson was a Nonconformist activist. A Congregationalist businessman with interests in cotton and iron smelting, he had been an opponent of the CD acts since 1870. He was also a pillar of Sheffield Nonconformist opposition to the 1870 Education Act, a temperance advocate, active on the Eastern Question in 1876 and 1877. After the passage of the 1885 Criminal Law Amendment Act, he was to become the treasurer of the National Vigilance Association formed to enforce the act. In 1885 he was elected as a Liberal MP.

Wilson discussed his plan for a new grouping with like-minded figures. Dr Hooppell offered advice, and Josephine Butler was heavily involved behind the scenes. Sufficient support for a more militant current was discovered, and the Northern Counties League for Repeal (NCL) emerged. Wilson became secretary at the formation of the league on 29 August 1872, with a Quaker businessman, Edward Backhouse, of Sunderland as chair and Joseph Edmondson of Halifax as treasurer.

The National Association was annoyed by this *de facto* challenge to its authority. Nevertheless it recognized the strength of the pressure for militant extra-parliamentary action and it appointed two electoral agents. By the end of the year the LNA had Fothergill in the field, who went straight from Pontefract to harry the Liberals at Preston, the National Association its two agents, and the NCL an additional two. Militant repealers in the Midlands regrouped on ll December 1872 to form the Midland Counties Electoral Union (MCEU), with Harriet Martineau's nephew R.F. Martineau as the leading light. The hopes of the militants were ill founded. Fowler was induced to bring in a private member's repeal bill, which failed on 21 May 1873 by the handsome margin of 128 votes to 251. The repealers ignored the actual vote and claimed they had won the debate. The militant repeal paper *The Shield* trumpeted that 'We have baffled the "conspiracy of silence", penetrated into the very heart of the enemy's country; stormed and for ever destroyed their earthworks of false statistic, and laid bare the true centre and key stone of their evil position – THE NECESSITY OF VICE'.

Such strong emotion blinded the repealers to their actual weakness. They could not carry Gladstone's Liberal government, and could expect nothing from the Tory Party, most of whose leaders and MPs backed the acts. The more politically astute began to realize this. In the month following the defeat of Fowler's bill, the repealers tried to stand J.C. Cox in the Bath by-election to dislodge the official Liberal. Cox enlisted the help of Coutts, an NA agent, but when H.J. Wilson went to the scene he checked carefully on potential support, came to the conclusion that Cox was heading for a serious and demoralizing defeat, and bullied him into withdrawing.

Wilson had come to realize he had been mistaken in agitating for militancy. His realism was not popular among repealers. When Robert Applegarth, the trade union leader who had served on the 1871 Royal Commission, commended the chair of the commission (W.N. Massey) to the working-class electors of Tiverton, he was denounced as a traitor by *The Shield*. Applegarth retorted that there were more things to campaign on than repeal of the CD acts, and that there was nothing to be gained by undermining the Liberal Party in favour of the Conservative Party.

This conclusion was not welcome among repealers. More typical was R.F. Martineau's belief in the success of the election tactic. 'How different election matters look everywhere now!' he wrote in a letter to H.J. Wilson in July 1873. 'No candidate appears but has to mention the subject, and there is always respect for our views, and if not entire adhesion, always concession.' The repealers were soon to undergo a rude awakening. The government was failing, and in January 1874 Gladstone went to the country. The Liberals were soundly beaten, the Conservatives gaining a decisive parliamentary majority of forty-eight.

The result came as a severe shock for the repealers. They now had to face the consequences of undermining a government which was potentially sympathetic and helping return a ministry wholly unsympathetic. The repeal campaign could not regard the election as anything but an unmitigated disaster. At the most optimistic estimate, the number of repeal MPs dropped to 144. Fowler lost his seat, and the campaign was unable to find anyone who would readily take his place. From February to July 1874, the committee of the NA, reinforced by representatives of the LNA, NCL, MCEU and Friends' Association for Repeal, met almost weekly in the search for a successor.

Meanwhile, the policy of undermining the Liberals had its last Pyrrhic fling. In March the former MP J.D. Lewis, having lost Devonport, tried to retain Oxford for the Liberals. Having declared that he would rather lose five seats than vote for repeal, his candidature was a red rag to the repealers. Repeal agents whipped up a campaign against him. Mrs Butler appealed to the women of Oxford to put pressure on their husbands, H.J. Wilson urged radicals to abstain (voting for the Tory was beyond the pale; he was a brewer), and Lewis was defeated. *The Shield* welcomed this as 'the most signal triumph' since Colchester. As the repeal leadership sought to find a replacement for Fowler, it dawned on them that many more such triumphs and their campaign would annihilate itself.

The repeal campaign now found itself in a position similar to that faced by the Campaign for Nuclear Disarmament (CND) a century later. It could expect nothing from the militaristic Conservative Party, and had perforce to rely on the other main party. But the Liberals, like Labour over nuclear disarmament, were deeply split over support for repeal. To secure Liberal sanction for repeal had proved a difficult enough task; and with the Tories comfortably ensconced in power in 1874, the repealers could now only look forward to several years of uphill struggle. Josephine Butler suffered something like a nervous breakdown.

The difficulties which moralists faced in securing legislative action against vice in the 1870s had been underlined by the almost farcical events surrounding the attempt to raise the age of consent. The age at which a girl could give consent to sexual intercourse in the early 1870s was twelve – and this was at a time when the age of puberty was generally much later. The moral reform lobby regarded this as outrageous. Josephine Butler had told the 1871 Royal Commission, 'At present for the purposes of seduction, and seduction only, our laws declare every female child a woman at 12 years of age. I am ashamed to have to confess to such a shameful state of the law before you gentlemen, but a child is a woman, for that purpose alone, at 12 years of age. I know from my experience amongst this class of women [i.e. prostitutes], how many have become so from that cause.'[52]

It was impossible to defend this situation, and the Royal Commission dealt with the issue in an admirably pithy paragraph. Its report stated

> Our attention has been drawn to the state of the law for the protection of female children. By the 24 & 25 Vict. c. 100, . . . carnal knowledge of a girl between the age of 10 and 12 years is a misdemeanour . . . The traffic in children for infamous purposes is notoriously considerable in London and other large towns. We think a child of 12 years can hardly be deemed capable of giving consent, and should not have the power of yielding up her person. We therefore recommend the absolute protection of female children to the age of 14 years, making the age of consent to commence at 14 instead of 12 years, as under the existing law.[53]

This view was incorporated as recommendation 10 – proposing to extend the age of consent from twelve to fourteen. Given this clear recommendation, it might have been thought that the government would have taken action. However, the half-hearted nature of the Bruce bill of 1872, and the speed with which it was dropped when opposition developed, showed that ministers had no stomach for reform where morality was concerned. These issues were therefore taken up by an obscure back-bench MP, Mr Charley, in an effort to humanize the morality laws.

Mr Charley's first concern was with the bastardy laws and the tragedy of infanticide. A select committee into these dark areas had uncovered much troubling evidence. The problem of deserted mothers was great, as Josephine Butler among others had stated, and provision for them seriously inadequate. The law required a sum of two shillings and sixpence (12½p) per week maximum for the support of a child. 'The evidence before the committee', Charley argued, 'showed that it was quite impossible to maintain an infant for a week upon so small a sum, and that rigid limitation led to infanticide. The mother had this alternative placed before her – either to maintain her child or to destroy it, for otherwise she could not possibly go to service' [i.e. obtain a job as a servant].[54]

While the treatment of unmarried mothers was Charley's main concern, he tacked on to his bill a proposal to raise the age of consent 'which happened to correspond with a proposal which the government had made, which was that the age of girls to which criminal liability for their seduction should attach should be raised from 12 to 14 years'.[55] If Charley believed this would ensure an easy passage for his bill, he was mistaken. While MPs, including James Stansfeld, generally welcomed his proposals to assist unmarried mothers, it became clear to Charley that the age of consent was a different matter. He dropped this proposal on 22 July in order to secure passage of the bastardy bill.

Charley tried again in the 1873 session. That spring, he moved the seduction laws amendment bill, which attempted to make fourteen the age of consent. He immediately ran into the opposition of Cavendish Bentinck, a reactionary Tory whose opposition to morality reform was to become notorious. Cavendish Bentinck tried a wrecking tactic arguing that he was not opposed to the bill, but was opposed to a back-bencher moving such a measure. The government should have moved the bill, as this would have allowed consultation with the law officers and avoided drafting errors which he claimed were in Charley's bill. This was relatively mild treatment by Cavendish Bentinck's later standards, and cut no ice with the attorney-general. That official rejected Cavendish Bentinck's criticisms of the government, and welcomed the proposal in the bill to raise the age below which sex with a girl was illegal from ten to twelve.

He did not agree with the proposal to raise the age of consent from twelve to fourteen, however. He argued that as the age at which marriage was possible was twelve for a girl (and fourteen for a boy), it was not possible to make sexual connection with a girl aged between twelve and fourteen illegal provided consent was obtained. He also made it clear that the government rejected any link between the age of consent and prostitution, and defended the CD acts, reproving the reform MP A.J. Mundella in very sharp terms:

The hon member for Sheffield [Mr Mundella] had fallen into an unintentional error in speaking of the age at which girls were constantly consigned to prostitution in our great towns. He had greatly exaggerated the extent to which girls were consigned to prostitution in our streets. In all the towns where the Contagious Diseases Acts had been in operation the traffic in girls of that age was absolutely at an end. He felt it was very important that this statement should be made.[56]

Important though he felt this statement to be, the attorney-general provided no evidence to support it.

In order to save his bill from total defeat, Charley struck out the proposal to raise the age of consent. His bill then went through, rendering sexual relations with girls under twelve illegal, whether or not consent was given. In the spring of 1874, however, he again attempted to have the age of consent raised to fourteen. His bill was lost as the new Conservative government imposed its own legislative programme. He tried again in 1875, by which time one can detect a degree of sympathy among MPs where Charley's thankless crusade was concerned. Despite this, fourteen was still a bridge too far for the House, but at the suggestion of the Recorder of London a compromise of thirteen was accepted by MPs, and at long last the bill passed to the Lords.

Charley's long crusade was not yet over. To his intense chagrin, as the 1875 session ground towards its close, the Lords considered his bill and deleted the clause dealing with the age of consent. Charley was incensed and the House of Commons supported him.[57] A committee of MPs was quickly formed and sent to the Lords, and the Lords were prevailed upon to agree to the compromise. The Offences against the Person Act was approved on 13 August 1875, raising the age at which a girl could consent to sexual intercourse from twelve to thirteen.

The problems which dogged the raising of the age of consent indicated very clearly the strength of opposition to moral legislation in Parliament in the 1870s. The repeal lobby had come to understand this very clearly in the shock of the Liberal defeat. Their first and most difficult task following the defeat was to find a new leader, and in the end, the campaign managed to find itself not one but two. The official leader, selected by repeal MPs and approved by the NA committee on 23 July, was a Whig baronet, Sir Harcourt Johnstone. The real leader, however, was the vice-president of the National Association, James Stansfeld, president of the Local Government Board in Gladstone's Cabinet, and a private advisor to Josephine Butler. Stansfeld was a member of the radical wing of the party, and complemented Johnstone, who represented Liberalism's right wing. Above all, they were strong figures who could not be brushed aside as the political lightweight Fowler had been. They also represented a growing realization that the attack on Liberalism had been fundamentally mistaken. Stansfeld warmly supported Fowler at the MCEU's annual meeting in December 1874 when the defeated leader attacked the policy of 'endeavouring to split up parties into small sections by undue pressure on candidates'.[58] This censure was entirely justified, and sank in.

Meanwhile, the hard core of repeal MPs staged an annual debate in the House of Commons with increasingly less effect. MPs simply became bored with the annual attempt to support a lost cause, and Tory MP Henry Lucy cruelly defined an empty House as 'Stansfeld on his legs delivering his annual speech on the

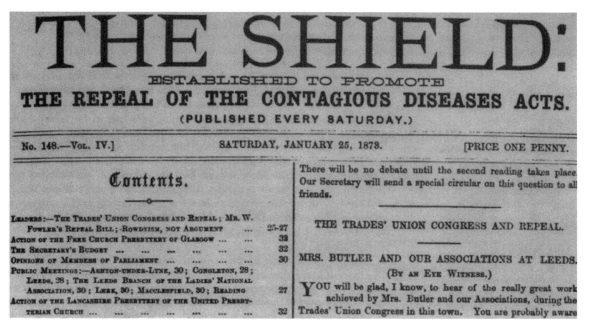

THE SHIELD:

ESTABLISHED TO PROMOTE

THE REPEAL OF THE CONTAGIOUS DISEASES ACTS.

(PUBLISHED EVERY SATURDAY.)

No. 148.—Vol. IV.]   SATURDAY, JANUARY 25, 1873.   [PRICE ONE PENNY.

Contents.

There will be no debate until the second reading takes place. Our Secretary will send a special circular on this question to all friends.

THE TRADES' UNION CONGRESS AND REPEAL.

MRS. BUTLER AND OUR ASSOCIATIONS AT LEEDS.
(BY AN EYE WITNESS.)

YOU will be glad, I know, to hear of the really great work achieved by Mrs. Butler and our Associations, during the Trades' Union Congress in this town. You are probably aware

The Shield, weekly journal of the Great Crusade, published from spring 1870 by Dr Hoopell. Josephine Butler travelled the country to gain support for the campaign, as indicated in this issue

rights of his fellow women'.[59] Campaigners were reduced to emotional appeals. Repealers played on the outrage felt at the suicide of Mrs Percy at Aldershot. Mrs Percy, a widow with three children to support, eked out a living as a singer around the town. The metropolitan police patrolling the town demanded constant submissions to medical examination from her and her sixteen-year-old daughter. When these were refused, the police harassed her and made it almost impossible for her to earn a living. In despair she poured out her troubles in a letter to the *Daily Telegraph* and then drowned herself in the Basingstoke canal. The reform campaign roused a storm over the issue, testifying to the virginity of the daughter, Jenny Percy, but to no avail. The police argued they had been working entirely within the acts. That, the reformers responded, was exactly the point.

Gladstone voted for repeal for the first time in 1875. His action underlined the fact that only the return of a Liberal ministry could open the door to repeal. This, however, was not on the cards in the mid-1870s – parliaments lasted for seven years in this period – but in 1879, after five weary years in the wilderness, repealers saw a chink of light in their darkness. In March 1879 the repealers moved the rejection of the army estimates, an annual ritual doomed to failure. The government, however, weary of constant harassment by the repeal lobby, offered a select committee to look into the operation of the acts. The reformers accepted this with alacrity. Both Johnstone and Stansfeld were appointed to the committee, which provided them with an excuse to abandon their annual purgatory of the Repeal Bill.

The select committee was, however, no repeal panacea. Repealers found themselves fighting an immensely tedious war of attrition with the extensionists. The repealers were in a minority – they initially mustered only five of the fifteen members – and must have suspected that the militant argument that the whole business was a diversionary tactic was true. It was, however, a priceless opportunity for the repealers to marshal their arguments and test them thoroughly against expert opposition. They exploited the opportunity to the full. Stansfeld, for example, extracted from the director-general of the army medical department the admission that he did not know the provisions of the acts.[60]

Meanwhile wider political developments sustained the spirits of repealers. The Liberals won the general election of April 1880 with a majority of 137 over the Conservatives. This did not mean automatic support for repeal of the CD acts. The cross-party lobby in favour of the acts remained exceedingly powerful. Both Lord Cavendish Bentinck, judge advocate general in Disraeli's government, and his Liberal successor George Osborne Morgan, supported the acts. Both men were meticulous attenders of the select committee – Cavendish Bentinck attended 66 of a possible 70 meetings, and Osborne Morgan 58 of a possible 61. Nevertheless, the return of the Liberals created a space in which to work. All five repealers on the select committee were returned but five Tory regulationists were defeated. The repealers calculated that the new parliament contained 179 repealers, 232 regulationists, and 241 MPs with unknown opinions. The LNA concluded that 'whatever our gains in the House, public opinion will ultimately decide the question'.[61] This was partly correct, but while the mobilization of public opinion was to be crucial to eventual repeal the change of government and pressure on MPs were essential to success.

Developments at Westminster certainly did not offer rapid progress. Stansfeld had been widely tipped for a Cabinet place in the new Liberal government, but was passed over by Gladstone in favour of Joseph Chamberlain. This left him with only the cause of repeal to champion, and in the early 1880s few were predicting success. Morale among the repealers slumped in 1881 as the select committee dragged on, preventing even a token private member's bill emerging. Stansfeld had to fight off an attempt by R.F. Martineau to form a new federal body aimed at imposing provincial control of the campaign over the London-based National Association. Stansfeld believed no progress could be made till the select committee had reported, and wanted no extra-parliamentary pressure upsetting the delicate balance at Westminster. His assessment of the situation was well founded. The only option available was to convince the government to support repeal, and the Liberal MPs would need careful handling. He ensured the militant wing of the movement was kept firmly under control, knowing that a repetition of the events of 1872–4 would be disastrous.

The test of Stansfeld's strategy finally arrived with the publication of the select committee report in August 1882. The committee made no attempt to arrive at a consensus position. It could only reflect the deep split in its ranks, and did so with a majority report supporting the acts and regretting only that they could not be extended, and a minority report condemning the acts on every ground.

Stansfeld drafted the minority report, which was signed by six members of the committee. The report was welcomed by all campaigners, was reprinted in great numbers, and formed the basis of the winter campaign of 1882–3. However, it also opened up the long festering wound between the militants and the moderates. The militants saw the majority report as a sign that the select committee had been a sham and that now a renewed campaign of militancy of the old style was the order of the day. *The Shield* commented that 'Repealers have reason to thank God that all skirmishing under false colours is ended, and ended also is the long truce forced upon us by the insidious tactics of our opponents. The Majority Report is a declaration of war . . . . Not only is the government not for us; it is against us, and it would be folly not to take full account of this fact in the coming struggle.'[62]

This was a signal that the leading militants on the NA executive intended to commit the campaign to an anti-Liberal offensive. The moderates, now led by Henry Wilson, moved rapidly to forestall this. Wilson urged a new delegate body be set up, preferably centred on Birmingham and incorporating the NA, but proceeding without the NA if necessary. Wilson gained enough support to establish an umbrella organization, the Political Committee, effectively outflanking the National Association. The stage was set for the decisive effort to swing the Liberal Party behind the repeal campaign.

The moderate repealers were now gambling everything on a concerted effort to capture the Liberal party organization. Wilson circularized his members to attend the National Liberal Federation's meeting on 19 December to turn official policy towards reform. The growing strength of the repeal movement among the Liberal rank and file was demonstrated when Josephine Butler's old ally, James Stuart, was chosen to second a vote of confidence in the government.[63] Stuart used the opportunity to warn the federation that the Liberal record on moral progress failed to match up to its record on social and political progress. Stuart was becoming increasingly influential in Liberal circles, and in February 1883 he dined with the two rising stars of the Liberal Party, Sir Charles Dilke and Joseph Chamberlain, at Trinity. Both pledged their support for repeal. At the same time, the reformers kept up an intense personal correspondence with individual Liberal MPs, while the NA made a significant contribution by organizing an immense tide of petitions and letters from the constituencies to Westminster.

The repeal campaign was now reaching a climax. A resolution against the acts was due to be moved in the Commons by the Liberal MP Hopwood on 27 February 1883. A resolution would be easier to get through than a private member's bill, and could lead to government action. With the balance of votes still undecided, it was the sharpest tactic to use, as long as uncommitted MPs could be brought to vote in favour or abstain. This was the crucial issue, and one which was wholly unpredictable. Pressure was therefore intense.

By February 1883, the agitation was reaching fever heat. On the night of 27 February the lobbies at Westminster were crowded with repealers, with Cardinal Manning present to rally the Irish MPs. The Westminster Palace Hotel housed an all-day women's prayer meeting. Yet at the decisive moment, the repeal campaign collapsed into anti-climax. Pressure of other business forced Hopwood's resolution off the agenda.

A group of MPs immediately balloted for time to introduce a motion, intending that another repeal resolution should be introduced. By good fortune, Stansfeld was the lucky man. He chose a simple but cunning resolution, to wit 'That this House disapproves of the compulsory examination of women under the Contagious Diseases Acts'. It was a brilliant stroke. Stansfeld did not ask for the repeal of the acts, but struck at the heart of their powers. Compulsion was the feature which most worried Liberals and, after the suicide of Mrs Percy, the provision which aroused most public unease.

The date agreed for the debate was 20 April and the repealers renewed the offensive. On 11 April sixty MPs (representing 200 pledged for repeal) met and wrote to Gladstone asking him to receive a deputation. On 12 April the general committee of the National Liberal Federation unanimously passed a motion calling for immediate repeal. Then on 13 April W.T. Stead, who had taken over as editor of the leading Liberal journal, the *Pall Mall Gazette*, six months earlier, wrote a powerful editorial pointing out that the acts had not been a great success and wondering 'whether the game is worth the candle'.

Under this intense pressure, the Cabinet cracked. At its meeting on 14 April it agreed to make Stansfeld's resolution an open question. With the government leaving the issue to the individual consciences of MPs, the repealers had a fighting chance, though most were pessimistic. Stansfeld, however, rose to the occasion. He moved his resolution with a clear and cogent summary of his minority report, carefully demolishing the arguments on hygiene, efficiency, moral improvement, public order, and the statistical record. He dealt at length with the failure of the acts to eliminate VD. His rational approach was far more effective than an emotional appeal to morality.

The regulationists were far less effective. Osborne Morgan, from the Liberal benches, attempted a standard public health defence of the acts. Cavendish Bentinck, from the Conservative side, was boorish and tendentious, attacking his opponents while making unsupported assertions on the benefits of the acts. Mundella had dismissed him in 1874 as 'a little, mean, drunken aristocrat, without the slightest capacity for business. He is notorious in the House of Commons for his muddled speeches, and unsteady gait after dinner.'[64] A more pointed critique of Cavendish Bentinck was provided by his prospective son-in-law, Sir Edward Walter Hamilton, who in 1886 commented that 'If national policy had been left to him, we should still be confronted with . . . press gangs, slave trades, total absence of educational provision, wholesale pauperism, abuses of labour in factories, . . . in short, retrogression of civilisation.'[65] Cavendish Bentinck may have been personally objectionable and politically reactionary, but he was nevertheless a man with formidable legal and political skills. He was the most implacable opponent of the moralists and the most effective defender of the double standard in the Commons in this period, but on this occasion he foulled his own nest.

Only two members of the government spoke. Hartington, the secretary of state for war, announced the Cabinet's decision not to defend the acts but to allow

Parliament to decide. He personally supported the acts, but the man who was Skittles's former lover had little moral influence. The home secretary, Harcourt, followed him in defending the acts, but the Cabinet knew the argument had been lost. As Josephine Butler led a deputation of women in prayer outside, the vote was taken. It gave a decisive majority for Stansfeld's resolution: 110 voted against, 182 in favour. Most MPs abstained, but this did not dim the exultation of the repealers. The regulationists had lost the vote, and their opponents claimed they had lost the argument. It remained to be seen how substantial Stansfeld's victory would prove.

THREE
White Slavery Revealed

PARLIAMENTARY STALEMATE

Stansfeld's victory in April 1883 was a very partial triumph. From the repeal perspective, the job was only half completed. The acts had been suspended, the government being forced to withdraw the police and suspend the compulsory examination of women. And as the supporters of the acts conceded, without compulsory examination the system of regulation was useless and might as well be abolished. Yet the acts remained on the statute book, and had influential supporters within the Liberal Party hierarchy, notably Hartington (secretary for war), Vernon Harcourt (home secretary) and Lord Northbrook (first lord of the admiralty), who were the ministers most intimately involved in the operation of the acts.

In the wake of Stansfeld's resolution, extensionists campaigned to have the issue reopened, while repealers pressed for complete abolition. The two sides were too evenly matched for either to gain a decisive advantage. Pressure on Gladstone to put government support behind the repeal campaign failed to move him. Gladstone's family were supporters of repeal, and in 1884 the premier's son and private secretary, Herbert, was privately offering advice to Josephine Butler on how to handle the Grand Old Man. But no amount of handling affected Gladstone, who had more important issues on his mind, notably the Irish crisis. Liberal ministers calculated that repeal of the CD acts was a minority issue even within the Liberal Party. In 1883 the Liberal cocoa manufacturer, Joseph Rowntree, recounted a conversation which he had had with a political acquaintance about politics in his home town: 'The gentleman had asked, "have you any fads in York?" I said, "Yes, any Liberal candidate must be against the CD Acts".'[66] Very many Liberals at this point regarded the repeal campaign as a 'fad', and the strength of Nonconformist puritanism in the early 1880s was not as overwhelmingly important for Gladstonian Liberalism as it became after the Home Rule split of 1886. Many Liberals regarded the repealers as cranks, and the repeal campaign as a minor political issue. The vast majority of Conservatives agreed.

Evidence to support this view was provided by the very triumph of Stansfeld's motion. Only 292 MPs had voted, out of a total of 658.[67] Thus 366 MPs, a very substantial majority, had not bothered to cast a vote. Considerable numbers of Liberal MPs were among this majority. Whether the abstainers were simply indifferent, intimidated by the strength of the repeal campaign, or repelled by discussing the distinctly unrespectable topic of prostitution, is hard to assess. But it is clear that while Stansfeld had won a majority for his motion, he had signally failed to win the support of a majority of MPs. Cavendish Bentinck never failed to remind repealers of this fact, and the repealers themselves were conscious that they depended substantially on the Liberals remaining in government. A Conservative administration could reverse the position they had secured, with the supporters of the CD acts able to catch the ear of the government in the same way as the repealers had just done.

It is certainly unwise to assume, as historians have sometimes done, that the battle against the Contagious Diseases Acts had been won in 1883. Judith Walkowitz, for example, argues that 'With the suspension of the compulsory examination clauses of the acts, their entire abolition seemed inevitable . . . . By and large . . . the opposition to repeal had been battered down, apparently exhausted by the petitions and "disgusting literature" that regularly appeared at their offices and on their breakfast tables.'[68] This assumes too much. The opposition to repeal, from both public health reformers and libertines, was very far from battered down.

Indeed, the very persistence of the reformers may have stiffened resistance. The effort expended by the repealers in lobbying, petitioning and circularizing is impressive. But it cannot be automatically assumed that it was effective. Espousing the cause of prostitutes was a deeply unrespectable thing to do. Even the most evangelical had to preface their speeches to the House of Commons with an apology to members for raising so unsavoury a topic. Before addressing the Commons about prostitution in 1857, for example, Gladstone apologized for doing so: 'I feel it very painful to be obliged to refer to such a subject, and I assure the House I do so with great reluctance; but we are forced into the discussion, and it cannot be avoided.'[69] For most respectable people the topic was unmentionable. John Bright was incensed when his wife and daughters received repeal propaganda through the post: though the veteran Liberal MP supported repeal, he was appalled when his family was sent what he regarded as offensive literature. After expressing his anger in a notable outburst at the Friends' Yearly Meeting in 1875, he was lost to the repeal movement.

Given the respectable abhorrence of discussing sexual matters, it is unlikely that respectable Victorians welcomed having these unsavoury issues forced before them. It is equally likely that those who did so aroused resentment, suspicion and opposition. Repeal propaganda may have turned respectable opinion against the campaign as much as towards it. It is certainly clear that in the early and middle 1880s the struggle against the Contagious Diseases Acts, and the double standard they embodied, was very far from won. It is also clear that in the years immediately following the victory of February 1883, the abolitionists struggled to make any further headway, while the extensionists behaved as though time was on their side. Cavendish Bentinck and his supporters looked on 1883 as a temporary reverse, with considerable justification. They could, and did, look to a reinstitution of state-regulated prostitution in the mid-1880s. Their defeat, and the consequent domination of late Victorian sexual politics by the moral puritans, was due to a wholly unexpected series of developments only loosely related to the deadlocked campaign to repeal the Contagious Diseases Acts.

INTERNATIONAL DIMENSIONS

Moral puritans of the 1870s had focused almost exclusively on the Contagious Diseases Acts. The tragi-comedy of Mr Charley's attempts to raise the age limit for permissible female sexuality had done little to make other issues seem worth pursuing. Indeed, the problems which Mr Charley had encountered in raising the age of consent from twelve to fourteen underlined the deep resistance of the legislators to changing the laws regarding sexual behaviour. This resistance horrified and demoralized the campaigners against prostitution, particularly when it was reinforced by the Liberal election defeat of 1874. The shock of the election result deflated Josephine Butler and her colleagues. She herself noted sadly that 'our cause seemed during this year to have touched its lowest level in regard to public notice'.[70] Failure at home, however, forced the repealers to look more closely at developments abroad.

The politics of prostitution were becoming international. A Public Health Congress held in Vienna in 1874 had called, logically, for a world-wide extension of regulation to control venereal disease. The oppositionists held a meeting at York in July and decided to meet the threat by extending their crusade to Europe. In December, Josephine Butler left for the Continent to carry out this decision. She found that while the tide of resistance to state prostitution was ebbing in Britain, it was gaining strength on the continent of Europe and in America. It found allies in the Roman Catholic Church, with Cardinal Manning joining the British campaign in January 1875, and Italy proved particularly fertile ground.

Support for the anti-regulation movement was sufficiently strong to encourage a new international organization. The British, Continental and General Federation for the Abolition of the Government Regulation of Prostitution was therefore founded in London in March 1875. The federation was firmly British led – Stansfeld was the first president, H.J. Wilson honorary treasurer, and Josephine Butler honorary secretary, but its council was composed of people of different nationalities. Garibaldi accepted nomination to the council. Josephine Butler's speeches of winter 1874–5, spoken in French, were published in French and German in autumn 1875, and her growing reputation on the Continent did much to bolster her reputation at home.

The anti-regulation movement was strong enough to hold an international conference of 500 delegates in 1877, which Josephine Butler hailed as 'the first International Congress . . . upon a question involving neither territorial aggrandisement, dynastic ambition, nor commercial development'.[71] The annual conference became an increasingly international affair, and was held in Liège in 1879. The decision to hold the conference in Europe was a sign of the growing importance of the struggle on the Continent, emphasized by events in France.

On 23 and 24 January 1879, the editor of the Parisian paper the *Lanterne* was prosecuted by the French government for printing a series of letters alleging abuses by the police, particularly the Police des Moeurs (vice police). Though the editor was sentenced to three months imprisonment and a 2,000 franc fine, the revelations of arbitrary and illegal behaviour by the French police led to the setting up of a committee of inquiry by the minister of the interior. This inquiry officially absolved the police from the charges made against them, but not before damaging evidence of police corruption had come to light. The reputation of the vice police suffered particularly badly. M Yves Guyot, who became leader of the French section of the federation, provided damning testimony to a committee of the Municipal Council of Paris on corruption in the vice police. Despite fresh legal action by the French government to defend the reputation of the state, the prefect of police, M Gigot, and leading members of his staff were forced to retire, and when this did not satisfy public opinion the minister of the interior, M Marcere, had to resign.

The resignations were still not enough, and the *Lanterne* continued its attacks on police corruption to great acclaim. In March 1880 Yves Guyot was elected member of the Municipal Council of Paris for the quartier de Notre Dame, and in the same year M Victor Schoelcher, French senator, accepted the position of honorary president of the Association for Abolition in France.[72] These developments were not merely of importance for the French. The growth of the campaign on the Continent continued to enhance Josephine Butler's reputation. Her command of events across the Channel had placed Josephine Butler in a unique position as an authority on European vice. That position was soon to be fully exploited, but not because of the anti–regulation campaign. That campaign, a minority issue on the Continent as in Britain, was overtaken by a much more sensational issue, the issue of white slavery.

Josephine Butler did not discover the white slavery scandal. The credit for uncovering an international trade in coerced women goes to one Alfred Dyer, an ascetic Quaker. Dyer ran a private publishing house with his brother at Amen Corner in Paternoster Row, London. The Dyer brothers poured out a stream of pamphlets preaching their obsessive fear of sex. But though Dyer was a puritan fanatic, where prostitution was concerned he was a courageous and thorough investigator, willing to probe into social spheres as remote to respectable Victorians as darkest Africa. An international trade in enslaved women was a topic which respectable opinion was happy not to know about. It was a subject where the wall of silence was profoundly impenetrable, and could only be broken by a blunt instrument wielded with fanatical force. That instrument was Alfred Dyer.

Dyer's crusade against white slavery began one Sunday late in 1879. On leaving the Friends' Meeting House in Clerkenwell, he was told by one of his friends that a young English girl was forcibly confined in a licensed house of prostitution in Brussels, and was contemplating suicide as the only means of escape. Dyer discovered that the source of the story was a respectable Englishman who had visited the brothel some weeks earlier, but who had left the girl to her fate fearing that any attempt to help her escape would lead to publicity harmful to his reputation.

Dyer followed up the story, tracing and interviewing the man. He discovered a classic example of white slavery. The woman's story was that she had been courted in London by a man of gentlemanly appearance, who promised her marriage if she would accompany him to Brussels for that purpose. Inexperienced and only nineteen years old, living away from her parents, she accepted the offer. On their arrival in Calais she was introduced to another man who spoke only French. Her 'lover' told her that he had spent all his money and would have to pawn his watch to return to England to obtain more. He would meet her in Brussels, to which city his friend would take her. She protested, but was forced on to a train with the stranger. He took her to Brussels, a city speaking a language of which she was wholly ignorant, and she was taken to a brothel where she was imprisoned and placed on the official register under a false name. She was then violated and found herself, in Dyer's words, 'as much a slave as was ever any negro upon Virginian soil'.[73]

This case was tragically typical of a phenomenon deeply rooted in the world of Victorian respectability. The decoying of respectable lower-class women into white slavery was the product of the sheltered upbringing of respectable womanhood and the lack of conventional career opportunities. The taboos which prevented sex being discussed in any form, and the restricted social intercourse of such women, kept the respectable woman wholly ignorant of the dangers involved in liaisons such as the one described. A French detective commented in 1859 that 'The education of English girls is usually of such a strictly prudish character that, in their simplicity and ignorance of the world, they offer themselves the easiest prey imaginable.'[74]

The gullibility of girls who were lured abroad with promises of marriage may seem absurd. It was, however, the logical outcome of an education system which taught that girls were slavishly subordinate to men and existed to supply their needs in the manner described by the Revd Hardy in the best-selling Victorian manual *Manners Maketh Man*: 'Sweetness is to woman what sugar is to fruit. It is her first business to be happy – a sunbeam in the house, making others happy . . . . Girls and women are willing enough to be agreeable to men if they do not happen to stand to them in relation of father, brother or husband; but it is not every woman who remembers that her raison d'etre is to give out pleasure to all as fire gives out heat.'[75]

The saccharine romanticism of this view provided no guidance to young women about the dangers they faced of sexual exploitation. It was all too easy to trap and enslave girls who, travelling abroad for the first time to secure an offer of marriage or a position of governess – a second major source of victims for white slavery – found themselves locked in a continental brothel ruled by violence. Pastor Borel of Geneva, in the first pamphlet to be published on European trade, commented: 'To what state of moral putrefaction must eight or twelve unhappy creatures sink, who are shut out from the world, without occupation, without interest in anything, cloistered in the twilight of filthy and infected rooms, reduced to a social intercourse consisting only of quarrels or obscene conversations; and at the first appearance of revolt are beaten like slaves by the mistress or her bully?'[76]

It was into this secret world of abduction, violence and deceit that Alfred Dyer marched in 1879. Dyer was a member of a committee of moralists based in the

City of London, dedicated to helping the campaign against the Contagious Diseases Acts. The chair was Benjamin Scott, chamberlain of the City, a quiet but effective campaigner whose contribution to the developing moral purity lobby was crucial. The committee provided Dyer with contacts in Brussels, one of whom, Pastor Leonard Anet, discovered the woman. Her name was Ellen Newland, and because she was under twenty-one she had been registered with the vice police under a false birth certificate, obtained from Somerset House. She had been unable to protest, the whole affair being conducted in French, a language she did not understand. Ellen Newland was returned home, where Dyer interviewed her on Boxing Day 1879.

Anet, however, had now discovered an even more scandalous story. On 16 October, an English lieutenant of artillery had been walking along the Rue des Sables in Brussels when he came across a crowd surrounding a young woman who was weeping hysterically. Dressed in a negligee, she declared that she had just escaped from a brothel at 28 Rue St Laurent, where she was being held against her will. The madam of the brothel was being restrained by the crowd from using force to recapture her. The lieutenant conducted her to a local hotel, where she was lodged.

That evening a man named Henri Perpete arrived at the hotel claiming to be from the police. He invited the woman, named Ada Higgleton, to accompany him to the police station to make a statement. Trusting the gentlemanly appearance of Perpete, Higgleton went with him – straight back to a brothel. Anet wrote bitterly, 'This individual proved to be another of the gentlemanly agents of the houses of prostitution, and took the girl straight off and securely lodged her in another house of infamy, where she now is'.[77] Dyer published this story in letters to the press in January 1880.

This led to a furious correspondence, notably from Edward Lenaers, chief of the Brussels morals police, who insisted that all women entering brothels in the city did so of their own free will, and had to state this formally to a police officer in their own language. This statement was backed by Thomas Jeffes, consular official in the British Legation in Brussels. Jeffes wrote, 'I can confidently assure the parents of all really virtuous girls that there is no fear whatever of finding their children in the same position as the girls referred to in Mr Dyer's letter.'[78]

Dyer and his group now concluded that they were not dealing simply with white slavers, but with collusion, conscious or unconscious, by the British and Belgian authorities. The belief that they were fighting a state conspiracy to promote vice was never far from the minds of moral campaigners in this period. Too often government and state officials acted in ways which confirmed their worst suspicions. Official reaction to the Dyer investigation into white slavery in Belgium was a case in point.

Dyer was disgusted by the apparent official indifference to his efforts. He therefore decided to visit Belgium and take direct action. Believing that his group alone took white slavery seriously, he set out for Brussels in February 1880. He took with him for support Charles Gillett, a fellow Quaker who was one of the most influential members of the Society of Friends. The two aimed to visit brothels and rescue Englishwomen detained against their will. Despite their noble aims, there is something absurdly comic about two strait-laced Quakers visiting Belgian brothels posing as men in need of women. Nevertheless, although it is easy to poke fun at Dyer and Gillett, there was very little humour in the situation they confronted.

Dyer and Gillett were advised that their crusade risked serious assault from the pimps, but undeterred, on an evening in early March, the two men, with a Belgian friend, entered a brothel on the Rue St Laurent. Dyer entered a room devoted to drinking, and ordered wine, which, as a total abstainer, he did not drink. Curious though this must have seemed to the proprietors, the action allowed him to get into conversation with an Englishwoman, Louisa Bond, who was overjoyed when Dyer offered to release her. But the plot foundered on an insuperable obstacle – Louisa had no street clothes.

Dyer and Gillett retired to consider. They decided to try the official channels, the Belgians having stated that they would support any Englishwoman who wanted to leave a brothel. The following morning they visited the procureur du roi, the official responsible for the morals police, in company with Alexis Splingard, a Brussels attorney. The men demanded Louisa Bond's release. The procureur referred them to the commissioner of police. The deputy commissioner agreed only to visit the brothel – alone – and interview the woman. He returned to report that Louisa now claimed to be completely happy and did not want to leave.

Dyer, Gillett and Splingard decided that such official obstruction left only frontal attack. They went back to the brothel and demanded to see Louisa. The madam refused, while the pimp threatened the men with violence. Beating a retreat, the three crusaders decided to call on the might of the British Empire. They visited the British legation and demanded to see the minister, Sir Saville Lumley. Lumley refused to see the party, and referred them to the vice-consul. Dyer was furious and warned 'If this young woman is the victim of violence, the responsibility will rest with the British Minister.' Lumley took the threat seriously enough to see the Belgian minister of justice, who ordered an inquiry into Louisa Bond's case. Dyer meanwhile was battering on any official door he could find. He visited the consular office, which he found closed. He found out where the vice-consul lived, and visited him at home. The vice-consul referred him to the pro-consul, Thomas Jeffes. Jeffes had already stated publicly that he was satisfied with the assurances given him by the Belgian authorities, and simply asked for an official investigation by the Belgians.

This took the form of a visit to the brothel by three Belgian officials to interview Louisa Bond. They were unaccompanied by any representative of the British embassy. Not surprisingly, they reported that Louisa now said that she no longer wished to leave the brothel. Dyer bitterly commented that 'this judicial farce was afterwards quoted by the Procureur du Roi in the *Journal de Bruxelles* as a conclusive refutation of my statement that the young woman was detained in a life of infamy against her will'.[79]

Dyer and Gillett had little success elsewhere. They discovered other English girls who wanted to escape, but these were too frightened by the appearance of strangers to take the offer of freedom. In the prostitutes' ward of the Hôpital St

Pierre they discovered Adeline Tanner, who was being detained against her will. Dyer complained to Thomas Jeffes. Jeffes tried to avoid a scandal by arranging for her to be sent home. However, the Belgian authorities decided to make an example of her to other troublesome prostitutes. She was prosecuted for making a false statement to the police, namely that being only nineteen she had signed the police register in a false name to appear to be over twenty-one. For this offence, she was sentenced to two weeks' imprisonment.

Dyer was outraged. He wrote, 'When this victim, at what was called her trial . . . tried to explain through the interpreter how she had been betrayed and deceived, the person occupying the seat of judge, spoke up in English and stopped her with the coarse remark that she need not come there to tell a parcel of lies, for no one would believe her. The British Pro-Consul [Jeffes] wrote to the girl's sister shortly after this pretended trial, and said that if it had not been for the false statements made in English newspapers (alluding to my letter to the *Daily News*, *Standard* and other journals) the girl would probably not have been sentenced to imprisonment.'[80]

Dyer's cup of bitterness was now overflowing. Although his organization managed to secure Adeline Tanner's return to England on her release, he was only too well aware that he had failed to secure the release of other women, that Adeline Tanner's prison sentence had been a very clear sign to other Englishwomen in the licensed brothels that the state was on the side of the brothel keepers. The bitterest pill was the wholly unsatisfactory behaviour of the consular officials. It is clear that the British officials simply dismissed Dyer and Gillett as troublesome fanatics, preferring to believe the statements of their Belgian counterparts. They certainly did not believe it was their job to seek to defend the interests of prostitutes.

Dyer retreated home, having lost the first battle. He was determined he would not lose the war. With his supporters he formed the London Committee for the Exposure and Suppression of the Traffic in English Girls for the Purposes of Continental Prostitution. The chair was again Benjamin Scott, chamberlain of the City of London. On 5 August 1880, the committee prepared for Earl Granville, the foreign secretary, a memorial which 'respectfully sheweth that there exists a system of systematic abduction, to Brussels and elsewhere on the Continent, of girls who are British subjects, for purposes of prostitution, and that the girls so abducted, being sold to the keepers of licensed houses of infamy, are generally confined and detained against their will in such houses'.[81] The memorial described, accurately and cogently, the system of white slavery.

The memorialists could not know that the Foreign Office was already aware of their concerns and had cautiously begun to probe the situation. Granville had, on 3 June, suggested to the Home Office that they send a police officer to Brussels to inquire into the state of affairs there. The Home Office sent a detective, Chief Inspector Greenham of the Metropolitan Police, whose subsequent report was a bland endorsement of the Belgian position that there was no cause for concern. Events overtook the report almost before the ink was dry.

When she heard about Dyer's fruitless campaign, Josephine Butler was inflamed, and decided to make a frontal attack. On 1 May 1880, she published an

THE

EUROPEAN SLAVE TRADE

IN

ENGLISH GIRLS.

A NARRATIVE OF FACTS.

BY

ALFRED S. DYER.

To which is appended a copy of a Memorial to Earl Granville, Secretary of State for Foreign Affairs, from the Committee formed in London for the purpose of exposing and suppressing the existing traffic in English, Scotch and Irish girls for the purpose of foreign prostitution.

LONDON :

DYER BROTHERS, AMEN CORNER,

PATERNOSTER ROW.

———

1880.

Title page of Alfred Dyer's pioneering exposé of the White Slave Trade, published in 1880 emotional attack on white slavery in the abolitionist journal *The Shield*, focusing on the most highly charged issue of all – child prostitution. The key allegation, Butler later recalled, was that

> In certain of the infamous houses in Brussels there are immured little children, English girls of from ten to fourteen years of age, who have been stolen, kidnapped, betrayed, carried off from English country villages by every artifice, and sold to these human shambles. The presence of these children is unknown to the ordinary visitors; it is secretly known only to the wealthy men who are able to pay large sums of money for the sacrifice of these innocents.[82]

The allegations caused outrage in Belgium. They were sweeping and emotional charges which Butler did not substantiate with any degree of authority. The Belgian authorities furiously demanded, via the procureur-général, that Butler repeat her allegations on oath before a magistrate. Josephine Butler and her advisors hesitated before complying, for the main evidence of child prostitution was hearsay from Alexis Splingard. Fortunately for Josephine Butler's reputation, campaigners had obtained evidence of police corruption involving collusion with the Brussels brothel owners. When Josephine Butler swore her deposition in November 1880 she was able to forward with it a sworn statement by a Belgian detective alleging police corruption. This immediately diverted attention from her allegations of child prostitution, and placed the abolitionist campaigners in the ascendancy. They decided to act. The international organization mounted a private prosecution in Brussels against brothel owners for prostituting girls under the age of twenty-one.

On 13 December in the main courthouse in Brussels, twelve brothel keepers were put on trial. Alexis Splingard led the prosecution. Four Englishwomen gave testimony, including Adeline Tanner and Ellen Newland, Dyer's original witness. The women spoke effectively, detailing the supply techniques, the physical and psychological tortures used to break the spirits of the women, and the prison-like conditions operating in the brothels. All the accused were convicted.

The Brussels Municipal Council then decided to hold an inquiry into the allegations of police complicity. Among the witnesses called was the editor of *La Nationale*, a major Belgian newspaper. This man wrote to Josephine Butler to ask her for evidence. Mrs Butler sent him her deposition. *La Nationale* published it in full, quoting names. It caused a sensation. The first print run of the paper, 60,000 copies, sold out and a second edition of 20,000 was sold on the following day. The editorial office was besieged by supporters and opponents, the brothel interest issued death threats, and the police threatened to take action for libel. Fortunately for Josephine Butler, the action was directed at the editor and not the author of the story, and she emerged bruised but unscathed.

In the event, the outcome was satisfactory. Lenaers, chief of the morals police in Brussels, and his second-in-command, Schroeder, instituted a prosecution for libel against *La Nationale*. This forced the issue, which was raised in the Belgian parliament amid public outrage. Lenaers and Schroeder were then dismissed. The abolitionists were triumphant – a fact which was duly noted in Whitehall.

Josephine Butler and her friends had clearly discovered an indefensible situation which rendered Chief Inspector Greenham's report irrelevant. Quietly, and without acknowledging any debt to the moral reform lobby, the Foreign Office decided to make its own investigation.

POLITICAL RESPONSES

In the winter of 1880–81, Whitehall appeared to be indifferent to the heated battles which had taken place in Belgium. The reform lobby gained the impression that government was unmoved by the Belgian revelations. Behind the scenes, however, the Foreign Office was anything but complacent. Granville had been unconvinced by the Greenham report. The foreign secretary decided a second investigation was needed – this time conducted by an official separate from the British police force, one who could not be accused of collusion with the continental police. In early December 1880, a conscientious barrister from the Middle Temple, Thomas Snagge, was quietly despatched to Belgium.

Snagge was thorough, incisive and skilled at cross-examination. Chosen for his full command of French, he was able to break down the prevarication and evasions of the morals police. By the time he returned, he had no doubt at all that British women were being held against their will in continental brothels. He had seen for himself that in the brothels of Brussels the street doors were so constructed that they could not be opened from within except by a key which was kept by the proprietor. He was struck by the distinctive dresses which the girls wore – a gaudy uniform which in the event of escape would make them easily recognizable. And he noted that, *pace* the Tanner case, 'Girls with false birth certificates live in constant terror. The threat of imprisonment is continually held over them.'[83]

Above all, he confirmed without reservation that the conditions in the brothels he investigated amounted to slavery. He commented 'Young English girls are a form of merchandise to be acquired by industry and disposed of at market prices per package . . . . From the point of view of the brothel keepers the girls form a costly portion of their stock-in-trade; they are like stock in a farm, kept in good condition more or less, and prevented from straying or escaping.'[84] Snagge called for legislative action to end the traffic.

Once this secret report had been studied in Whitehall, there could be no doubt left among the officials responsible that white slavery was not a figment of the fevered imagination of religious zealots or feminist campaigners. White slavery was a real scandal of major proportions, which cried out for government action.

The government, however, made little public show of concern. In the spring of 1881 Benjamin Scott wrote to Granville, deploring the fact that the Belgian convictions had failed to 'arouse the attention of public men in promoting action in this country'. He received no more than a formal acknowledgement. This seemed to Josephine Butler yet further proof of official indifference. In May 1881 she drew up a petition calling for 'Such changes . . . in the English laws as should make it impossible for any young girl or child in our country to be deprived of her liberty by fraud or force, and to be kept in a foreign city in bondage for the basest purposes'.[85] She secured a thousand signatures to the petition, and presented it in person to Earl Granville, threatening to besiege his office until he saw her. She found she was pushing at an open door. Granville received her, and told her that the government was preparing to move for a select committee of the House of Lords to investigate white slavery.

The select committee was a historic development. It was the first official acknowledgement that white slavery was an issue, and it has been hailed by historians as an outcome of Josephine Butler's personal efforts.[86] This is too simple. Granville had had the Snagge report for four months. He had called for the Greenham report over a year earlier. The matter had been a live issue in the Foreign Office, and in the embassies concerned, for the whole of that time. The politicians did not need Scott and Butler to tell them the problem existed, and they were not prepared to acknowledge the role of the troublesome and un-respectable anti-vice lobby in bringing it to their notice, particularly when so prominent a role had been played by the extremist Alfred Dyer. Moreover, to confront white slavery, the government would be confronting the powerful male interests which supported legalized prostitution in its various forms. The government preferred to move more slowly than Scott, Butler and their allies wished in so delicate a matter.

Thus when the Earl of Dalhousie moved 'that a Select Committee be appointed to inquire into the state of the law relative to the protection of young girls from Artifices to induce them to lead a corrupt life, and into the means of amending the same', he took great care not to mention the anti-vice lobby. In presenting his case to the House of Lords on 30 May 1881, he was careful to argue as if the matter had arisen simply from concerns emanating from official channels. He referred to a letter of 1874 from a prostitute in Antwerp which had arrived at Scotland Yard pleading for help. He mentioned a case of 1876 where an English chaplain had stepped in to save English girls decoyed to Antwerp. He reported the trial of a white slaver, Klyber, in Antwerp in 1879, and the request of the foreign secretary to the Home Office of 3 June 1880 that a police investigation take place, as if the two were connected. Stating that the police investigator (unnamed) had discovered only two girls who had been decoyed away under false pretences – one of whom was clearly Adeline Tanner – he moved without comment on to the Snagge inquiry.

Dalhousie noted that 'In September . . . the Secretary of State for Foreign Affairs suggested to the Home Secretary that an inquiry should be made by some person unconnected either with the police or with any government office'.[87] He dwelt at length on the Snagge report, Snagge being named and commended. Dalhousie concluded by commenting, 'It is no longer a matter of doubt that for many years past large numbers of English girls, some of whom were perfectly innocent, have been annually exported to supply the demand of foreign brothels . . . there can be no doubt that, during the last 15 years, many Englishwomen have, against their will, endured a life of worse than living death, from which there was no escape, within the walls of a foreign brothel'.[88]

Dalhousie was right to argue that the existence of the white slave traffic was now indisputable. However, when he concluded by saying, 'I feel sure that your

Lordships will be of the opinion that no time should be lost in putting a stop to a practice . . . which surpassed all that they knew of any other trade in human beings', he was distinctly hopeful. Dalhousie was, after all, only proposing a select committee, not a change in the law. Moreover, the House of Lords knew that Dalhousie was not a Cabinet minister, and that while he spoke for the government white slavery was not a major priority for Gladstone's ministry.

The terms of reference of the select committee deliberately did not restrict it to investigating only white slavery, and it took as its remit prostitution in all its forms. The committee's thorough investigation into the subject was impressive, and played a particularly important role in bringing to public attention the issue of child prostitution. Dalhousie commented when moving the continuation of the committee, on 28 February 1882, that witnesses believed this had increased in the previous four years. The 1871 Royal Commission had endorsed concern at child prostitution, and recommended raising the age of consent to fourteen, but without thorough investigation. The Lords select committee attempted a serious investigation.

On 10 July 1882 the committee published its recommendations for changes in the law, along lines which the anti-vice lobby could only welcome. The chief proposals were that attempts to solicit or to procure English girls to leave their homes in order to enter foreign brothels (regardless of the girls' willingness) should be treated as a serious misdemeanour; that the age of consent should be raised to sixteen; that the age up to which it should be illegal to abduct for purposes of carnal knowledge should be raised to twenty-one; that it should be illegal for anyone to receive into their home a girl under the age of sixteen for the purposes of her having sexual intercourse with any particular man; and that a police magistrate should be empowered to issue a general warrant of entry to a police officer for purposes of searching a house where the officer had reason to believe a girl under sixteen was being harboured for the purposes of sexual intercourse.

However welcome the proposals were to the anti-vice lobby, they were only proposals. Legislation to embody them into law was likely to be difficult to secure, for Gladstone's second ministry was preoccupied with Irish and imperial affairs, and did not regard prostitution as a major issue. Nevertheless, a bill was drafted on the lines suggested by the select committee, and on 31 May 1883, the Earl of Rosebery introduced the Criminal Law Amendment Bill into the Lords for its first reading. Rosebery was a rising star in the Liberal Party, who would be brought into the Cabinet as lord privy seal two years later. In 1883 he was well set on the upward path, and his introduction of the bill was a sign that it had support at the highest level; not, however, an overwhelming degree of support. When the bill came back for its crucial second reading, it was the much less important Earl of Dalhousie who took on the unenviable task of steering the bill towards the statute book. The fortunes of this bill were to confirm the worst fears of the anti-vice lobby about the strength of the opposition facing them.

On 18 June Dalhousie moved the second reading. It was chiefly directed against children being employed as prostitutes. The age of consent was to be raised from thirteen to sixteen to secure this end. Furthermore, anyone procuring a woman to become a prostitute was to be guilty of a misdemeanour. The bill also gave increased police powers, *inter alia* to take action against brothels, and to prevent loitering and solicitation by women.

The bill was immediately subjected to a savage attack by the Earl of Milltown, notably because in his view it would be used for purposes of extortion. The fear that under-age women would blackmail men by offering sexual favours was one which would surface again and again as the most plausible reason for opposing the bill. The bill had vocal support, with the lord chancellor, the archbishop of York, and the bishop of Peterborough all speaking in favour. However, Lord Salisbury, the leader of the Conservative Party, endorsed Milltown's fear of extortion and sounded an ominous note – namely, that the government was in danger of listening to well-organized pressure groups and not the majority public opinion. 'The public opinion represented by eager petitioners is not the kind of public opinion which must execute the Act you are now asked to pass. You must pass an act which the public opinion represented by 12 average jurymen . . . is prepared to enforce.'[89] Salisbury called for another select committee. This was a bad omen. Salisbury was Conservative leader, and had been a member of the original select committee. With the Liberals unsure of their own supporters on a morality issue, Dalhousie could have little doubt that he faced a long uphill struggle.

If he had any hopes that this could be avoided, they were ended on 29 June when the bill came for its report stage. Opposition was considerable. Earl Fitzgerald was obstructive, moving that the the proposed new age of consent should be lowered from sixteen to fourteen, and Salisbury backed the amendment. The Liberals won the votes on each challenge, securing the passage of the bill on the third reading on 5 July by the comfortable margin of 82 (118 to 36), but then decided to cancel and reconsider. Their reasoning appears to have been that the roughness of the ride in the Lords, which had its own select committee report to back the initiative, suggested an even rougher ride in the Commons. The government decided on a tactical retreat. Dalhousie was sent off to redraft the bill.

He returned with a redrafted bill in the spring of 1884. He moved the second reading by calling attention to the fact that 'it was a much milder measure than the Bill which passed through their Lordships' house last year'.[90] 'The Government', he said, 'in framing the measure, had endeavoured not to go beyond public opinion, . . . it had been their object to keep their efforts within such limits as would be approved by public opinion as represented by 12 jurymen.'[91] The attempt to win over Lord Salisbury was clear. It was a successful tactic. Salisbury was more conciliatory and, when Milltown attempted to lower the age of consent from sixteen to fourteen, Salisbury spoke against him. Milltown attempted to refer the bill to a select committee, but this time he could not gain support. The bill passed its second and third readings. The long effort to secure a measure of protection for young women had cleared its hurdles in the Lords, and now passed to the Commons. However, before the bill left the Lords, the obscure Lord Oranmore and Brown sounded an ominous note. As *Hansard* reported: 'He believed that there were very few of their Lordships who had not,

'A Sketch from Nature', Punch, *12 July 1884. This cartoon is typical of the mild humour of the time before the storm broke*

when young men, been guilty of immorality. He hoped that they would pause before passing a clause within the range of which their sons might come . . . the more they attempted to prevent the indulgence of natural passion, the more they would face unnatural crime.'[92] His lordship had unwittingly expressed precisely the endorsement of vice which aroused the morality lobby to greatest fury.

The bill now began an embattled passage through the Commons. On 3 July 1884 the home secretary, Sir William Harcourt, moved the formality of the first reading. But for the second time, the hopes of the campaigners were dashed. On 10 July the Liberals dropped the bill without debate. With the government struggling to cope with business at the end of a fifth parliamentary session, it seemed there were more important demands on Commons time than white slavery.

And so the Earl Dalhousie was forced to bring a Criminal Law Amendment Bill to the House of Lords for a third time in the spring of 1885. His lordship must have felt akin to Sisyphus. In moving the second reading for a third time, on 13 April 1885, Dalhousie spoke in distinctly apologetic terms: 'The Government were anxious in a matter of this kind not to legislate in advance of public opinion . . . .The Bill differed from its predecessors inasmuch as it did not go so far . . . . For instance, the age at which protection was extended . . . was reduced from 16 to 15 years . . . this change was made in the hope of securing unanimity in the passing of the Bill.'[93]

Milltown immediately attacked the conduct of the government in persisting with the bill, arguing that 'it was perfectly notorious that in the present state of Business in the other House there was not the smallest chance of the measure being carried into law this year'. He criticized the Liberals for making 'this House a kind of theatre to exhibit a solemn farce year after year'.[94] His fellow lords may have agreed with him, but none could be bothered to argue. The bill, in a stronger form, had already passed the Lords, and the third attempt went through to the Commons with relatively little trouble.

Dalhousie had done his job, and Harcourt now had to carry the burden through the lobbies of the House of Commons. He took up the challenge on 22 May 1885, the day before Whitsun, when most members had already adjourned for the holiday. Harcourt moved the second reading in the briefest possible terms. Cavendish Bentinck objected that the House was inquorate, forty members not being in attendance. The House was counted, and it was shown that exactly the minimum number of forty members were in the chamber. The debate continued in an atmosphere of profound lethargy and bad-tempered, end-of-term bickering.

The end came at ten minutes to seven, when the Speaker decided to put an end to a remarkably pointless proceeding. Cavendish Bentinck was showing every sign of being prepared to filibuster the measure. He had the last word in typical style, ranting that he 'protested against the measure being brought on that afternoon, when there was a scant attendance, and when the Law Officers of the Government were absent. He did not know what the principle of the Bill was. It had so many principles, and you could not select the principal principle.' As Cavendish Bentinck drew breath to continue his rant, the Speaker decided enough was enough, and closed the debate.[95]

Watching the debate from the strangers' gallery, Benjamin Scott was profoundly disillusioned. Gladstone's ministry clearly had little interest in the bill, and was simply going through the motions. There was no groundswell of opinion among MPs which might force them to change their mind. Milltown's comment on government business had struck a chord. Political observers knew perfectly well that Gladstone's government was in trouble, and that far more important issues than white slavery were occupying ministerial minds. Scott left the chamber deeply depressed. Unless a drastic change of course could be wrought, the chances of securing a measure against the white slave trade were negligible. It was even possible that the Contagious Diseases Acts could be re-activated, especially if the Conservatives won the election which was now clearly on the horizon. He was well aware that most opinion formers were profoundly indifferent, as exemplified by the scant attention paid to the parliamentary debates by the press.

However, there was one significant exception, the Liberal-inclined *Pall Mall Gazette*. On the day after the debate, the editor, W.T. Stead, had commented in his 'Occasional Notes' that

Once more we regret to see that the protection of our young girls has been sacrificed to the loquacity of our legislators. Mr Bentinck talked out the Criminal Law Amendment Act yesterday, and we fear that the chances of proceeding with this measure before the General Election are the slightest . . . . A House of Commons in which women were represented would not display such indifference to a question which is really one of life or death to immense numbers of young girls.[96]

Scott noted these comments. W.T. Stead was a rare voice supporting the anti-vice campaign. Scott shrewdly concluded that Stead was a figure capable of bolstering the failing morality lobby. Benjamin Scott made it his business to meet W.T. Stead.

FOUR

The Maiden Tribute of Modern Babylon

AN EXPLOSION OF FEELING

As the passage of the Criminal Law Amendment Bill ground to a halt at Whitsun 1885, Benjamin Scott and his colleagues faced a bleak future. The anti-vice lobby had created a formidable pressure group, forcing Gladstone's Liberal government to suspend the Contagious Diseases Acts. But further than this it could not go. From the high point of Stansfeld's victory in 1883 it had fallen back, unable to sustain the pressure of that spring, and wholly unable to convince a majority of MPs. Indeed, Cavendish Bentinck made it his business to write to the *Pall Mall Gazette* arguing that a majority of members were opposed to the anti-vice crusade, and that a vote to reintroduce the Contagious Diseases Acts would probably succeed. He wrote: 'If the vote of the House of Commons, even now, could be taken by ballot upon the main issues, the repealers of the Acts would not carry a hundred members with them, notwithstanding all the assistance which they might derive from the efforts of ignorant, superstitious and fanatical agitators.' [97]

Cavendish Bentinck was probably right. The Contagious Diseases Acts had provoked a most formidable agitation. The campaigners had published 520 books and pamphlets on prostitution and venereal disease. Between 1870 and 1885 they produced 17,367 petitions against the acts, with 2,606,429 signatures, and held over 900 public meetings. [98]

Yet all the campaign had achieved was to embed itself on the margins of the Liberal Party, without achieving any purchase on the Conservative Party at all. The campaigners were painfully aware that the potential for a parliamentary cross-party alliance to reinstate the CD acts was considerable. And if there was any doubt about the lack of interest among parliamentarians on morality issues, the great difficulties legislators had experienced in securing the passage of the Criminal Law Amendment Bill told its own story. With Gladstone's second ministry beset with difficulties that summer, the chances of the bill passing the Commons seemed increasingly slight. Politicians looked forward to a general election. The anti-vice crusade, unable to demonstrate any degree of popular appeal with the electorate, did not.

Far from the abolition of the CD acts being 'inevitable', as historians such as Judith Walkowitz have suggested, the opponents of the CD acts had every reason to look forward with trepidation at that time. They knew that the politics of conventional pressure-group activity had stalled, as the fate of the Criminal Law Amendment Bill showed. But if conventional pressure-group politics had failed, the resources of the lobby were not yet exhausted. One common pattern among reforming campaigns shows that when conventional petitioning and arguing fails, campaigners can be so driven by anger that they resort to more extreme measures to achieve what they desire. In the summer of 1885, the anti-vice campaign was forced into this route. The paradox for historians is that the events of that summer have usually been interpreted as stemming from the strength of the campaign. This is not so. They stemmed from weakness.

This is shown clearly by the Jeffries affair, the final straw which drove the moral reformers to rebellion. Mrs Mary Jeffries ran a series of discreet and very expensive brothels in Church Street (now Old Church Street), Chelsea, catering for the rich and powerful. According to Charles Terrot, Mrs Jeffries had four brothels, numbers 125, 127, 129 and 155, in the street itself, a flogging house called Rose Cottage in Hampstead, a house of assorted perversions near the Gray's Inn Road, and a white slave clearing house for the Continent on the river near Kew Gardens. Exceedingly wealthy, she avoided the attentions of the police by extensive bribery. In April 1882, however, the detective Jeremiah Minahan was appointed an inspector in T division of the Metropolitan Police, the division covering Chelsea. Minahan was a narrow and puritanical figure in the Dyer and Scott mould. An honest man with principles, he worked with unwavering zeal and a remarkable lack of tact.

Shortly after taking up his duties, Minahan noted many comings and goings of men using hansom cabs to houses owned by Mrs Jeffries. Mrs Jeffries made his acquaintance and, to Minahan's disgust, offered him gold coin. Minahan reported the attempted bribe to his superior, Superintendent Fisher. Fisher warned him to be careful of what he was saying and took no action. The other officers, Minahan later testified, made him a laughing-stock for refusing the bribe. Minahan was used to being an outcast. He had been transferred from his previous division for making allegations against his brother officers that were officially considered to be unfounded.

Minahan bided his time, spending the next six months compiling a dossier of the comings and goings at Mrs Jeffries' houses. In April 1883 he submitted an official report in writing, keeping a notebook with the results of his surveillance in his desk drawer. Minahan's dossier outraged Scotland Yard. He was demoted to the rank of sergeant, ostensibly for making unfounded charges against police officers. Minahan protested, appealing over the heads of the police chiefs to the home secretary. The member for Chelsea (Charles Dilke) took up the case and communicated with the home secretary, Sir William Harcourt. Harcourt replied that 'After the most careful enquiry by the Assistant Commissioner and District Superintendent into a series of charges which he (Minahan) brought against the Superintendent of the Division and other offficers, all of which were proved to be without foundation, I see no ground to review the decision of the

Commissioners.' Harcourt quoted this letter, written on 28 January 1884, in replying to Stuart's questions about the Jeffries case on 21 May 1885.[99] Minahan resigned from the force in protest, and sent a copy of his investigations to three daily papers. All ignored his document. He then decided to have the paper published privately, and took it to the Dyer brothers.

For the Dyer brothers, the Minahan document was a gift from heaven. Arriving at a time when the Criminal Law Amendment Bill was already encountering stiff opposition, the Minahan document provided apparently solid evidence not only of sexual immorality and white slavery in London, but of collusion by the police to serve the very aristocrats who were opposing the bill in the Lords. Moreover, Minahan was now unemployed, and his detective skills could be turned to good use. Dyer contacted Benjamin Scott, and in March 1884 Minahan was employed by the London Committee for the Suppression of Traffic in English Girls. Minahan's brief was to get evidence on which to base a legal action against Mrs Jeffries.

Neither white slavery nor catering to sexual perversions were illegal under the law as it then stood. Minahan therefore concentrated on discovering evidence that Mrs Jeffries kept a disorderly house. And in this he succeeded. Minahan unearthed several of Mrs Jeffries' former servants who were willing to testify against her. Minahan also took evidence from the neighbours, and compiled an explosive list of clients – including Lord Fife, Lord Douglas Gordon, Lord Lennox, Lord Hailford and, most sensational of all, Edward, Prince of Wales, later King Edward VII. Mrs Jeffries always denied vehemently that His Royal Highness was one of her clients.

By March 1885 the campaigners had enough evidence to mount a prosecution. The magistrates were reluctant to act even on Minahan's now substantial dossier, but Scott's committee applied to Westminster Court under Statute 25 George II, which gave the magistrates no alternative provided that two ratepayers of the parish furnished evidence. With great difficulty, two ratepayers were found who were prepared to testify, and on 25 March a police inspector served Mrs Jeffries with a warrant for her arrest. At the magistrates' court on 10 April, Minahan made his allegations of police collusion with Mrs Jeffries, and in the *Pall Mall Gazette* the following day W.T. Stead argued, 'This alleged encouragement of vice and connivance in bribery on the part of highly-placed oficers of the police must be probed to the bottom'.[100] No such probe occurred.

The trial took place on 5 May 1885 at the Middlesex Sessions as the Queen versus Jeffries. As the Crown now took over the prosecution, they provided the prosecuting counsel. And at this point, the proceedings took a very different course from that which Benjamin Scott's committee had envisaged. The authorities were aware of the possible implications of the case. Powerful men at the highest levels of society were implicated, and though the magistrates had banned the use of names of clients, that of the King of the Belgians had already slipped out in evidence, causing a diplomatic incident.

The events of 5 May were carefully stage-managed to dispose of the Jeffries case as smoothly as possible. As soon as the case opened, Montagu Williams asked Edward Besley, the prosecuting counsel, to retire for a private consultation. When

Williams returned, he told Mrs Jeffries to 'Say you are guilty' – which she promptly did. The *Daily News* reported that the defence was that while there was a technical breach of the law, the prosecution was malevolent. Dyer, sitting in the body of the court, was furious, but helpless. As Mrs Jeffries had pleaded guilty no witnesses would be taken. All the long months of compiling evidence had been circumvented by a clever legal tactic.

Worse was to come. Besley then made a prosecution speech which was in effect a defence both of Mrs Jeffries and her clients. 'The case really resolves itself', he argued, 'into allowing people to assemble together for improper purposes. Undoubtedly they were free from scandal in the ordinary sense of the word.'[101] After this extraordinary statement, it was not surprising that the judge behaved with great leniency. He fined Mrs Jeffries £200 and bound her over to keep the peace for two years. The sentence was itself scandalous. This was an offence for which imprisonment was not uncommon. And if any observer had missed the point, the judge in the trial, P.H. Edlin, underlined it one week later. He presided at the Middlesex Sessions in the trial of a man named Barrett for keeping a brothel. Barrett had no influential friends, and Edlin sentenced him to six months' imprisonment. On 21 May, James Stuart MP tabled the question already referred to in the House of Commons asking the home secretary to set up a committee of the House to investigate the discrepancies in the two sentences and the circumstances attending the dismissal of Minahan from the police force.[102] Harcourt replied that Barrett had previous sentences for warehouse breaking and keeping a brothel and other offences, and this might account for the discrepancies in the sentences. He absolutely refused to have an inquiry into the Minahan case.

Harcourt's words were still fresh in the minds of anti-vice campaigners when Harcourt moved the second Commons reading of the Criminal Law Amendment Bill on the following day, 22 May, in decidedly perfunctory terms. The debate which followed was the farce that has already been described. The following day, MPs dispersed for the Whitsun break.

They did so at a time when the political temperature was beginning to rise dangerously among anti-vice campaigners. Even the mainstream press was beginning to stir uneasily. The Jeffries sentence provoked sharp criticism in the London press, which could normally be relied on to ignore prostitution as an issue unfit for civilized discourse. The *Morning Mail* attacked the sentence as a 'mere mockery of justice', and described the way in which it had been hushed up as 'A disgrace to all concerned'. The *Daily Echo* demanded that the government set up an 'impartial investigation' into Minahan's charges of collusion by the police. The government took no action.

The anti-vice campaigners were beside themselves with rage. Dyer lashed out in the *Sentinel*, arguing that 'The inferences point to a state of moral corruption, heartless cruelty and prostitution of authority, almost sufficient even in this country to goad the industrial classes into revolution . . .'. This was an overstatement, but the clear political dangers, in a country where republicanism was far from dead, were underlined a few days later when the *Sentinel* published an account of a speech by one James B. Wookey.

W.T. Stead as the campaigning editor of the Pall Mall Gazette. *A man of strong principles, he was a steadfast supporter of the anti-vice lobby*

Wookey, an activist in the fundamentalist Gospel Purity Association, had addressed a packed meeting in Luton. His text was 'Corruption in High Places', thundering against 'Male traitors . . . allowed to walk amongst the pure as if there was nothing in their soul and body murdering life of which they need be ashamed . . . .They are oft times found sitting in Parliament making laws by which we have to abide. They have occupied the chief places of justice . . . '.[103]

This was strong meat, but Wookey was merely warming to his theme. Claiming to have seen Minahan's dossier, he told his listeners that among the list of male debauchees were many of the highest rank, ending with the strident punchline that the most eminent name on the list was that of the heir to the throne – Edward, Prince of Wales himself. This caused a sensation among the crowd in the Luton Corn Exchange. When Dyer published the speech in the *Sentinel*, the impact was felt throughout the country. That edition of the paper is said to have sold 200,000 copies.[104]

Feeling among anti-vice campaigners was now running dangerously high. From their point of view, they had fought for a decade and a half against a powerful and hypocritical male political establishment. By the end of May 1885, events had demonstrated to their satisfaction the power of that establishment to frustrate and pervert the law and control the legislature. The Jeffries case, and the fate of the Criminal Law Amendment Bill, seemed almost calculated to prove to the anti-vice lobby that it was powerless either in the courts or Parliament. It was at this point that the elderly Benjamin Scott decided on a course which had the most momentous results. Scott could only see one way to arouse public opinion, and that was to focus on child prostitution, with its overtones of abduction and rape. And to do this, he had only one card to play – W.T. Stead's editorship of the *Pall Mall Gazette*. On 23 May 1885 he went to see Stead at the *Gazette* office and explained the impasse facing the anti-vice campaign. 'All our work', Scott stated, 'will be wasted unless you can rouse public opinion and compel the new government to take up the Bill and pass it into law . . . if you cannot no one else will help us. You might be able to force the Bill through. Will you try?'[105]

Scott had chosen his man well. Stead was the son of a Congregationalist minister, who had been brought up in a house which regarded sin as an ever-present gateway to hell. He had become a Sunday-school teacher with a strong sense of social injustice and, gifted with great literary skills, then joined the *Northern Echo* in Darlington and became its editor. A staunch Liberal, Stead secured national attention over his support of Gladstone in the Eastern Question agitation of 1876, Gladstone complimenting him with the words 'I have read your articles with much admiration of the high public spirit as well as the ability with which they are written'.[106] More importantly from Scott's point of view, Stead was a long-standing supporter of the anti-vice campaign. Although Scott had not met Stead before 23 May 1885, he knew that Stead had personal contact with Josephine Butler and the leaders of the Salvation Army. He had been active in the campaign against the CD acts as early as 1872, when Henry Wilson's wife had met him at the Richmond by-election. From 1876 onward he had begun corresponding with Butler, offering her the support of the *Northern Echo*. In 1879 he became aware of the Salvation Army's work to reclaim sinners in the slums of Darlington, but disapproved of its policy of sending young women into the most violent and dangerous areas. He wrote to the head of the army, General William Booth, to warn of the danger to the health of the local Salvation Army worker, a Miss Clapham. Booth replied on 19 July 1879 that 'We are glad to find that not merely the true character of our work but the desperate self sacrifice it demands is coming to be understood and appreciated. I am sorry to say it is no easy matter suitably to relieve her without entirely overtaxing someone else.'[107] This courteous and reasonable response led to a warm friendship between Stead and the Booth family, of great importance to events in 1885.

In 1880, Stead was offered the deputy editorship of a leading Liberal daily, the *Pall Mall Gazette*, then under the editorship of John Morley. When Morley went off to become Gladstone's secretary of state for Ireland, Stead gained his opportunity to achieve the ambition of which he had written in his diary on taking the appointment, of becoming 'one of the half dozen men in London whose advice is listened to by the rulers of the Empire'.[108] Although Stead was almost ideally suited for the campaign which Scott was planning, initially Stead hesitated. He later wrote of Scott's visit, 'I naturally wanted to try, but every instinct of prejudice and self-preservation restrained me. The subject was tabooed by the press. The very horror of the crime was the chief seat of its persistence.'[109] However, according to Stead's own statement in his defence at the Old Bailey, he did ask Scott what he could do without imperilling his paper. 'Mr Scott said, "Why don't you appoint a committee to investigate the thing and bring it to light?" "Well", I said, "I would think about it. Can you", I asked him, "suggest any help I might get?" He said, well, he had been talking to Mr Bramwell Booth about the matter, and I said I would go down with him and see Mr Bramwell Booth at once.'[110]

In this way, what became known as the 'Secret Commission' came into being. The Salvation Army had been involved in the reclamation of prostitutes since 1884, when the impossibility of saving the souls of street women without saving their bodies had become obvious to William Booth and his family. Appalled by the stories of procuring and abuse which the women told, Booth's son, Bramwell himself, had investigated. He was turned into an activist by interviewing a fourteen-year-old girl who had been picked up off the streets. When Stead and Scott came to see him, he had the evidence ready to hand. Booth produced three girls under sixteen who had been on the streets, one of whom was pregnant though only fourteen years old. Stead was not convinced that the evidence was strong enough, realizing that the allegations of three street girls would carry little weight.

Stead pursued his investigation through both official and unofficial channels. He communicated with Sir E. Henderson, head of the Metropolitan Police, and with the Liberal home secretary, Sir William Harcourt, without success. Stead was acquainted with Howard Vincent, however, through the latter's CID work. Stead asked if innocent girls could be procured for money in brothels in London. 'He said, "Oh! yes." I said to him, "But is it true that if I am well introduced, and I have a five pound note or a ten pound note in my pocket I can go and order a girl to be brought to me in the same way in which a man would go and order a sheep to be brought to him in the market?" I said to him that such a state of facts was enough to "raise hell". He said it did not raise the neighbours. I said, "Well, if I can get to know these facts of my own knowledge – if I can prove that this thing can be done for me it will not raise the neighbours but it will raise all England."'[111]

Even at this point, Stead might have been bent on a conventional journalistic investigation, but a final episode turned him into a crusader. Stead decided to visit Benjamin Waugh, the founder of the National Society for the Prevention of Cruelty to Children. Stead asked Waugh to show him some actual children who had been abused in brothels. Waugh then took him to one of the society's shelters, where he was shown two little girls recently picked up by the society's inspectors. One of them, seven years of age, had been abducted and raped in a fashionable brothel. Her persecutors could not be brought to justice because no magistrate would accept her statement on oath.

The second girl, who was aged four-and-a-half, had been lured into a brothel one evening and had been raped twelve times in succession. Again, because the laws of evidence in Victorian England required a person taking the oath to understand its meaning, her assailants had been discharged from court unconvicted. When the large, bearded figure of the editor approached the girl, she began to scream hysterically, imploring him not to hurt her. Stead broke down with genuine emotion, crying, 'I'll turn my paper into a tub! I'll turn stump orator! I'll damn, and damn, and damn!'[112] After this experience, any chance of objectivity in Stead's investigations vanished.

The campaigning editor was imbued with a particularly sharp sense of urgency because of the imminence of a general election. Gladstone's government had collapsed in the early summer of 1885. The crisis happened on 8 June 1885, when an admendment to the Budget was carried against the government by a majority of 264 to 252, with 76 Liberal MPs abstaining. Gladstone took this as a vote of no confidence, and resigned next day. A general election did not take place immediately, Lord Salisbury deciding to form a minority government. The Conservatives took office on 24 June 1885, in an administration which lasted exactly seven months.

Stead grasped that the formation of a minority government provided a window of opportunity for passing the Criminal Law Amendment Bill. While the parliament remained in session, legislation already in the pipeline could proceed. Once a general election was called, bills not passed would be cancelled and the whole process of getting legislation through the two Houses would have to start from scratch. Hence it was vital to secure the completion of the second and third Commons reading before Salisbury went to the country. Stead knew that the date of the election was unpredictable, but might be only weeks away. He also knew that the Conservatives had no intention of completing the passage of the bill. A sensation would be required to force them to change their minds. Stead set about producing a sensation.

Thus by the time Salisbury entered 10 Downing Street, Stead's so-called Secret Commission was well under way. The Salvation Army was providing much useful information, infiltrating one of its officers into a brothel to pose as a prostitute. The girl survived for ten days before being discovered. She failed, however, to discover evidence of child prostitution. Stead also interviewed a notorious Belgian procurer, Jean Sallecartes, who disputed official contentions that white slavery had ceased in Brussels because of tighter regulations. The Secret Commission compiled an extensive dossier on child prostitution and white slavery, but none conclusive enough, or sensational enough, to be used to force the parliamentary impasse.

Stead decided on a desperate throw. He concluded that the only way to prove that children could be bought and sent into enforced prostitution was to do the deed himself. Josephine Butler came to his assistance. She had discovered an alleged procuress, Rebecca Jarrett, in a refuge for reclaimed women in Winchester, where Butler's husband was now canon at the cathedral. Jarrett claimed that she had herself procured young girls when she was a brothel keeper. She was ideally cast to play the part of procurer for W.T. Stead.

Stead bullied Jarrett into acting as procurer for him: 'I said to her, "But I cannot believe it" . . . . She said, "It is true; I have done it myself:" and I said to her, "If you have done it yourself you deserve to be hanged in this world and damned in the next, and if you want to make some reparation . . . help me try to expose it . . . ." And she said, "How shall I do it?" I said, . . . "You must come and buy girls for me and bring them to me in a brothel, that I may see you can do it . . . ." She demurred, she shrank from it. I was very, very hard upon her. I think I may have done wrong; but when a woman tells you that she has taken young girls at the age of thirteen and beguiled them away . . . administered sleeping potions, and then turned loose her good customer upon them unsuspectingly, a man may be pardoned if he does feel somewhat hot. I insisted; I was as ruthless as death.'

Under this intense pressure, Jarrett caved in and agreed to help Stead. Stead knew that his plan bordered on abduction, and consulted the solicitor of the Association for Enforcing the Laws for the Protection of Women, Shaen, of Shaen and Roscoe.[113] He advised Stead that there could be no crime without a criminal intent, and that to establish that he did not have a criminal intent Stead should tell a public figure of impeccable credentials of his intentions before proceeding. Stead took his advice, and explained his plan to the Archbishop of Canterbury, Benson. Benson disliked the plan, but Stead was implacable.[114]

Stead proceeded. His plan was to purchase a girl of thirteen, have her examined professionally to ensure she was a virgin (standard practice in the brothel trade), introduce her into a London brothel, then send her abroad – to the Salvation Army headquarters in Paris. Rebecca Jarrett was vital to the successful execution of this plan. Unfortunately for Stead, she consented to play the part Stead had designed for her, but not as well as he had planned.

By early June she had made contact with an old friend, Nancy Broughton, from the Marylebone area, and asked her to to seek out likely girls. Eventually she selected a bright, dark-haired girl, Eliza Armstrong, who was given to understand she was going to be a servant. Jarrett claimed that both Nancy Broughton and the mother were told explicitly of the real purpose of the transaction. Stead claimed he taxed Jarrett on this crucial point, claiming in his defence: 'I said to Jarrett, "Now are you quite sure that they understood why you have got this girl?" "Yes", she said, "Because I distinctly told her, and I told Mrs Broughton that I wanted her for a man, and she must be pure, and I gave the mother a sovereign, and I gave Mrs Broughton two, and I have to send the rest of the money to Mrs Broughton after she has been proved pure".' Rebecca bought Eliza new clothes, and when she returned gave the mother the sovereign she had been promised.

Jarrett then took Eliza Armstrong to an apartment in Albany Street, where she met Stead and Mrs Reynolds of the Salvation Army. The party then went to Madame Louise Mourey, of Milton Street, an acknowledged expert in the brothel trade in the proving of virgins. Mourey confirmed that Eliza was a virgin. Jarrett then took Eliza to an accommodation house in Poland Street, followed in a cab by Stead and a man called Sampson Jacques. Jarrett undressed Eliza and prepared her for bed. She tried to chloroform Eliza but was unsuccessful. Eliza was therefore awake when Stead entered the room and locked the door behind him, playing the part of lecher. Eliza cried out and Jarrett 'rescued' her. The party then took Eliza to Dr Heywood Smith in Harley Street, who certified she was still a virgin – Stead did not want his reputation sullied. The girl was then taken to a private hotel for the rest of the night. The pantomime was over.

The next morning Rebecca and Eliza went to Charing Cross to catch a train to France, for as Stead put it in his defence, 'There was another thing to be proved, and that was that the girl who had been so used, and who might have been so abused, could be sent out of the country . . . Mr Booth, having a place at Paris, consented to take her there; and there, so far as I personally was concerned, my responsibility, immediate and direct, ceases.' Jarrett and Eliza stayed in Paris for several days, during which time Jarrett mailed two £1 postal orders to Mrs Broughton as final payment. Eliza Armstrong was then placed in the safe keeping of the Salvation Army, and Rebecca Jarrett went back to Josephine Butler's refuge for fallen women in Winchester.

Neither Jarrett nor the girl had any real idea of the motives for the pantomime in which they had just starred. But they were about to emerge blinking into the glare of a political world they hardly knew existed. W.T. Stead now had the evidence he needed for his most sensational campaign.

THE PASSING OF THE ACT

When W.T. Stead penned the articles which appeared under the heading 'The Maiden Tribute of Modern Babylon' in the week beginning 6 July 1885, he was out to shock. The previous Saturday the *Gazette* had warned squeamish readers to avert their eyes. 'All those who are squeamish, and all those who are prudish, and all those who prefer to live in a fool's paradise of imaginary innocence and purity, selfishly oblivious of the horrible realities which torment those whose lives are passed in the London inferno, will do well not to read the *Pall Mall Gazette* of Monday and the following days', Stead wrote in his editorial. Despite the warning, the middle-class Victorians who read the paper could hardly anticipate that Stead would expose them to the moral sewers of contemporary society. But this he did. Stead observed few of the proprieties of respectable journalism. Driven by a moral fervour which disdained proprieties, Stead presented his audience with a sink of immorality which he compared to the raising of the Campo Stone of Naples, covering a mass of festering corpses. In four long articles that week he revealed in copious detail the world of the brothel trade – the decoying of girls and young women, the traffic with the Continent, the rapes, the brutality suffered by those who tried to escape, the indifference and culpability of the authorities. Stead had no desire to spare the sensibilities of his readers.

Above all, Stead tore into the hypocrisy of the age, comparing the trade in children with the mythical sacrifice of virgins to the half-man, half-bull, Minotaur of classical legend. Stead was not attacking an abuse; he was attacking a society which he regarded as riddled with corruption. He wrote:

> London's lust annually uses up many thousands of women . . . . That may be inevitable . . . but I do ask that those doomed to the houses of ill fame shall not be trapped into it unwillingly . . . . If the daughters of the people must be served up as dainty morsels to the passions of the rich, let them at least attain an age when they can understand the nature of the sacrifice which they are asked to make. And if we must cast maidens . . . nightly into the jaws of vice, let us at least see to it that they consent to their own immolation, and are not unwilling sacrifices procured by force or fraud. That is not too much to ask from the dissolute rich.[115]

This language was markedly overstated. Claiming that 'thousands of women' were being 'literally killed and made away with' was indefensible exaggeration.

THE

PALL MALL GAZETTE

An Evening Newspaper and Review.

No. 6335.—Vol. XLII.   *SATURDAY, JULY* 4, 1885.   *Price One Penny.*

THE NEW TORY PROGRAMME.

LORD SALISBURY'S first speech as Prime Minister is not a bad one so far as it goes, but we doubt whether it will do him or his party much good. If his new Ministry is going to stake the fate of Conservatism at the next General Election on the establishment of the Scotch Kirk the hopes inspired by their recent electoral victories will fade rapidly away. The best thing that a wary Conservative leader could do for the Establishment is to avoid all attempts to make it the battle horse of a political party. If the Church were growing weaker there might be some reason for forcing on a fight, but as by universal confession the Church has of late years lived down and worked down much of the antipathy with which she was formerly regarded, every year gained before the final assault is delivered is a year to the good. Lord SALISBURY, however, has decided otherwise. He insists upon precipitating the State Church battle all along the line, instead of employing his ingenuity in drawing sufficient red herrings across the track to divert the attention of Scotch Radicals from the Kirk. It is a mistake from the point of view both of the party and of the Church, but Lord SALISBURY has made his choice, and he will abide by it.

With the exception of that false step Lord SALISBURY'S speech was not unworthy of the occasion. It is quite inspiriting to see the leaders of the two great parties in the State vieing with each other as to which is the most zealous in the work of Decentralization. Lord SALISBURY condemned, and rightly condemned, the assumption that the Liberals have a monopoly of the question of Local Government Reform. This is a field in which the Conservatives may legitimately assert a natural claim, as well as for their defects as for their virtues. Lord SALISBURY was perfectly correct when he explained the origin of our excessive centralization as follows :—

It was the result of the earnest and patriotic efforts of numbers of well-intentioned and earnest public servants. It was one of those evils which arose automatically. The constant efforts of Departments in London to gather to themselves all the power they could, the greater strength of the cultured forces of the metropolis over the divided, scattered, and comparatively feeble resistance of the provinces, resulted year after year in a concentration of power in this town, and a constant accumulation of duties upon the offices and authorities which this town contains, until at last the administrative offices in London, and still more the parliamentary machine which works them, staggered under the load that is placed upon them. They are unable to perform the duties which they have ambitiously concentrated upon themselves, and the body politic suffers by an ambition which you cannot blame, but which yet it is our duty to remedy and terminate.

It is the natural rôle of the Conservative party to defend local liberties—and local abuses. In France the dominant Republicans insist upon maintaining the centralization condemned by the wisest of their number, because it enables the intelligence of Paris to lay down the law to the reactionary rurals. And we may depend upon it that sooner or later a similar line of cleavage will appear in English politics. The Reformer, impatient of delay, will insist upon strengthening the power of central Departments over the local authorities, while the Conservative will have a congenial task in insisting that localities shall be allowed to make fools of themselves if they please without interference from the central power. At present Liberals are all throwing up their caps for decentralization, local self-government, and a more or less veiled Home Rule. But as soon as these excellent ideas get translated into facts, they will discover that there is a good deal more to be said in favour of centralization than it is at present the fashion to admit.

The great problem before the nation is how to define the limitations which must be placed on the authority of local authorities by the Imperial Legislature. At present neither party has any idea of how to define the functions of the central power on the one hand or of the local governing authority on the other, and the only thing which is quite certain is that both parties will find much to try their faith in decentralization if once they take it up in earnest.

How will the Nonconformists, for instance, relish the establishment and endowment of the Roman Catholic religion in most of the schools of Ireland, which is one of the most obvious corollaries of any system of Home Rule ? It is to be feared that they will like it as little as English Churchmen will like the equally inevitable disestablishment of the Scotch Kirk which would result from allowing the Scotch to manage Scotch affairs in accordance with Scotch ideas. But whether we are Whigs or Tories we have got to make up our minds what are the limits within which the discretion of local authority should be absolute, and then resolutely to determine not to interfere although the local authorities act in a fashion which we know to be most opposed to sound principle and common sense. On the whole the Conservatives have the most to gain by giving the local authorities a free hand, but Conservatives have so little faith in their own strength, and so abject a dread of allowing any representative body to do anything that might interfere with some of their superstitions or their interests, that it is more than doubtful whether they will have the nerve to take a resolute stand in favour of a principle which, logically applied, might, for instance, enable the corporation of Birmingham to become the sole landlord of the town.

THE Criminal Law Amendment Bill, it is said, will be abandoned, owing to the late period of the session and the difficulty of finding time to carry it through the Commons. That measure deals with a subject the importance of which has been admitted by both parties, and is based upon the urgent recommendation of a House of Lords Committee of which the Marquis of Salisbury was a prominent member. It has thrice been passed through the House of Lords, and now for the third time it is threatened with extinction in the House of Commons. The public, it is said, is not interested in the subject, and the bill, therefore, may safely be abandoned. That we are told is the calculation in high quarters. But if Ministers think of allowing the bill to drop because the public is not keenly alive to its importance, it is necessary to open the eyes of the public, in order that a measure the urgency of which has been repeatedly admitted may pass into law this session. We have, therefore, determined, with a full sense of the responsibility attaching to such a publication, to publish the report of a Special and Secret Commission of Inquiry which we appointed to examine into the whole subject. It is a long, detailed report, dealing with those phases of sexual criminality which the Criminal Law Amendment Bill was framed to repress. Nothing but the most imperious sense of public duty would justify its publication. But as we are assured on every hand, on the best authority, that without its publication the bill will be abandoned for the third time, we dare not face the responsibility of its suppression. We shall, therefore, begin its publication on Monday, and continue to publish it *de die in diem* until the whole infernal narrative is complete. But although we are thus compelled, in the public interest, to publish the case for the bill, or rather for those portions of it which are universally admitted to be necessary, we have no desire to inflict upon unwilling eyes the ghastly story of the criminal developments of modern vice. Therefore we say quite frankly to-day that all those who are squeamish, and all those who are prudish, and all those who prefer to live in a fools' paradise of imaginary innocence and purity, selfishly oblivious of the horrible realities which torment those whose lives are passed in the London Inferno, will do well not to read the *Pall Mall Gazette* of Monday and the three following days. The story of an actual pilgrimage into a real hell is not pleasant reading, and is not meant to be. It is, however, an authentic record of unimpeachable facts, "abominable, unutterable, and worse than fables yet have feigned or fear conceived." But it is true, and its publication is necessary.

Stead's warning to readers on the front page of the Pall Mall Gazette, *4 July 1885*

Stead was riding a wave of near-hysterical emotion not untypical of the extremist elements of the morality lobby. He attacked parents who neglected 'even to warn their children of the existence of dangers', the press that 'recoils in pious horror from the duty of shedding a light into dark places', and the Church which had failed to take action. Most startlingly, he castigated the rich. Stead railed: 'In all the annals of crime can there be found a more shameful abuse of the power of wealth than that by which . . . princes and dukes and ministers and judges and the rich of all classes are purchasing for damnation . . . the as yet uncorrupted daughters of the poor?' The morality lobby had long blamed plutocratic lust for the tolerance of prostitution, but this was the first time the readers of a respectable Liberal paper had been exposed to such an offensive. The accusation that the rich were abusing the daughters of the poor seemed to many respectable Victorians more shocking than the immorality Stead was attacking. But it echoed the attacks on the rich made by the infant socialist movement, and undoubtedly added to the impact Stead's articles made in Whitehall.

At the heart of his exposé stood the Eliza story. Stead may be credited with inventing a new form of journalistic device – the 'faction' story, part-fact, part-fiction, all sensational. It was an unfortunate development, particularly as in his haste to create an impact Stead was cavalier with the facts. He described the outline of the story accurately, but he made serious errors. He described Broughton's one-room home in Charles Street as a brothel – patently untrue. He portrayed Mrs Armstrong as a woman 'indifferent to anything but drink', who pressed her daughter on the procuress, whereas Rebecca Jarrett had told him the mother had refused to let her go for twenty-four hours. Damagingly, he wrote that the father was at home 'drunk and indifferent', a statement which was to be held against him in court.

Most seriously, he did not reveal that he himself was the purchaser, nor that he was employing the procuress, and laid himself open to the charge of manipulation by declaring, 'I can personally vouch for the absolute accuracy of every fact in the narrative'. To give credence to his sensational stories, he offered to reveal his evidence to any of six named figures in return for an undertaking that the information would not be used to bring charges against those involved in the procuring of the girl, whom he called 'Lily'. The six included the Archbishop of Canterbury, Cardinal Manning, and the Earl of Shaftesbury.

The sensation produced by Stead's articles was all that he could have wished. Demand was so great that by the end of the first day the paper had developed a soaring street price. Respectability, however, was shocked. W.H. Smith, the biggest chain of newsagents in the country, refused to sell it. Stead's office improvised a chain of impromptu newsvendors, using the large crowd cramming the area outside the offices of the *Gazette* in Northumberland Street and the Salvation Army network. Reputedly George Bernard Shaw, who was one of the paper's reviewers, threw himself into the campaign and set up a post in the Strand to sell copies to passers-by. Michael Holroyd records that Shaw wrote to Stead stating that 'I am quite willing to take as many quires of the paper as I can carry and sell them'.[116]

Respectable people were appalled. The *St James Gazette* attacked Stead on the Tuesday with the comment that 'Newspaper sensationalism had been carried very far before this present week of grace, but yesterday it reached its utmost possible point in the production of the vilest parcel of obscenity that has ever yet issued from the public press . . . . The man who invented the "sensation" . . . has flung all decency aside, openly dealing with the worst abominations in the plainest and foulest language.' For the *St James Gazette*, the offence was clearly not the abduction and rape of young girls, but raising the topic in public. Cavendish Bentinck took the same view. At Question Time that Tuesday, he asked the home secretary 'Whether his attention had been directed to publications relating to objectionable subjects . . . printed and circulated throughout the metropolis by . . . the *Pall Mall Gazette*; and whether any means exist of subjecting the authors and publishers of these publications to criminal proceedings.'[117] The Conservative home secretary, Sir Richard Cross, responded non-committally that 'I am advised that the publication of any obscene writing is a misdemeanour, that the publication can be dealt with by indictment in the usual way. The question whether any particular writing is obscene is one for a jury to decide.'[118] Cross was treading very carefully, aware a major scandal was developing.

Stead was not deterred. He followed up his revelations of Monday on Tuesday 7 July with a detailed description of the seduction system used by the brothels, including a vivid personal interview with a girl who escaped from a Pimlico brothel to the Salvation Army headquarters. By Wednesday the situation around Stead's offices in central London was beginning to pose a serious threat to public order. The City of London solicitor had arrested twelve newsboys selling the *Gazette* on an obscenity charge. The Lord Mayor of London, presiding at the Mansion House, dismissed the charge. Stead, he thought, had been influenced by 'high and honourable views'. The crowd outside the Northumberland Street office was so massive it spilled over into the Strand, bringing traffic to a halt. Whether from sheer frustration at not getting hold of the paper, or because they were hired by the brothel interest to smash up Stead's office (as the purity lobby later alleged), a riot broke out. Stead's office staff had to manhandle desks and cabinets against the outer doors to avoid being overwhelmed.

Stead knew his campaign was alarming the authorities, and that the government was considering prosecuting him. On 8 July he challenged the government on the front page to prosecute him. 'Mrs Jeffries pleaded guilty in order to save her noble and Royal patrons from exposure. There would be no such abrupt termination to any proceedings that might be commenced against us . . . . We await the commencement of those talked of proceedings with a composure that most certainly is not shared by those whom . . . we should be compelled to expose in the witness box.' The Home Office took Stead's threat seriously. Cross could not take the risk of putting so emotionally unstable a man in a court from which he could reach a national and international audience with allegations which could well implicate the highest in the land. The Cabinet decided the only way to stop Stead wreaking untold damage was to proceed as rapidly as possible with the Criminal Law Amendment Bill. The following day, 9 July, Cross rose in the Commons to move the second reading adjourned at Whitsun.

He did not, of course, refer to the storm centred on the offices of the *Pall Mall Gazette*, but discussed the bill purely in terms of the parliamentary debate. He argued with less than complete honesty that 'The whole subject is thoroughly ripe for legislation . . . . We have not only put the Government star upon it, but, as hon and right hon gentlemen will see, we have taken the earliest opportunity of bringing the question before the House.' Cross concluded a distinctly short speech by stating, 'There is a great amount of public opinion in its support. From what I found at the Home Office, I do not believe that public opinion would be satisfied unless the Bill is not only read a second time, but even passed, it might be with some alterations, but at all events passed into law.'[119] This somewhat breathless statement suggests a politician concerned that he might not succeed in his endeavour.

The subsequent debate was not distinguished. Henry Broadhurst praised Stead, though not by name, holding that 'the man who held up to scorn the existing hideous state of things deserved well of the nation'.[120] Samuel Morley 'knew enough of the editor of that paper to be satisfied that he was utterly incapable of publishing the statements in question for any other than a pure motive'.[121] Mr Wharton shrewdly pointed out that Cross had, when merely Mr Assheton Cross, supported an amendment to lower the age of consent from a proposed fourteen to thirteen, and so it was inconsistent for him now to support this bill, which raised it to fifteen. But the opponents of the bill were losing the battle, and even Cavendish Bentinck confined himself to a minor procedural intervention. The attorney-general wound up by arguing that 'If one thing had been established, it was that there had been for some time, and to a large extent, a disgusting trade in young girls . . . and that alone was sufficient ground for legislation.'[122] And with this, the bill was sent to committee.

In the weeks before the committee debate, with the attorney-general's department slaving over the clauses of an increasingly complex piece of legislation, Stead and his allies maintained intense public pressure. Interest in the campaign had spread abroad, with American papers reproducing the 'Maiden Tribute'. The articles were published in French, German and Portuguese.[123] Stead had finished the series on 10 July with a sweeping attack on police corruption and complicity in the operations of the white slavers. The campaign then took off across the nation with a series of massive public meetings, notably in Manchester, Sheffield, Leeds, Portsmouth and Newcastle upon Tyne.

Stead skilfully kept the political atmosphere at fever pitch. He persuaded a committee of influential men, including Samuel Morley, the Archbishop of Canterbury, the Cardinal Archbishop of Westminster (Cardinal Manning) and the Bishop of London, to examine the evidence contained in his articles. At the end of July they reported that 'without guaranteeing the accuracy of every particular, we are satisfied that, taken as a whole, the statements in the *Pall Mall Gazette* on this question are substantially true'.

Meanwhile, the Salvation Army was using its extensive network of centres across the nation to collect a huge petition in support of the bill. In seventeen days 393,000 signatures were collected, which when made into a huge scroll measured two and a half miles long. On the day the committee debate on the bill was due to take place, 30 July, hundreds of Salvation Army officers marched in procession with the petition from the Clapton HQ to Westminster. A fifty-strong brass band led the way, one hundred and fifty life guards accompanied the petition, and four white horses drew the carriage on which it rested. When it arrived at Westminster, Professor Stuart presented it to the Commons.

The major debate on the bill took place against the background of this intense agitation. Cross, opening the debate, left no doubt about the determination of the government to push the bill through to the statute book. Cross emphasized that 'We shall go on with the consideration of the measure from day to day until the Committee is closed. This is a question which has stirred England from one end to the other . . . . The feeling has gone abroad that the purity of their households and the honour of their daughters has been and is liable to be violated, and they have made up their minds that this shall no longer be the case.'[124]

This statement was an extraordinary back-handed tribute to the political effectiveness of Stead and his supporters. The leading politicians of both parties were nevertheless at pains to deny that the passage of the bill was dictated by the furore stirred up by the *Pall Mall Gazette*. Sir William Harcourt, Gladstone's home secretary, denied the 'suggestion that this Bill was the off-spring of a sudden panic due to recent occurrences. This is not so. This bill was framed three years ago . . . .'[125] Sir William did not explain why the bill had taken three years to arrive at the committee stage of the House of Commons, having failed twice to pass its second reading.

Cavendish Bentinck was nearer the mark in taking Harcourt to task.

To the statement of the right hon Gentleman opposite [Sir William Harcourt] denying that they were asked to legislate under the influence of panic, he desired to give the most absolute contradiction . . . the late Home Secretary had been guilty of grave official negligence in not bringing the Bill on at an earlier period of the session, when it could have received a discussion which was at present impossible. But for the publications to which reference had been made, he did not believe that the House would have been so full as it was on the present occasion.[126]

Cavendish Bentinck's points were well made. To bring on a major bill at so late a stage in the session, when both holidays and a general election were pending, was bad political practice, particularly for a minority government. And the contrast between the fullness of the House now, and its emptiness at Whitsun, told its own story.

But Cavendish Bentinck could no longer make any difference. He and those who felt like him had lost the battle. Faced with the intensity of the campaign outside the Commons, both the Conservative and Liberal front benches were determined that the Criminal Law Amendment Bill would pass, and in a form that would satisfy the most implacable member of the purity lobby. The committee debate was rigorous and thorough. The House was in no mood to tolerate deviations, and when the member for Stockport, Mr Hopwood, moved an amendment to send the bill back for more investigation, he could not find a seconder. Equally significantly, when Henry Labouchere and Cavendish Bentinck attempted a wrecking amendment to raise the age of consent to twenty-one, the House voted against them 221 to 2.

It was clear that MPs no longer wished to stall the Criminal Law Amendment Bill. The bill passed the committee stage and the second reading, went through the third reading on 6 and 7 August, passed the Lords finally on 10 August, and received the royal assent on 14 August. In less than two months, the Criminal Law Amendment Bill had been rescued from almost certain oblivion and made the law of the land. When W.T. Stead claimed the credit for this transformation, he was undoubtedly justified. He had achieved the success which had eluded campaigners for raising the age of consent for a decade and a half. By any standard, it was a remarkable result.

The legislation known as the Criminal Law Amendment Act of 1885, officially entitled 'An Act to make provision for the Protection of Women and Girls, the suppression of brothels, and other purposes' (48 and 49 Victoria, Chapter 69), was comprehensive. The act contained clauses against procuration, particularly by threats, fraud, or administering drugs, and defilement of girls under thirteen years of age; raised the age of consent to sixteen; punished householders allowing sex with under-age girls; banned the abduction of girls under eighteen for the purposes of sex, and similarly made unlawful the detention of any woman or girl against her will with intent to have carnal knowledge; gave justices of the peace the power to issue warrants to any person searching for a missing female conferring the right to search a suspected place; conferred the power on a court to remove a girl under sixteen from her legal guardians if they condoned her seduction; and provided for summary proceedings against brothels. It also contained, as Clause 11, Labouchere's notorious catch–all measure against male homosexuality, which will be discussed later.

The act as passed was a complete victory for the anti–vice crusade. While the crusade had yet to achieve victory over the Contagious Diseases Acts, it had made the decisive breakthrough in its struggle to regulate morality in Britain. As far as legislation and official politics was concerned, the purity campaign was now firmly in the ascendant. It was from this point onward that puritanism dominated the sexual politics of Victorian Britain.

That this was so is largely the achievement of one man and one press campaign. It is true that W.T. Stead and 'The Maiden Tribute of Modern Babylon' could not have succeeded without the work of others, notably Benjamin Scott, Bramwell Booth and Josephine Butler. But it was the explosive contribution of the campaigning editor which was decisive. Stead was clearly emotionally unstable, and his tactics were highly questionable. To this day, opinion on the man is split between strong supporters and equally strong critics. But however much Stead can be criticized for bullying, scheming and manipulating, the judgement of the *British Medical Journal*, made at the time, still has weight. The editor wrote:

Of one thing we feel certain, and that is that a great end will be served by this exposure, undertaken as we feel assured it was, with intense sincerity, and with an overruling hatred and fierce anger of practices which have too long secretly prevailed in our midst, and have too long passed unscathed by public indignation. Desperate diseases need strong remedies. A cancer such as this, which is eating away the vital morality of whole classes of society, spreading wildly, ravaging the unprotected classes, calls for the knife. It has been applied publicly, red hot, and with an unsparing hand.[127]

From 14 August 1885, the law protected children and young girls against abduction and forced prostitution. Those men whose tastes ran to sex with immature females, particularly virgins, could no longer do so with impunity. And whatever may be said about W.T. Stead's methods in securing the passage of the act, no government has ever attempted to repeal its essential clauses. The anti-vice crusade had crossed its Rubicon in August 1885. Its victory would resound for years to come.

FIVE

The Puritan Triumph

THE EMERGENCE OF NATIONAL VIGILANCE

The passage of the Criminal Law Amendment Act was the watershed in the development of the anti-vice agitation in late Victorian Britain. The campaigners were, however, deeply cynical about the will of the authorities to enforce the provisions of the act, and determined to mount a sustained effort to prevent it becoming a dead letter. Accordingly the morality lobby resolved to sustain the momentum of the 'Maiden Tribute' campaign by setting up a permanent initiative, and were planning to do so even before the act had completed its passage into law.

The leaders of the campaign decided to establish an organized anti-vice lobby. This was to be launched at a conference on 21 August, to be followed immediately by a public demonstration to build and develop public support. The conference was to take place in St James' Hall, London, and the demonstration in Hyde Park the following day. The moral purity lobby hoped to consolidate the very wide coalition which had supported the Maiden Tribute campaign. Stead in particular had been impressed by the willingness of socialists and working-class leaders such as the trade union MP Henry Broadhurst to back his efforts. In the first of the Maiden Tribute articles Stead had proclaimed 'The future belongs to the combined forces of socialism and democracy'[128] and he was able to convince his co-workers for the moment to take this line.

This wider movement temporarily included the infant socialist groups. Fabian intellectuals such as Shaw and William Morris backed the crusade, albeit with many reservations. Morris was deeply worried that the campaign would stimulate a puritanical revival.[129] The socialists also had reservations about the dangers of a purely moral campaign diverting attention from their emphasis on the socioeconomic causes of prostitution and sexual exploitation. Stead quoted the Fabians as considering sexual exploitation as but one 'result of the exploitation of man by man which is the curse of modern society'.[130] Nevertheless, the socialists threw in their lot with the moralists for a time. The small Marxist Social Democratic Federation, though its paper *Justice*, also backed the campaign, as did the working-class radical paper *Reynolds News*. None of this support was to survive Stead's sensational trial later in the year.

In the August of 1885, however, the moral purity lobby had enormous working-class support in London, and made strenuous attempts to capitalize on it. The great demonstration held in Hyde Park on 22 August was hugely successful. The *Pall Mall Gazette* estimated attendance at between 100,000 and 150,000,[131] but the number was uncountable: the paper stated that some estimates claimed the attendance was a quarter of a million. At all events, the *Gazette* stated, 'there has been no such gathering of Londoners since the Hyde Park railings went down in 1867' (during the demonstrations for the second Reform Bill).

It was an especially impressive show of strength since the event had only been planned since 1 August. Observers noted the large numbers of working-class men and women in the crowd, the *Daily News* calling it 'essentially a working men and women's demonstration'. A particularly striking vignette was provided by members of the Women's Trades Union who were employees of the Army Clothing Establishments. Led by Henrietta Mueller their detachment marched into the park followed by a wagon full of young girls dressed in white, flying a banner proclaiming 'Innocents will they be slaughtered'. In the park itself, since it was impossible to assemble all the huge crowd to focus on one platform, no less than twelve platforms were provided, each with speakers addressing the people as they surged past. Ten columns had converged on the park, the East End and Pimlico contingents via enemy territory, the clubland of Belgravia and the West End. It was all in all an impressive indication of the impact of the Maiden Tribute campaign on the working-class population of London.

Yet the demonstration was not the start of a broad popular alliance, despite Stead's hopes. The day before the demonstration, Friday 21 August, a highly successful meeting had been held in the St James' Hall to form a continuing initiative to back up the Criminal Law Amendment Act. Seven resolutions were passed unanimously, the most important being that moved by James Stansfeld. This stated 'That this conference recommend the formation of a National Vigilance Association of men and women for the enforcement and improvement of the laws for the repression of criminal vice and public immorality'.[132] The puritans, by moral outrage, furious campaigning, and sheer good fortune, had secured a legislative triumph. They were determined never to let go of the initiative, and the formation of a National Vigilance Association was designed to ensure that they would not.

But the National Vigilance Association was not interested in a broad radical alliance against upper-class vice and the economic forces blamed by the socialists for forcing women to prostitution. It focused on pornography, popular entertainments and campaigns for further legislation to clear the streets of visible vice. Many working-class people, both male and female, came to regard it as another effort by middle-class reformers to control their few available pleasures, and organized working-class support drifted away. Within a year the overriding working-class concern shifted to unemployment. There was massive unrest in London, culminating in violent clashes with the police on 7 February 1886 in Trafalgar Square, and 21 February 1886 in Hyde Park. The Marxist Social Democratic Federation had supplied two representatives to the St James' Hall conference; it lost interest, becoming fully occupied with organizing the unemployed. On 13 November 1887 a police decision to ban a demonstration on unemployment led to the extreme violence, known as 'Bloody Sunday', in which two people died. Against this background the interest of socialists and trade unions in the anti-vice campaign ceased to exist, and the anti-vice campaign reciprocated by losing interest in the working classes.

The intellectuals around the Fabian Society also withdrew their support. Shaw and his fellow socialists came to regard Stead's tactics as deeply questionable. Shaw in particular detested the narrow puritanism of the campaign and, after failing in a conscious effort to convert Stead to his view that economic exploitation was the root of prostitution, withdrew from writing for the *Pall Mall Gazette* to concentrate on writing plays. He put his theory about economics and prostitution in the play *Mrs Warren's Profession*. Most Fabians, though by no means all, followed Shaw's lead, and Stead personally never lost interest in Labour (but not socialist) affairs. He was to become a valued ally of Annie Besant during the famous Bryant and May matchgirls strike of 1888. But for the most part, socialists and anti-vice campaigners went separate ways.

So too, surprisingly, did Josephine Butler and her closest supporters. It is paradoxical but unquestionable that Josephine Butler found little place for herself in the movement which she had done so much to bring about. Butler was a John Stuart Mill Liberal, passionately concerned for individual rights, the rights of women, and above all the rights of female prostitutes. As such she had a clear philosophical perspective about the need to protect liberty against arbitrary action by the state, and this had been the basis of her opposition to the Contagious Diseases Acts.

Her role in the repeal campaign has been well documented; her activities in defence of individual liberty are less well known. She had helped form an association to this end in 1871 called the National Vigilance Association for the Defence of Personal Rights. From 1881 on, the association had produced a journal, whose motto was 'The price of liberty is eternal vigilance'. Josephine Butler was deeply unhappy at the puritan indifference to individual liberty, while the Personal Rights Association was furious when, in August 1885, the puritans stole its title for their new organization. In an editorial entitled 'Our Name', it complained: 'The new Association which has just been formed, with branches all over the country, for the purpose of enforcing the provisions of the Criminal Law Amendment Act has, very unnecessarily we think, "filched from us our good name", and, without enriching itself, for another would have done just as well, has put us in a position of considerable inconvenience.' The editorial concluded: 'With the aims of the new society, the repression of criminal vice, especially where the very young are the victims, we heartily sympathise; but it is quite possible that methods of doing this may be adopted which we could not approve.'

The Personal Rights Association had good grounds for its fears. Joseph Edmondson and Henry Wilson had in 1875 drawn up a scheme to outlaw fornication – and had been vigorously resisted by Josephine Butler.[133] The Rescue Society (founded by Lord Shaftesbury to rescue prostitutes) had in its 1880 report argued that 'prostitution should be completely suppressed and houses of ill fame utterly rooted out'.[134] More worryingly still for civil libertarians, the veteran purity campaigner Ellice Hopkins had in 1880 sponsored the Industrial Schools Amendment Act. This had denied the right of custody of children under the age

Josephine Butler, leader of the Great Crusade, photographed in later life by Elliott & Fry

of sixteen if they were living in a brothel.[135] With this background, personal rights campaigners had good cause to fear the new National Vigilance Association.

But Josephine Butler and her views were no longer influential in the anti-vice campaign. It was the voices of Stead, Edmondson, Wilson, Hopkins and their like that would dictate the course of events from now on. Josphine Butler retired to the sidelines after 15 years of sustained campaigning, worn out and increasingly disillusioned by the ruthless onward march of the hard-liners in the vigilance campaign. She had helped Stead secure the Maiden Tribute victory, only to see the victory exploited to create an initiative whose indifference to personal rights she could not endorse. Moreover, she realized that her ability to influence and restrain Stead and his co-workers was minimal. She was deeply disturbed by the events which followed the Maiden Tribute campaign, particularly the imprisonment of Rebecca Jarrett in the famous trial of the Secret Commission in the autumn of 1885. Indeed, as the events of that autumn ground onward, it was increasingly clear that there was no room for Josephine Butler and her fellow libertarians in the movement they had done so much to create.

THE MAIDEN TRIBUTE UNDERMINED

The Hyde Park demonstration on 22 August marked the high point of popular support for the anti-vice campaign. Even as the crowds surged through the park, however, feeling had begun to turn against the puritans. Stead and his Secret Commission had cut corners to secure their sensation. Their methods were now being used against them, in ways that would lead Stead to become hero-martyr to the moral campaigners, and a dangerously irresponsible figure to others.

The 'Lily' story of the purchase of a child had become controversial. In writing up the Maiden Tribute campaign, Stead had used Rebecca Jarrett and the child she had procured for him to point up the argument about child prostitution. This was a vital factor in creating the enormous popular impact that the campaign had achieved, but the tale now backfired. Stead appears to have assumed that once the purchase of the girl had been achieved, the family of the child would simply disappear into the teeming slums into which he had so briefly delved. This assumption was wrong.

Rebecca Jarrett had only dealt with Eliza's mother, giving her to believe that she wanted Eliza merely to go into service – or so the mother later claimed. The titular father, Charles Armstrong, known locally as 'Basher' from his habitual violence, was not consulted. When he returned home that night, and found the girl gone, there was a violent argument, during which Armstrong assaulted his wife. Mr Armstrong had discovered that his wife did not know who had taken his step-daughter, or where she had gone, and did not have a forwarding address. The neighbours in the tight-knit slum community of Charles Street, Marylebone, joined in the row, taking Armstrong's side.

Mrs Armstrong went off to the local pub, the Marquis of Anglesey, and got so drunk that the police arrested her. It was Derby day (3 June) and the coincidence of the arrest and the date of the race marked the occasion clearly in the minds of the inhabitants of Charles Street. Mrs Armstrong now experienced severe community pressure. This pressure was temporarily relieved when a letter arrived from Rebecca Jarrett in Winchester to Nancy Broughton, the go-between, claiming that Eliza was with her in Winchester and happy. This became public knowledge because one Jane Farrer, an inhabitant of the street, read it to Nancy Broughton, who was illiterate.

And there matters stood until the first week of July, when the Maiden Tribute articles appeared. The inhabitants of Charles Street were not slow to make comparisons between Eliza and 'Lily'. Both girls were the same age. They had disappeared on the same day – 3 June – and both had been taken on school outings to Richmond and Epping Forest. Lily's mother was characterized as a drunken woman. Furthermore, the 'brothel keeper' who had introduced the procuress to the mother had been paid two sovereigns. Nancy Broughton had been paid money by Rebecca in the presence of Jane Farrer, though she claimed it was only one sovereign and was payment for past debts. She also denied she was a brothel keeper – a valid point. This cut little ice in Charles Street. Charles Armstrong found himself penned in his own house by crowds of neighbours chanting 'Gazette! Gazette!'

These events caused a bitter row between Mrs Armstrong and Nancy Broughton. Feeling that attack was the best form of defence, Mrs Armstrong accused Mrs Broughton before a crowd of neighbours of being 'a drunken brothel keeper', and selling her child for £5. More importantly, the day after she had read Stead's article in the *Gazette*, Mrs Armstrong applied to the Marylebone magistrates' court for help. Crying bitterly, she stated that Eliza's employer had promised to write regularly but in a month she had not heard a word. The court instructed the police to investigate.

At this point, the issue began to surface in the press. *Lloyd's Weekly London News* picked up the story through a court reporter, and ran it on 12 July under the heading 'A Mother Seeking Her Lost Child'. It appeared a commonplace lost child story. *Lloyd's* did not immediately follow up the story. Police Inspector Borner had questioned Mrs Armstrong and Mrs Broughton, then took a train to Winchester to check the address on Rebecca Jarrett's letter. He was directed to Josephine Butler, who refused to give him any information and directed him to Bramwell Booth. Borner returned to London and visited Booth. Booth claimed not to know precisely where Eliza was but informed the officer that she was well, and promised to investigate her whereabouts and pass the address on to Assistant Commissioner Monro at Scotland Yard, with whom he was acquainted. Borner drew the conclusion that the matter was out of his hands, and made plans to go on holiday. The police told Mrs Armstrong that Eliza was well 'and that she had better let the matter drop'. This was passed to the *Lloyd's* reporter following the case, and the story appeared to die.

Mrs Armstrong, however, had gained an important ally, one Edward Thomas of the London Female and Preventive Reformatory Institute. He was in court on a different case the day Mrs Armstrong appeared before the magistrates. He knew Rebecca Jarrett, believed her to be a liar, and advised Mrs Armstrong to attend the opening hearing of the committee of investigation into the Maiden Tribute allegations, to be held at the Mansion House on 15 July. Thomas's motives for involving himself in the Armstrong case are unclear. Stead later saw him as an 'éminence grise' for the brothels lobby, forming Mrs Armstrong into a weapon against him, but Thomas denied this hotly in a letter to *The Times*.

Mrs Armstrong was dismissed by the commission of inquiry as an evil woman who had sold her child. Thomas then directed her to approach Bramwell Booth, and she did so. Booth refused to see her. Thomas then suggested she return to the magistrates' court, and the magistrate ordered the police to renew their inquiry. Borner returned to Salvation Army headquarters, where he had a sharper exchange with Bramwell Booth. Booth admitted he knew where Eliza was, but would not return her home, where he believed her to be in moral danger. If any such move were made, he would apply to have her made a ward of court. 'I've investigated,' he told the inspector. 'The mother is a drunken woman and the neighbourhood a bad one.'[136] He could no longer refuse to see Mrs Armstrong, however, and the following day the inspector returned to Salvation Army HQ with the woman.

The interview was again curt, but this time Booth could not refuse to give the address of the daughter to her legal guardian. He revealed that she was in Loriol, a town some 100 miles south of Paris, working as a servant. The news was conveyed to the magistrate, and picked up by the *Lloyd's* reporter. The *Lloyd's* report, which highlighted the fact that the Salvation Army had been involved in spiriting away a thirteen-year-old girl to France, attracted much attention. Emboldened, *Lloyd's* sent a reporter to Winchester, who discovered that the woman who had spirited Eliza away was 'a professedly religious woman' who was 'matron of a Winchester home'. This was a clear opening for Cavendish Bentinck. He asked the home secretary whether he had seen the *Lloyd*'s article and whether he had directed any inquiries to be made. Another MP promptly asked whether the decoying of a child under fourteen was not a felony.[137] Immediately, the legal position of the Secret Commission became extremely insecure.

These attacks bore directly on the Salvation Army, whose leaders were acutely aware that they were vulnerable. The army was far from the respectable body of men and women it became in the twentieth century. In Victorian society it was deeply suspect to more conventional churches and bitterly opposed by the brewing and vice interests. Conventional middle-class Christianity saw commitment to converting the lumpenproletariat as deeply threatening. The commercial interests saw Salvationism as an even deeper threat, and repeatedly resorted to quite astonishing levels of violence aroused by the advance of the army in the early 1880s.

The tension between the army and wider society led to a deeply ambivalent attitude towards Salvationism. Stuart Mews has commented, 'Within an astonishingly short space of time, the army could be, on the one hand, praised, patronised and even courted by other religious leaders, and almost overnight, castigated like a precursor of the Moonies for brainwashing teenagers, keeping them beyond their parents' reach, expropriating their money, and marrying them off at the earliest legal age to other sect members'.[138] Mews refers particularly to an unpleasant controversy in 1883 in which an Anglican clergyman, Charlesworth, alleged that his fifteen-year-old daughter had been secretly enlisted by the army

THE SKELETON IN THE CUPBOARD!

Mistress. "I THOUGHT I HEARD A MAN'S VOICE DOWN HERE, JANE. I DO TRUST, AFTER ALL I TOLD YOU ABOUT THE LAST COOK AND HER SALVATION ARMY FRIENDS, THAT YOU 'VE NOT ADMITTED ANY——"

Cook. "OH LOR, MU'M! THAT YOU SHOULD EVER THINK THAT OF ME!—WHICH I CAN'T ABIDE THE SALVATIONISTS, MU'M—AND MY YOUNG MAN A 'SKELINTON,' AND AT THIS MINUTE AT WORTHINK A FIGHTIN' THE 'ORRID WRETCHES!"

'The Skeleton in the Cupboard', Punch, *27 September 1884. The anti-Salvationist hooligans of the period were known as 'skeletons'*

against his wishes. In 1885 the controversy still rankled and Salvation Army headquarters feared that the tide of public opinion could turn rapidly against the army. They were entirely justified.

By early August, the position of the Secret Commission was becoming extremely vulnerable, and most of the heat was turned on the Salvation Army. Booth wrote to Stead for support, suggesting 'You might say a word to-morrow to the effect that we took charge of the girl after having rescued her from what might have been a terrible fate'.[139] Stead himself was starting to feel under pressure. He had ordered a check on the situation in Charles Street as early as the end of July. He was told that Mrs Broughton did not run a brothel as alleged, and Rebecca Jarrett claimed she had never said she did. Stead, realizing the consequences of admitting flaws in the story of 'Lily', held firm to the truth of the tale.

By Sunday 16 August, *Lloyd's* was confident enough of its position to run the story prominently. It had located the driver of the hansom cab which had taken Eliza and Rebecca to the brothel after her examination by Madame Mourey. He had been suspicious of the party, especially when taken to a known brothel in Poland Street, followed by two men in another cab. When *Lloyd's* began running the story, he had contacted the paper. Booth, under intense pressure, wrote to the editor of *Lloyd's* offering to hand over the child to the editor or Mr Lloyd himself if they would take responsibility for her. The offer was declined. The paper reported that detectives had called on Mrs Armstrong on Saturday directing her to attend at Scotland Yard on Monday. The report added that 'afterwards she would have to go before the Public Prosecutor'.[140] A net was beginning to close around the Secret Commission.

When *Lloyd's* took up the story the following Sunday, it reported that Eliza had still not been returned to her parents, and that when inquiries had been made at the address given by Bramwell Booth in Loriol the girl could not be found. Scotland Yard had despatched an inspector to Loriol, taking with him Charles Armstrong. The Salvation Army had already sent Eliza home, aware that it could no longer hold on to her. The unexplained absence of the child caused great public concern, however, *Lloyd's* commenting ominously, 'We have no wish at this juncture to make charges against any individuals, but looking to the statements publicly made by Mrs Josephine Butler, Mr Stead, and General Booth, it is impossible to avoid the conclusion that the case is not being openly and fairly dealt with'.

By the middle of August, the story of 'Lily' was clearly backfiring on the Secret Commission. The day before the great Hyde Park demonstration, Stead was barracked as he spoke at a meeting in London with the chant 'Armstrong! Armstrong!' 'I'll tell you about Armstrong,' he responded. 'We took that child from a place that was steeped in vice, from a mother who has admitted she was going to a brothel as she thought and instead . . . we placed her in good and Christian guardianship.'[141] The significance of Stead's argument was less his claim that Mrs Armstrong thought Eliza was going to a brothel than the fact he made it at all. Stead was preparing his defence.

Stead and Booth realized that they could hold on to Eliza no longer. On 25 August, the *Pall Mall Gazette* carried a brief report about Eliza Armstrong 'who was yesterday handed over to her mother by my instructions'. Stead did not report that after Mrs Armstrong had signed a formal receipt for the girl, she and Police Inspector Borner – who had travelled to Wimbledon with the mother – had visited the public prosecutor. Stead then left for his long overdue holiday. If he was unaware that he was about to be prosecuted, he was to find out very soon.

THE MARTYRDOM OF STEAD

The week after Eliza Armstrong had been returned to the family home, a warrant was issued for the arrest of Rebecca Jarrett. Stead was on holiday in Switzerland when he heard of the charges. He wired the *Pall Mall Gazette* immediately to say: 'I alone am responsible. Rebecca Jarrett was only my unwilling agent. I am returning by the first express to claim the sole responsibility for the alleged abduction and to demand, if condemned, the sole punishment. Meanwhile, I am delighted at the opportunity thus afforded, of publicly vindicating the proceedings of the Secret Commission.'[142] Stead's bounding confidence and desire for martyrdom are typical of the man. Unfortunately for the others involved, he was in no position to demand sole punishment.

When Stead arrived back in London, he too was charged with the abduction of Eliza Armstrong. On Monday 7 September 1885 he found himself in the dock at

Bow Street Police Court, together with Bramwell Booth, Rebecca Jarrett, Sampson Jacques, Madame Mourey (the midwife who had certified Eliza's virginity) and Madame Combe (the Swiss Salvationist who had taken Eliza to Paris). The main charge was abduction, but there was a secondary charge against Stead, Madame Mourey and the others involved in the examination of Eliza, of technical assault. Stead's supporters were outraged. The *Methodist Times* asked

> Do the government intend to prosecute the Pall Mall Commission and no-body else? Are public money and all the resources of the state to be used in attacking those who have exposed an infamous traffic, while those who engage in the traffic, and find their base pleasures in it, are to go scot-free? . . . Why did they not take the brave advice of Mr Cavendish-Bentinck and prosecute the *Pall Mall Gazette* as an obscene publication? Was it because in that case Mr Stead would have been able to place in the witness box those whom Mrs Jeffries calls 'persons in the highest ranks of life', and to confront them with their obscure victims?[143]

These entirely valid questions went unanswered. The authorities were now able to ignore their critics. As Rebecca Jarrett was only too well aware, she had not obtained the permission of 'Basher' Armstrong. And in the law of Victoria's day, a father had comprehensive legal rights over under-age children. Technically, Stead and his associates were indeed guilty of abduction.

The magistrate's hearing at Bow Street took place amid extraordinary scenes of mob violence. The public had undergone a complete mood swing, which Stead's supporters claimed was orchestrated by the brothel interest. The London crowd now regarded Stead as a villain who had exploited a young girl. The latent anti-Salvation Army feeling added fuel to the fire, and the result was a howling mob which surged outside the court building. Nor did the crowd stop at abuse. On the second day of the hearing Bramwell Booth, disdaining police protection, walked away from the courtroom at the end of the hearing and was attacked. His wife wrote in her diary on her twenty-fourth birthday: 'Quite forgot this morning that it was my birthday . . . . Came out of Court at 4.30 and thinking it a pity to wait while Bramwell had consultations with the lawyers, came home. Darling one came home with a very bad blow on the nose – had been wretchedly mobbed coming out of Court by the magistrate's door.'[144]

The change in mood was particularly startling where Stead was concerned. The crowd carried wax effigies of the main defendants, and he was not safe even at home. On one occasion a mob surged through the grounds of his Wimbledon home, flourishing the waxworks at his windows and caterwauling. On another, he woke to find an effigy of himself dangling from a tree. Stead's daughter, Estelle, later told Charles Terrot that the family was persecuted for months on end. The 'respectable' people of Wimbledon – a considerable distance from Bow Street, and from the slums of central London – ostracized the family. Life was hell for Stead's wife. She could not even go shopping without being followed by a jeering mob.[145] This level of intimidation is remarkable even by the standards of the violent 1880s.

Stead set out his defence at length in a prepared statement which hinged on the argument that his motives were pure and thus justified his actions. He attempted to read out this statement on 27 September, but as soon as he reached the point where he began to discuss motive the magistrate ruled, quite correctly, that this was irrelevant in law. He later reprinted his statement in full as *The Armstrong Case; Mr Stead's Defence in Full*, in a privately printed pamphlet. What remained of his defence once he was barred from discussing motive was a technical argument that no offence had been committed because the mother's consent had been given, and an attempt at a public interest defence. He argued, "I submit there is no case to submit to a jury . . . .There can be no abduction where there is consent, and the consent of the mother was admittedly given for the departure of the child. Even if she did not, as she says, consent to her going with Jarrett for an immoral purpose, that is beside the question, for the child was not taken away for an immoral purpose.' This was no defence in law, because the father's consent had not been obtained. The second line of defence was more important, as an attempt to salvage his reputation. Stead argued, 'The circumstances were extraordinary, and nothing short of some such demonstration would have convinced a sceptical public of the ease and impunity with which crimes of the nature I have endeavoured to express could be perpetrated. Even if Jarrett did deceive me, she only took upon her own shoulders the crime of procuring a child for a brothel.'[146] Politically, this was the heart of the case. If Stead could prove that Eliza had been knowingly sold into prostitution by the mother, then he might even survive the technical charge of abduction. But in conceding that Jarrett might have deceived him, he was tacitly admitting the difficulty of doing this.

At the end of the proceedings the magistrate, Mr Vaughan, committed the defendants to trial on criminal charges. Vaughan dismissed the defence that Eliza had been taken for pure motives. He ruled that:

Mr Stead's motive may have been lofty, it may have been a pure one, but that can be no legal justification at all for the offence for which he is charged. But it may have been a different motive. There may have been a motive existing in his mind, a desire to get together material for the concoction of that deplorable and nauseous article which appeared in the *Pall Mall Gazette* on the sixth of July – an article which has certainly given great pain and sorrow to very many good people, and has greatly lowered the English people in the eyes of foreign nations.

Samson Jacques interrupted from the dock 'that shows your animus', and he was right.[147] But despite the animus of the magistrate, his reading of the law was entirely correct.

The trial began on Friday 23 October 1885. It was reported across the Western world, and was very near to a political show trial. The prosecution was undertaken by Sir Richard Webster, the attorney-general, backed by the legal resources of the Conservative government. Webster had had to toil through the summer to prepare the Criminal Law Amendment Bill for the statute book. It is difficult not to believe he was seeking revenge. The defendants were offered the services of the cream of the Liberal legal corps, and largely accepted. Rebecca Jarrett was defended by Mr Charles Russell QC, MP (later Lord Russell of Killowen). Bramwell Booth was defended by Mr S.D. Waddy QC, a future County Court judge.

Stead, with typical arrogance, chose to defend himself. He still based his defence on the argument that his intention in organizing the Eliza Armstrong affair was based on noble motives. Stead's room to manoeuvre was limited, given the magistrate's ruling that to take the child without the father's consent was illegal. Stead knew that this consent had never been obtained and that if the High Court judge upheld this ruling then his only hope of acquittal would be to have the court accept that his motives had been honourable and motivated by a desire to save the child from a vice-ridden household.

The judge, Mr Justice Lopes, did indeed uphold the magistrate's ruling. Shaen, the solicitor Stead had consulted before taking action, testified that he had advised Stead on the Eliza Armstrong episode. He recalled his advice that, provided Stead could show he had no criminal intent, he would not be committing a criminal act. Lopes retorted, 'I don't agree with that view of the law at all. I shall tell the jury that the taking of the child away against the will of the father was a criminal offence.'[148] Once this ruling had been made, Stead's only hope of acquittal was to convince the court that despite the technical offence, he was justified because he was saving the girl from being sold into prostitution. The defence had to convince the jury that Mrs Armstrong had sold the child to Rebecca Jarrett knowing she was bound for a brothel. The prosecution case was that the mother had no intention of selling the child into vice, and that Stead was deceived by Jarrett. The prosecution's objective was to tar Stead as a gullible man taken in by lies, and destroy his reputation.

The trial thus turned on the issue of whether Mrs Armstrong knowingly sold her child believing her to be bound for white slavery, or was an honourable but foolish woman attempting to set her child into a career as a servant. The clash of testimony here was crucial. Eliza Armstrong gave testimony that she thought she was going into service, and that she had been treated kindly by Rebecca Jarrett. Many witnesses gave evidence, notably Nancy Broughton and Charles Armstrong, but the key witnesses were the mother and Rebecca Jarrett. The performance of the two women decided the outcome of the trial.

Mrs Armstrong clung to the story that she had not sold her child into vice. She asserted that she believed that she was arranging for her child to become a servant. She had been led to believe that Rebecca Jarrett was a fellow-servant of Nancy Broughton's at Claridge's. As Claridge's was a respectable establishment, she thought Jarrett a safe person to take charge of her daughter. She denied being paid more than one shilling for the transaction. Mrs Armstrong was a far from satisfactory witness. The defence established without difficulty that she was arrested on 3 June for being drunk and disorderly, and she was cross-examined about where she obtained the money for this drinking spree. Her explanations were not satisfactory, and she emerged from the witness box with the suspicion that she might well have received more than one shilling for allowing Jarrett to go off with her daughter. Unfortunately for Stead, his legal team could not push home this advantage. Mrs Armstrong survived as a disreputable, but not dishonest, woman who had her daughter's interests at heart.

In contrast, Rebecca Jarrett's testimony was totally disastrous. Jarrett was essentially a simple woman, semi-literate and easily confused. She was a born-again Christian and was sustained during the trial by hymns sung outside her prison cell by Evangeline Booth (the general's daughter) and two Salvation Army cadets. Hymns, however, were poor weapons with which to counter the onslaught she faced inside the Old Bailey. Sir Richard Webster was an outstanding advocate, later to become lord chief justice. He was determined to break Jarrett and paint her as an immoral, deceitful and manipulative woman who had led Stead into breaking the law. Rebecca Jarrett was wholly unable to defend herself against Webster's tactics, playing into his hands by lying pathetically on oath.

Jarrett's only hope of surviving the case unscathed was to convince the court that she had told the truth in claiming Mrs Armstrong knew of the likely fate of her daughter, and that she was a minor player in the drama under the control of Stead. Her standing as a witness was, however, destroyed by Webster's forensic skill. He was aware that Jarrett was not a former brothel keeper, and had misled Stead in order to bolster her standing as a fallen woman who had repented. His strategy was not to cross-examine her as to whether Mrs Armstrong had known Eliza was bound for prostitution – the chances of proving the point either way were slight – but so to destroy her credibility that no-one would trust her whatever she said. And in this he was completely successful.

On the first day of his cross-examination, Webster's savagery was unremitting. Under constant harrying, Jarrett went completely to pieces. On the verge of hysteria, she contradicted herself and in a desperate attempt to distance herself from the Maiden Tribute tried to deny that her taking of Eliza had anything to do with the story. She caused a sensation by claiming: 'I have a doubt as to whether Lily was Eliza Armstrong. I do not know it. Honestly I believe it is another child whose history we have . . . there is another little girl whom I believe will be produced before you. Her name I think was Grace.'[148] Stead was horrified by these lies, but Jarrett made things worse when cross-examined by Stead by saying, 'I heard you say that Lily was not Eliza Armstrong but she was made up of two girls, Eliza and Grace, who were outraged in a brothel.'[149]

Webster cleverly exploited Rebecca Jarrett's inadequacies. He took her through her history of involvement in vice, and in cross-examining on her history as a brothel keeper obtained an address for a brothel she claimed to have kept. When the court adjourned for the weekend, he had the address checked. It was false. On resuming on the following Monday, 2 November, he went straight on to the attack. 'You said on Friday that you kept a gay house at 23 High Street, Marylebone at the end of 1882 and the beginning of 1883. Do you adhere to that statement?' Jarrett suddenly realized that to answer yes was to perjure herself, while to answer in the negative would destroy what little credibility she had left. She replied: 'I am not going to tell you where I did live.' The judge ordered her to answer the question. Webster repeated, 'Do you adhere to the reply you gave me that you kept a bad house at 23 High Street, Marylebone . . . ?' And Jarrett replied, 'I allow you forced that lie out of me.' Webster continued, 'Do you adhere to that statement?' Jarrett blurted out: 'I am not going to answer that. Anything concerning the case I will answer faithfully and truthfully, but I am not going to answer anything concerning my past life. I am not going to.' And she refused to answer any further questions.[150]

Jarrett's character was completely destroyed. No-one in the court would believe her word against Mrs Armstrong's. Webster referred to her in his summing-up as:

> One of those women who had been led to exaggerate her guilt for the purpose of glorifying herself and exaggerating her merit at the present time . . . . Jarrett's position depended on her power of keeping up the story she had told Stead . . . . Jarrett started out to buy girls who were in stock and it was essential she should get a girl else she would soon have been discarded by Mr Stead and possibly discarded by Mrs Butler as well . . . . Her position as a Magdalen was at stake and so she went to her old friend in Lisson Grove . . . [151]

It was a damning indictment, which succeeded in its purpose of destroying Jarrett and her role in the Maiden Tribute.

But if Webster hoped to destroy Stead, he failed. Stead rescued his own reputation with his final speech to the jury. Stead could have defended himself by blaming the whole affair on Jarrett and her untruthfulness. He chose not to do so. He took the responsibility on himself, and defended his key actor. 'I am told', he said, 'that Jarrett is discredited but . . . I believe she told me a true story. She may have been a stupid witness, but she is not a fraudulent witness. I honour her, driven and harassed as she was in her evidence here, for refusing to answer questions that would incriminate her old friends . . . '.[152]

By taking this line, Stead recaptured the moral high ground. He went on to make an exceptionally fine speech, ignoring the legal questions to stake out the appeal to morality. He argued that if in the course of rescuing mariners from a sinking ship, he stole a boat with which to do it, he would admit that a crime had been committed, but that it was justified in achieving a higher good. Stead made no attempt to defend himself against the abduction charge, on which he was clearly technically guilty, but hammered away at the question of motive. His conclusion was a masterly attempt to turn the tables on Webster's claim to be defending the children of the poor. He argued:

> Mr Attorney said, 'We must protect the children of the poor'. Was not this the object which I did all this for? . . . You KNOW it was! You know that was why Rebecca did it – and Jacques did it – and Booth did it – and we ALL did it! It was not in order to abduct a girl, but to rescue a girl from what we believed to be her inevitable doom. And, gentlemen, if in the exercise of your judgement, you come to the conclusion that you can take NO note of motive, NO note of interest, NO note of the scope of the operations – all I have to say, gentlemen, is that when you return your verdict I shall make no appeal to any other tribunal . . . . If in the opinion of twelve men – twelve Englishmen born of English mothers – with English fathers – and possibly fathers of English girls – if they say to me you are guilty, I take my punishment and do not flinch.[153]

W.T. Stead as portrayed in the Sentinel,
February 1886, on his release from prison

As he finished, a spontaneous burst of applause broke out in the court. It was Stead's finest moment, and in its mixture of sentiment, principle, logic and egotism summed up all the strengths and weaknesses of Stead's character.

Judge Lopes was moved by this speech to pay a reluctant tribute to Stead, beginning his summing up by accepting that 'A speech more impressive I think few of us have ever heard. Although I was unable to agree with many of the observations made, I am bound to say I cannot but admire the power and ability with which he declaimed his address.'[154] It made no difference to the judge's directions to the jury, but made enough impact on the jury to stage a final dramatic twist to the proceedings.

The jury could not agree, and returned to ask for guidance from the judge. The foreman reported that, 'Our difficulty is this; that if Jarrett obtained the child by false pretences, we feel it was directly contrary to Stead's intentions. We find it therefore, difficult as businessmen to hold him criminally responsible for that which, if he had known it, he would have repudiated.' This led to a further burst of applause from the public gallery. Judge Lopes was profoundly irritated, and insisted that the only relevant question was, 'Did Stead and Jarrett, or either of them, take Eliza Armstrong out of the possession of the father and against his will?'[155]

The jury retired again, and finally returned with an agreed statement which was read by the foreman. 'We find that Stead did not have the consent of the father to use the child for the use to which he put her, but that Stead was misled by Jarrett. There's a further recommendation, m'lord, and that is this – "That the jury trust that the Government will secure the efficient administration of the Act recently passed for the protection of children".'[156] There was another burst of applause for this.

Lopes could only agree with this, and interpreted the result as a guilty verdict against Stead and Jarrett on the abduction charge, Booth and Jacques being acquitted. Madame Combe had been discharged earlier in the trial. A further trial was immediately held on the assault charge, and at the end of this Stead was imprisoned for three months without hard labour, Jarrett for six months without hard labour, Jacques for one month, and Madame Mourey for six months with hard labour. She died in prison.

The immediate result of the trials was victory for the prosecution. The London press was almost wholly against Stead and his co-defendants. The verdicts helped prevent the wide-ranging anti-vice alliance which Stead had hoped for in August. The socialists and the Labour movement now distrusted Stead. He also lost credibility with the powerful, and hence his chance of influencing imperial affairs. He remained influential in the Liberal Party, and figures as various as Cardinal Manning, Arthur Balfour and Lord Rosebery remained on friendly terms with him, but the trial revealed such serious errors of judgement that no serious politician would trust Stead. He became an increasingly marginal figure in British political history.

Yet in the development of puritan morality, the Eliza Armstrong trial was anything but a reversal. Stead was crowned with the laurels of martyrdom. His own sense of self-righteousness spread to the movement he had helped to create. The purity lobby developed an even stronger sense of confronting a powerful, ruthless, hypocritical establishment which had to be fought without quarter. The contrast between prosecution of the Secret Commission for what was little more than a technical offence, and the law on vice being laxly enforced, was an outrage to the puritans. In the year of the trial of Mrs Jeffries, few clearer lessons in official hypocrisy could have been taught. The anti-vice lobby never forgot it.

SIX

The Impact of Vigilance

A VIGILANT ASSOCIATION

The formation of the National Vigilance Association on 21 August 1885 marked an ambitious attempt to pull together the different strands of the moral purity campaign and bring them together in one umbrella organization. This was never fully achieved, but nonetheless the NVA was a formidable grouping. It incorporated the Society for the Suppression of Vice, the Minors Protection Society, the Belgian Traffic Committee (chair Benjamin Scott) and later the Central Vigilance Society. After the repeal of the Contagious Diseases Acts, many veterans of that campaign went over to the NVA.

The main immediate object of the NVA was to ensure that the authorities carried out the 1885 Criminal Law Amendment Act. The long-serving organizing secretary, W.A. Coote, later recalled in his pamphlet, *A Romance of Philanthropy*:

> There was during that period [the late 1880s] a wide felt distrust on the part of officialism in relation to the Act. The press described it as panic legislation, queried the need for it, and tried to discredit the means by which it had been passed. Consequently . . . it often happened that owing to the unsympathetic attitude of the authorities a case broke down and the culprit escaped his due punishment.[157]

Coote dedicated the pamphlet to Stead, who had financed him as honorary secretary till the organization had raised enough funds to employ him full time. The major activity of the NVA in its early years was therefore undertaking prosecutions. In its first twelve months 105 prosecutions were undertaken, dealing with the prosecution of (a) disorderly houses (brothels), (b) men for offences against women and (c) dealers in indecent books.

The activities of the National Vigilance Association produced a marked change in the attitude of the authorities in the direction of censoriousness and repression. In 1916 Coote referred with satisfaction to the 'great change which now appertains to the authorities in this direction. To-day, they do their work so thoroughly and enthusiastically that very little legal work is left to the Association.'[158] Coote was correct. A growing puritanism in the moral stance of the state took place in the last decade and a half of Victoria's reign, largely as a result of the work of the moral purity crusade.

This was not, however, especially the result of the work of W.T. Stead. Stead was released from Holloway Gaol on Monday 18 January 1886, after serving two months and seven days of his three-month sentence. He returned to resume his former career unchastened and unbowed. For most of his supporters in the purity lobby, Stead was a martyr-hero, and they demonstrated their undiminished regard for him at a great meeting on the very evening of his release. The Exeter Hall in London had been booked, and it was packed by a huge crowd determined to welcome Stead with honour. The purity lobby regarded the prosecution of the Secret Commission as the act of a vindictive and hypocritical government. Dame Millicent Fawcett spoke for many when she wrote to Mrs Stead shortly after the trial that: 'My heart burns within me at this hideous injustice and all that it means. One good has already come out of this wicked trial and that is that whoever has read his conscience must recognise your husband in his true light – the hero saint who in every age of the world's history has been picked out for special persecution.'[159]

These sentiments were shared by the people who crowded the Exeter Hall. James Stansfeld opened the meeting with a ringing welcome to Stead, coupled with a denunciation of vice. He told the crowd they were met to welcome, on his release from imprisonment, one of the most fearless and devoted men whom it had ever been his lot to know. To such a man, the best welcome they could give was to determine to prosecute his work (cheers). He denied that Mr Stead had exaggerated the vices and the crimes against which they were bound to act (loud cheers). Hideous and abnormal, those vices and crimes honeycombed the very substance of social life. 'He believed there was no safety except in truth and light.'[160] Stansfeld proclaimed Stead to be responsible for the passage of the Criminal Law Amendment Act, to more cheering.

The Revd Hugh Price Hughes then moved a resolution of welcome to Stead, stating that they welcomed him back as an innocent man. This was met with prolonged cheering. Hughes opined that the purity lobby had in the previous six months learnt the power of the press. Hughes then set down a principle which was to have a profound influence on public morality for the next half century. He stated:

> Hitherto it had been held that a man's public life had no connection with his private life, though the latter might be that of the fornicator, the man whose selfishness had changed his heart into a heart of stone, and whose impurity had destroyed the balance of his reason. In this reform they must begin at the fountain head. They must begin by cleansing the House of Commons (loud cheers). They should lay it down, as a great political principle, that no man who believed that the daughters of the poor must be sacrificed to the lusts of his own sex was fit to make the laws of England . . . . They must raise the purity of public opinion until it became impossible for an immoral man to occupy any public position in this country, from the village police station to the throne of England (loud cheers).[161]

But despite the warmth of his welcome, Stead's position in the movement was not as strong as it appeared. In spite of the outrage which had greeted his trial, his conviction weakened his position within the purity movement. Stead's mistakes could be glossed over, but mistakes they were. And whatever Stead's supporters might say on the lines of the ends justifying the means, this was not a line of argument which the morality lobby could find comfortable. Privately many leaders of the movement agreed with Bishop Lightfoot's comment that 'it was indeed sad that Mr Stead should spoil an especially good cause by such inconceivably bad taste and lack of judgement'.[162]

Stead's spell in prison hardly justified Fawcett's description of Stead as 'hero-saint'. Stead was treated with great consideration by the authorities, which appear to have regarded him as too powerful to be treated as a common criminal. Stead showed astonishing arrogance in publishing an account of his imprisonment as *My First Imprisonment*. In this, he recounts a conversation with a prisoner, who on learning of Stead's sentence commented, 'You've got off cheap';[163] and indeed he had. Stead was also foolish enough to confess that 'Never had I a pleasanter holiday, a more charming season of repose . . . . Here, as in an enchanted castle, jealously guarded by liveried retainers, I was kept secure from the strife of tongues, and afforded the rare luxury of journalistic leisure. From the Governor, Colonel Milman, to the poor fellow who scrubbed out my room, everyone was as kind as kind could be.'[164] Stead was allowed visitors every day, and wrote articles for the *Pall Mall Gazette* from his cell. At Christmas, he had a special card printed featuring the prison and sent it to old friends, including Cardinal Manning. When Stead was finally released from prison, he took his prison uniform with him and wore it to work on the anniversary of his sentence. Such arrogance was not the ideal qualification for leading the forces which were now assembling under the purity banner.

Outside the purity movement, Stead was regarded with deep suspicion. Shaw came to distrust the man profoundly, and in 1922 told Frederick Whyte:

> Stead was impossible as a colleague; he had to work single handed because he was incapable of keeping faith when excited; and as his hyperaesthesia was chronic he generally WAS excited. Nobody ever trusted him after the discovery that the case of Eliza Armstrong in the Maiden Tribute was a put up job, and that he himself had put it up. We all felt that if ever a man deserved six months imprisonment Stead deserved it for such a betrayal of our confidence in him . . . it is hard to say that Stead's deficiencies did not often serve as assets; but they certainly limited and frustrated him sufficiently to prevent him from realizing anything like his potential social value.[165]

Shaw's judgement seems just. Without Stead's obsessional energy, he could never have carried out the Maiden Tribute campaign, and the Criminal Law Amendment Act would almost certainly have failed. But given his deficiencies he could not be trusted, and his hopes of becoming a power in the land were doomed. After his prison sentence, he was to be no more than a minor political influence with dwindling stature even inside the purity lobby.

His lasting legacy to the lobby was, however, immense. Stead had forced the passage of the Criminal Law Amendment Act with the Maiden Tribute campaign, and thus acted as midwife to the National Vigilance Association. He had decisively altered the political climate of the country and immeasurably increased the influence of the puritan current. The next decade would show how powerful the puritans had now become.

THE ACHIEVEMENT OF REPEAL

The events of 1885 had produced a powerful and well-organized moral purity group in the National Vigilance Association, but there were strict limits to its political influence. Although Josephine Butler's great crusade had proved strong enough to have the Contagious Diseases Acts suspended in 1883, final repeal had eluded the campaigners. After the success of 1885, the purity lobby looked to their growing influence within the Liberal Party to secure repeal – assuming Gladstone could win the impending general election, and they could then convince the Cabinet that their campaign was of prime political importance. It was not a foregone conclusion that either condition would be met. Paradoxically, the Irish crisis which ripped the Liberal Party apart in the summer of 1886 forced repeal through even as Gladstone's government collapsed.

In that traumatic year, the political stage was wholly dominated by the Irish Problem as Gladstone fought to gain Home Rule for Ireland. The long struggle of the Catholic Irish to overcome domination by Anglo-Scottish Protestantism had profoundly affected the prime minister. The middle years of the century had been marked by passionate rebellion, spearheaded by Fenian terrorism, and when Gladstone became prime minister for the first time after the 1868 election, he immediately stated, 'My mission is to pacify Ireland'. So saying, he placed a millstone around his neck.

In Gladstone's first ministry (1868–74) he had sought to pacify the Irish by legal measures aimed at removing the privileges of the Protestant landowning class in Ireland. The limitations of Gladstone's measures were ruthlessly demonstrated by the violence which attended the agricultural depression of the late 1870s. This amounted to virtual civil war between Protestant landowner and Catholic tenant farmer in rural Ireland.

The land war powerfully stimulated the Irish Home Rule Party, which now fell under the control of its militant wing, led by Charles Stewart Parnell. Parnell's Land League exploited the agrarian crisis of the late 1870s by organizing rent strikes, and the government arrested its leadership. The Cabinet realized this was no solution when rural violence escalated without the controlling influence of the leaders. Gladstone's Cabinet was negotiating with Parnell for a peace treaty when the dark side of Irish nationalism overwhelmed them. On 6 May 1882, Lord Frederick Cavendish, the chief secretary for Ireland, was walking with Mr Burke, the under-secretary, in Phoenix Park, Dublin. They were surprised by members of an Irish terrorist group, the Invincibles, and hacked to death with long surgical knives. The shock waves of these brutal murders wrecked the treaty, and forced the Liberals to put through a coercion bill putting Ireland under police rule for three years.

It was the expiry of this act which dominated Gladstone's mind in the summer of 1885. He was privately grateful for being allowed a period out of office that summer to consider his options. Gladstone quietly came to the conclusion that the only solution short of permanent coercion was to give Ireland Home Rule. He was, however, well aware that Home Rule was unpopular with many Liberals, particularly the Whigs, led by Lord Hartington. Gladstone decided to keep quiet about his conversion to Home Rule till after the result of the election had been announced. It was a fateful decision.

The election started on 23 November, and by late December it was clear that the Liberals had the majority of seats in the Commons, but not an absolute majority over Tories and Home Rulers combined. If the Parnellites voted with the Tories, the Liberals could be denied power. On 15 December, Herbert Gladstone, son of the Grand Old Man, foolishly let slip his father's conversion to Home Rule. This created the impression that Gladstone had switched to Home Rule as a result of the election, and was trying to tempt Parnell to support the Liberals to secure power. The Tories immediately abandoned tentative discussions with Parnell, and announced they were totally opposed to Home Rule. Gladstone was left to mend fences with his aggrieved colleagues as best he could.

Thus when the new Parliament met in January 1886, the political atmosphere was very highly charged. Gladstone became prime minister for the third time on 3 February. Hartington refused to join the Cabinet, while Joseph Chamberlain did so only with strong reservations about Home Rule. It was very clear that with Gladstone bent on introducing a Home Rule bill in the spring, it would be impossible to retain Chamberlain in the government, and Gladstone looked round for a replacement. With the Home Rule drama unfolding, the fate of the Contagious Diseases Acts was hardly an issue for anyone at Westminster. Fortunately for the repealers, one of the few people for whom it was a major issue was James Stansfeld, and he was earmarked by Gladstone as an obvious replacement for Joseph Chamberlain if Chamberlain carried out his threat to resign in opposition to Home Rule. But Stansfeld had pledged that he would not take high office until the CD acts were repealed. Thus by sheer accident Stansfeld's refusal to seek promotion till the acts were removed suddenly became a key issue for the Liberal government, and Gladstone suddenly found that repealing the CD acts had become an urgent necessity.

On the day that Parliament opened, Henry Wilson and Professor Stuart, both now Liberal MPs, announced that they would move resolutions adverse to the CD acts, Wilson naming 16 February as the day. It was, however, Stansfeld who moved the resolution, 'That in the opinion of this House the Contagious Diseases Acts 1866–69 ought to be repealed'. Sir J. Kennaway then moved an amendment to add the words, 'due provision at the same time being made for the continued maintenance of hospital accommodation, with adequate treatment of women voluntarily seeking admission and medical care'. This apparently friendly amendment was immediately denounced by repealers as a blind designed to preserve the Lock Hospitals – and still more odiously, to protect the men who frequented prostitutes and thus allow vice to continue by providing 'clean' women. This was unacceptable to the repealers, and the amendment was lost by 245 votes against 131.[166]

Faced with this defeat, the opposition collapsed. When the bill came up for its second reading, even Cavendish Bentinck could not organize support for his

THE SENTINEL

THE END OF A NATIONAL DISGRACE.

THE long struggle against the State regulation of vice within the limits of the United Kingdom has now practically ended. At twenty-five minutes past one, a.m., on Friday, March 26th, the Second Reading of the Rt. Hon. James Stansfeld's Bill for the total repeal of the Contagious Diseases Acts, passed the House of Commons without a division. Mr. Cavendish Bentinck had moved the rejection of the Bill, but when the time came for voting, the opposition collapsed. Thus closes, with profound gratitude to God on the part of thousands, a struggle that has extended over seventeen years.

The case with which the victory was gained on the 26th is explained by what took place ten days before.

The debate upon Mr. Stansfeld's resolution on March 16th, was distinguished by the Pro-Acts party raising and voting upon a side issue. Mr. Stansfeld's motion was, " that in the opinion of this House the Contagious Diseases Acts, 1866-9, ought to be repealed."

Sir J. Kennaway's amendment, to add to the motion the words, " due provision at the same time being made for the continued maintenance of hospital accommodation, with adequate treatment of women voluntarily seeking admission and medical care," was altogether foreign to the question. It is the climax of a detestable hypocrisy to pretend that the C. D. Acts were enacted with any reference to the interests of suffering fallen women. Their purpose was to secure immunity in their vices to profligate men. Mr. Stansfeld proposed that this horrible system, which was literally smuggled through Parliament, and which, according to Mr. Gladstone, was " never brought before the Cabinet," should be utterly abolished. Sir J. Kennaway, with men at his back who mock at virtue, thereupon moved an amendment ostensibly with a philanthropic motive as regards women. A few good men fell victims to the deceit. Perhaps they had forgotten that in the hospitals established under the C. D. Acts, the intention is not to cure diseased women for their own sake, but to protect from disease the vile men who habitually consort with them. There can be no mistake as to the object of the majority of those who followed Sir J. Kennaway into the lobby. They desired, by any means, fair or foul, to retain if only a vestige of the iniquitous system that for twenty years has dishonoured the name of Britain, in order that at the first opportunity the unclean structure might again be raised upon that foundation. They were defeated. The majority was decisive—245 against 131. After such a majority the hopelessness of a further division was self-evident.

A GOOD WORK AT MANCHESTER.

The third Annual Meeting of the Manchester Society for the prevention of the degradation of women and children was held in the Free Trade Hall on March 2nd. Mr. F. W. Crossley, J.P., the Hon. Secretary, read the Report, which stated that the work of the Society, speaking broadly, was divided into two sections—(1) repression of traffic in vice, and (2) rendering assistance to the injured. A special Act obtained for the benefit of Manchester had for a number of years given very great facility for putting down disorderly houses. Their officer had lodged no less than 304 petitions against these places, or otherwise aided in suppressing them, since his engagement, a little more than two years ago, 274 persons having in consequence been convicted, fined, or imprisoned.

The Rev. Alexander M'Laren, D.D., Mrs. Ormiston Chant, the Rev. Prebendary Grier, M.A., and Mrs. Booth, were among the speakers at the meeting.

The Sentinel, *April 1886, celebrating victory*

attempt to have the bill rejected. It passed at twenty-five minutes past one in the morning, on Friday 26 March. Later that day, Chamberlain resigned from the Cabinet and Stansfeld was at last free to accept Gladstone's subsequent offer to join the government. The CD acts were ended, not by the puritan campaign, but by parliamentary manoeuvre.

For Josephine Butler, the victory was bitter-sweet. After sixteen years of struggle, she was exhausted and disillusioned. The triumph did not move her to great exultation. It was a paradox that in the course of securing the victory, a powerful puritan current had been created which cut across the individualistic Liberalism which had motivated her to take up the issue in 1869. The future course of the politics of morality, she realized, would take a direction which she would find increasingly unsatisfactory. Her great crusade had ended in victory, but in a form from which she could derive little pleasure.

For the moral purity lobby, the events surrounding the repeal of the Contagious Diseases Acts were also bitter-sweet. The Home Rule controversy of 1886 ended with the total defeat of Gladstone's Liberal government and its replacement by a Conservative administration largely unsympathetic to moral purity. Though the National Vigilance Association could not know that it would be two decades before the Liberal Party again secured an absolute majority, it was certainly clear that the immediate aftermath of the events of 1886 ended conventional pressure-group politics for moral purity for some time. The forces of moral purity began to seek other ways to influence the politics of morality. They began to discover that parliamentary lobbying was not the only weapon in their armoury.

THE FALL OF CHARLES DILKE: A TRIAL FOR DIVORCE

In the development of late Victorian puritanism, the Criminal Law Amendment Act and repeal of the Contagious Diseases laws had provided the call to arms. After the fall of Gladstone's government in 1886, however, parliamentary politics ceased to be the central focus of puritan activity. Thwarted by their inability to secure legislative changes, the energies of the puritans flowed towards a more general purification of public life.

Fundamentally, the puritans wanted changes in attitudes and behaviour. Immorality was to be eliminated by a crusade to cleanse public life of behaviour of which the puritans disapproved. When the hard-line Methodist preacher Hugh Price Hughes spoke to the meeting welcoming Stead back from prison, he openly called for a puritan crusade with the call that, 'We must begin by cleansing the House of Commons. We should lay it down, as a great political principle, that no man who believes that the daughters of the poor must be sacrificed to the lusts of his own sex is fit to make the laws of England . . . . We must raise the purity of public opinion until it becomes impossible for an immoral man to occupy any public position in this country . . . .' This was greeted with great enthusiasm. It marked a tightening of the standards demanded of politicians which was to have the greatest effect on the political life of Britain, for it contributed powerfully to the downfall of two of the most important politicians of the era – Sir Charles Dilke and the Home Rule leader, Charles Stuart Parnell.

When Price Hughes spoke in the Exeter Hall, he might well have had the case of Sir Charles Dilke uppermost in his mind. In the winter of 1885–6, Sir Charles Dilke was fighting to save his political career from the disgrace of being named in a divorce action. In July 1885, Dilke had been heir-apparent to Gladstone as leader of the Liberal Party. By the summer of 1886, Dilke was politically ruined.

In the early 1880s, Sir Charles Wentworth Dilke (1843–1911) vied with Joseph Chamberlain as the rising star of the Liberal Party. Both were leaders of the

Sir Charles Wentworth Dilke (1843–1911), before the Crawford case

radical wing of the party, a wing growing in strength as the power of the aristocratic Whigs declined. One or the other, many supposed, would succeed Gladstone when the Grand Old Man retired, as he was imminently expected to do. (Gladstone was born in 1809 and was 71 when he became prime minister in 1880.) And Dilke was markedly ahead of Chamberlain. Disraeli had commented, on seeing Dilke's parliamentary career develop in the 1870s, that 'Sir Charles Dilke was the most useful and influential member, among the young men' that he had ever known. In 1879 he went further, prophesying that he was almost certain to become prime minister.[167]

Dilke had successfully overcome early controversy. He had nearly wrecked his career in the autumn of 1871 when, as an inexperienced radical MP (he had been elected in 1868 at the age of twenty-five), he attacked the royal family and espoused republicanism. The storm roused by this was so severe that when Dilke had moved for a select committee into the Civil List on 19 March 1872, he was deserted by his followers in a hostile House and was defeated by 276 votes to 2. Yet by 1877, Dilke had so far put his republicanism behind him that he was invited by the Prince of Wales to dine at Marlborough House, becoming a member of the Marlborough House set.

Dilke also conducted a complex personal life with tact and discretion. After the death of his first wife, Katherine, in 1874, Dilke began an intense friendship with Emilia Pattison, the wife of Mark Pattison, the elderly rector of Lincoln College,

Oxford. Pattison was thirty years older than his wife, and the pair were ill matched. (The characters of Edward Casaubon and Dorothea Brooke in *Middlemarch* are considered to be based on Mark Pattison and his wife.[168]) The marriage was soon a union in name only, and from 1875 Mrs Pattison, a serious and high-minded high churchwoman, entered into a strong but platonic relationship with Dilke which was to lead to their marriage ten years later. The relationship was, however, conducted largely by letter, and Dilke behaved with complete Victorian propriety while Mark Pattison was alive.

Dilke was considered entirely respectable by the early 1880s, and was moving steadily up the parliamentary ladder. Gladstone forgave him his earlier republican views by making him under-secretary at the Foreign Office in 1880. Dilke moved in the highest circles, cultivated by the Prince of Wales, acquainted with Lord Rosebery, future Liberal prime minister, and intimate with the Marquess of Hartington, to whose ancestral mansion Hardwick Hall he was invited in January 1884. Gladstone promoted Dilke to head the Local Government Board in December 1882. This was a Cabinet appointment, and Dilke became a member of the Privy Council. He was the youngest member of the government at thirty-nine.

Dilke used his position at the Local Government Board to set up the Royal Commission into the Housing of the Working Class in January 1884. Lord Salisbury, the Roman Catholic leader Cardinal Manning, and the Prince of Wales all sat on the commission. Later in the year, Dilke succeeded in securing positions for women on the Metropolitan Asylums Board, enhancing his reputation as a radical politician of the first rank. In July 1884, Mark Pattison died and Dilke became engaged to his widow. Mrs Pattison was to spend the summer of 1885 in Madras as the guest of the governor, and marry Dilke on her return in the October. Fortune seemed to shine on Sir Charles Dilke.

Yet there were undercurrents in Dilke's life. Dilke kept his engagement secret, apparently convinced that someone was plotting against him. He had been receiving anonymous letters, and feared an attempt to disrupt his marriage. On 10 June 1885 he wrote to his fiancée that 'I had another of those dreadful letters a day or two ago. They always suggest conspiracy but why should those who conspire let me know. I fancy it must be some lunatic.'[169] Dilke was also involved in a family crisis involving a distant relation. He wrote to Mrs Pattison on 6 March that 'Maye [Mrs Ashton Dilke, his sister-in-law] has discovered that her sister, Mrs Crawford, is carrying on a correspondence with an officer now in Dublin and is in half trouble already with Crawford and likely to get into worse trouble'.[170] But Dilke could not spare much time for his sister-in-law's affairs; the politics of the failing Liberal government occupied his attention fully in the spring of 1885. The radicals of Cabinet rank – Dilke, Chamberlain, Trevelyan, Shaw Lefevre and Morley – were meeting weekly and were presided over by Dilke. Chamberlain deferred to Dilke as a more acceptable radical leader than himself.

Yet just as his career reached new heights, Dilke's upward progress stalled. On Saturday 18 July the Reform Club staged a banquet in his honour. He returned home late, planning to spend the following day on the river. At home he

Sir Charles Dilke at the despatch box,
Illustrated London News, *16 February 1884*

discovered a note from Mrs Rogerson, a close friend, asking him to call on her the following morning as she had some grave information to give him. He went early, and was told that Mrs Donald Crawford, the sister of his brother's widow, had announced to her husband that Dilke had been her lover since shortly after her marriage. Crawford was about to sue for divorce, naming Dilke as the co-respondent.

Dilke had no illusions about the seriousness of this threat. Divorce had only been legal since 1857, and the bill setting up civil divorce had been deeply controversial. To be adjudged the guilty party by the divorce court ended respectable status, and divorce actions were rare and sensational. Two or three hundred per year was the norm – as against an average of 170,000 marriages annually in the late nineteenth century. In the three decades since the Divorce Act had been passed, no politician had been adjudged a guilty party. The politician who had come closest to the edge had been the lecherous Lord Palmerston, who had been named co-respondent by Timothy Joseph O'Kane in seeking divorce from his wife Margaret Matilda in 1864. Mrs O'Kane was thirty and attractive, and had certainly visited the prime minister. No immorality was proved, and Lady Palmerston thought the suit an extortion. The case was dismissed, the judge supporting Palmerston in the strongest terms.

Dilke knew that unless he cleared his name, his political career would be irreparably damaged. His initial reaction was to retire from public life, and he wrote to Mrs Pattison, then in India, to that effect on the day the blow fell. He changed his mind, but he had no illusions about his likely success. Four days after receiving the bad news, he wrote in his diary, 'Such a charge, even if disproved, which is not easy against perjured evidence picked up with care, is fatal to supreme usefulness in politics. In the case of a public man a charge is always believed by many, even though disproved, and I should be weighted by it through life. I prefer, therefore, at once to contemplate leaving public life.'[171]

Crawford filed his divorce suit on 5 August, but the case was not to be heard till early 1886. Mrs Pattison stood by Dilke and they were married in Oxford on 3 October 1885. Dilke retained his Chelsea seat in the election of November 1885, having written to his electors denying the charges against him. But although the Liberals won the election and Gladstone formed a government, there was no place for Dilke within it. With the Crawford divorce action unresolved, Gladstone could not afford to associate with a potential scandal. The political world knew that if Dilke wished to continue his political career, he had to clear his name.

The case of Crawford v. Crawford and Dilke was heard before Mr Justice Butt on 12 February 1886. Dilke retained Sir Henry James and Sir Charles Russell, the new attorney-general, acting in a private capacity. Russell was regarded as the foremost advocate of the day, and charged the then phenomenal fee of 300 guineas. Chamberlain was also in court to offer advice. Mrs Crawford was not in court.

In order to save Dilke's public reputation, it was essential that the court clear him of the charge of adultery with Mrs Crawford. Dilke knew this. What Dilke does not seem to have appreciated was that the public expected that he would repeat on oath his denial of the charges against him. He had already done this in writing to his electors in Chelsea. This was not sufficient. The public expected him to go into the dock, as the Prince of Wales had done in the Mordaunt case. The Prince of Wales had been involved in the divorce action brought by Sir Charles Mordaunt, MP for South Warwickshire, against his wife in 1870. Harriet Mordaunt had confessed to affairs with several men, including the Prince of Wales. The evidence against him was little more than that he had paid visits to Harriet which her husband had disliked because of his bad character. Nevertheless, letters from him to Harriet appeared in the press and his advisors pressed him to clear his name by appearing in court and testifying on oath. He thus duly appeared in the witness box, was asked if any criminal acts had occurred with Harriet, and replied (according to *The Times*, 'in a very firm tone'), 'There has not', and was discharged from the case.[172] It was this precedent of denying the charges on oath which informed opinion expected Dilke to follow in the Crawford case.

The divorce court was packed on 12 February 1886. Mr Inderwick QC led for Crawford, Mr Lockwood QC for Mrs Crawford, and Russell for Dilke.[173] Inderwick opened the action, outlining the case for his client. Crawford and his wife had been married on 27 July 1881, the lady apparently being under age. Crawford was a Liberal MP. In April 1882, when at the Home Office, Crawford received an anonymous letter directed to his office cautioning him to 'beware the member for Chelsea'. Crawford thought nothing of the letter and destroyed it, but not before showing it to his wife. She became very excited, and asked Crawford what he would do with her money if they became divorced.

In February 1884, while visiting London, Mrs Crawford became acquainted with one Captain Forster, and a flirtation took place between them. Mrs Crawford received a letter from Captain Forster, which her husband did not see. He taxed her on this, and though she told him the letter was harmless he was dissatisfied. His wife's sister, Mrs Ashton Dilke (Sir Charles' sister-in-law), effected a reconciliation. They went to Scotland at the end of the parliamentary session, returning to London in February 1885. Mrs Crawford came back earlier than her husband, and stayed with Mrs Rogerson – Dilke's friend.

In March 1885, Crawford received a second anonymous letter. The letter stated, 'The first person who ruined your wife was Sir Charles Dilke. She has passed nights in his house and is well known to his servants.' He took the letter home and showed it to his wife. She was much excited, and said she believed the letter had been written by her mother. Crawford destroyed this second letter. On 10 June Crawford received a third anonymous letter addressed to him at the Home Office. This stated that 'Your wife was seen at the Metropole on Monday with Captain Forster. Are you a fool?' Crawford taxed his wife with this, and though she denied it he was uneasy and kept the letter. On 17 July, he returned home from his club at 11 o'clock at night and found a letter addressed to him on the hall table. This was a fourth anonymous epistle in a disguised hand. It read, 'Fool, looking for the cuckoo when he has flown, having defiled your nest. You have been foully deceived, but dare not touch the real traitor.' He went upstairs to confront his wife in the bedroom. There followed a scene out of Victorian melodrama.

Inderwick told the court that Crawford addressed his wife, 'I must know one way or the other. Is it true you have defiled my bed as stated in the letter?' His wife replied, 'It is perfectly true. I was sure that I should have to tell some time or the other.' She told her husband that he was wrong to suspect Captain Forster. 'The real man who did me the injury is Charles Dilke.' She went on to give a long statement, the nub of this being that in 1882 Dilke had begun to pay attentions to her. She had first gone to an assignation house in the Tottenham Court Road, but later had gone to Dilke's own house and had been seen by the servants there. Dilke had also visited her in her own household. On an occasion when she had come to town several days before her husband, she had spent two nights with Dilke, the first returning to her own house at 4 a.m., and the second between 7 and 8 in the morning. She denied adultery with Captain Forster. She had broken off relations with Dilke in 1884 following a promise made to Mrs Rogerson.

Inderwick stated that the evidence of Mrs Rogerson had been sought, but she had been taken ill and medical evidence would be given that she was too sick even to make a deposition. It would be shown that Mrs Crawford's statement that Sir Charles Dilke was in the habit of calling on her was true, and that he was on several occasions alone with her. She was indeed in London alone on 12, 13 and 14 February 1882, and had left the house after dinner. She told the servants she had been to stay with her sister. In her engagement diary for 23 February was the entry CWD.

Inderwick concluded his remarks by saying, 'That is substantially the case against Mrs Crawford', and he held it was a very strong one. As to the case of the co-respondent, he could not say there was such certain evidence against him as would justify his lordship in granting a decree against him. But the law required that in every case of alleged adultery a co-respondent should be cited unless the court should otherwise direct. He could not take it upon himself to say that there was no evidence against Sir Charles Dilke. 'There was undoubtedly some evidence against him, and he had accordingly been cited in this case.' With this extraordinary comment, Inderwick sat down.

Donald Crawford then took the witness stand to confirm the story told by Inderwick, essentially that adultery had taken beween Dilke and his wife from 1882 to August 1884. But Crawford added a sensational detail which caused Dilke enormous damage. Crawford stated that his wife told him that Sir Charles Dilke made her go to bed with a servant called Fanny, who lay beside them. He asked her who Fanny was, and she replied that Fanny was a woman he had there as his mistress. She said she did not like it at first, but she did it because he wished it; and she believed she would have stood on her head in the street if he wished it. She said he had taught her every French vice, and that Sir Charles Dilke told her he took her because she was so like her mother and that he used to say when they were together, 'How like you are to your mother just now'.

Crawford finished his evidence with inconclusive statements about the places where the alleged adultery had taken place. Mrs Crawford could not remember the address of the alleged assignation house, but believed she could point it out. The footman and Dilke's servant, Sarah, had seen her at Dilke's house in the morning, and Sarah had dressed her. There had been little written communication between them, and the assignations had all been made verbally. When Crawford had finished his evidence, Russell applied to postpone cross-examination of him, as there appeared to be no evidence against Dilke. Mr Inderwick had no objection, and Mr Justice Butt allowed the application. He agreed with Russell that at that moment there was no evidence against Dilke.

Ann Jameson, parlourmaid for Mr Crawford, then gave evidence. Her testimony confirmed that Mrs Crawford spent most of the night out on two nights in 1883 when her husband was away from London. In 1883 and 1884 Sir Charles Dilke had paid visits to Mrs Crawford in a carriage. His carriage came once per fortnight for a short time about 12 or 12.30 in the midday. The carriage used to wait for him. Mrs Crawford told her not to admit anyone when Sir Charles was there. Russell cross-examined Ann Jameson. She stated that when Dilke visited he was announced, entered in the ordinary way, and was shown to the drawing room on the ground floor. The visits lasted about half an hour and she treated them as those of an ordinary visitor. Before Mrs Crawford left home in July 1885 she told her to tell Mr Crawford about Dilke's visits. Up to that point Mr Crawford had not asked her about Dilke, but had asked her about Captain Forster. Captain Forster had visited in 1883, and in 1884 Mrs Crawford received letters from Captain Forster. Ann Jameson had posted letters to Captain Forster. She had seen letters addressed to Forster as late as July 1885. She had never posted letters to Sir Charles Dilke. Captain Forster was sometimes at Mrs Crawford's house. Russell established that there were large windows to, and a through light in, the drawing room referred to by the witness. After Ann Jameson had completed her evidence, the court adjourned for lunch.

The events of the morning posed painful dilemmas for Dilke's legal team. The case against Dilke was very thin. Russell, in fact, opened in the afternoon by addressing the judge with the bald statement 'My Lord, I submit to your Lordship that there is no case whatever which Sir Charles Dilke is called upon to answer. There is nothing to answer.' Given this, the most logical move would be to put Dilke in the witness box to deny that he had committed adultery. But there were serious dangers in doing this. The first was that his legal team feared he would be open to cross-examination about his relations with Mrs Crawford's mother, Mrs Eustace Smith. The second was that he would be cross-examined about his relations with the mysterious third party, Fanny, and the issue of 'French vice'. The allegations of sexual misconduct with the third party, Fanny, were extremely damaging. Yet even if Dilke went into the witness box and denied the allegations, his denial would not carry weight unless Fanny herself testified.[174] Fanny could not be found. It was accordingly decided by Russell and James, with Chamberlain reluctantly concurring, that Dilke should not go into the witness box to deny the charges. They would rest their case on the absence of solid evidence against Dilke. Dilke, who was waiting in a separate room, was told of the decision.

This later proved to be a disastrous mistake, but at the time it appeared to be a wise move. At law, it was certainly well founded. Russell reminded the court of the case of Robinson v. Robinson, in which a confession by a woman respondent in a divorce action based on entries in a diary was held to be no evidence. The judge concurred in the strongest possible terms, saying, 'I cannot see any case whatever against Sir Charles Dilke. By the law of England, a statement made by one party in a suit – a statement made not in the presence of the other – cannot be evidence against that other. I cannot see a shadow of a case.'

This was what Russell wanted to hear, and he stated, 'That opinion of your Lordship is a great relief to myself and my learned friends . . . in the responsibility we have taken upon ourselves in not putting our client in the box'. He dismissed the evidence of Dilke's meetings with Mrs Crawford as no more than normal social intercourse. 'Sir Charles Dilke's visits were made in an open manner, he driving up to the house in a brougham, and seeing Mrs Crawford in a ground floor drawing room, lighted by windows at either end, it would be an extraordinary inference to draw that such visits were made with a view to impropriety of any kind.'

Unfortunately for his client, Russell then clouded the issue, by arguing, 'Ought we to take upon ourselves the responsibility of putting Sir Charles Dilke in the witness box, where he might be put through the events of his whole life, and in the life of any man there may have been found to have been indiscretions – ought we to take upon ourselves that responsibility? After an anxious consideration of that matter we have come to the determination to leave the case where it stands.' This latter comment was deeply unfortunate for Dilke, suggesting as it did that Dilke's former life would not stand up to close examination. Nevertheless, in the atmosphere of the courtroom, the decision appeared wholly reasonable. Inderwick concurred. He stated:

He had opened the case as he would open any similar one, and while expressing the opinion that there was a very strong case against Mrs Crawford . . . he had admitted that there was no case against Sir Charles Dilke upon evidence directly applicable to him. In these circumstances, he could not object to his learned friends' application to have Sir Charles Dilkes' name struck out of the petition.

It was then up to the judge to make a decision, and the decision that he made was deeply perverse. Having dismissed Dilke from the petition, the logical conclusion was that Dilke had not committed adultery with Mrs Crawford, and that Crawford's petition for divorce on the grounds of that adultery should fall. Crawford would then have had to petition for divorce on other grounds. However, the judge did not come to this logical conclusion. Instead, he summed up the position with the following comment:

> I am compelled to come to the conclusion that the adultery charged was committed and to grant the petitioner the decree and relief which he craves for. With regard to the co-respondent, Sir Charles Dilke, my decision is in accordance with what I have already indicated – namely that there is no evidence worthy of the name against him and the petition against him must be dismissed, with costs.

His lordship then pronounced a decree nisi against Mrs Crawford.

This decision may have been correct in law, but it seemed wholly illogical to the general public. The verdict appeared to be that Mrs Crawford had committed adultery with Dilke, but Dilke had not done so with her. Nevertheless, Dilke's conclusion on the night of the verdict was that he had escaped. He wrote in his diary:

> My case tried. I left myself absolutely in the hands of counsel and they took the right course in saying with the judge 'no case'. But Russell did it clumsily and (without my permission) talked of 'indiscretions' . . . . But for this blunder the case stood well. Nothing could be stronger than the judge's words, and 'costs' mean that Crawford had no ground for 'reasonable suspicion', as in similar cases where there had been such ground costs had been left to be paid by each side.[175]

But Dilke was wrong to think that the trial had cleared him. In the eyes of the public, he had not been cleared, and the harsher trials were yet to come.

THE FALL OF DILKE – THE SECOND TRIAL

Dilke's belief that he had been cleared by the decision of the judge was widely shared in the days following the trial. Chamberlain sent an express message to Downing Street saying, 'Case against Dilke dismissed with costs, but the petitioner has got his divorce against his wife'. Mr Gladstone answered, 'My

Dear Chamberlain, I have received your prompt report with the utmost pleasure'.[176] Sir William Harcourt wrote to Dilke: 'Dear Dilke, so glad to hear of the result and of your relief from your great trouble – yours ever WVH.'[177] But by the time Dilke received these plaudits, he knew that the trouble was far from over.

The verdict came under fire both from Liberal and Conservative sources. The leading Conservative newspaper, *The Times*, did not share the view that Dilke had been vindicated. On the morning after the trial, alongside a blow-by-blow account from the courtroom, *The Times* published a damning leader article. The editorial described the result as 'Very singular, and to ordinary minds not very comprehensible'. It focused on the decision of the judge to exonerate Dilke while finding Mrs Crawford guilty of adultery. *The Times* commented:

> The petitioner went into the witness box and related minute circumstantial confessions by his wife which, if true, implicated SIR CHARLES DILKE only . . . . Mrs Crawford admitted the correctness of her husband's evidence by not appearing to deny any part of it, and by letting, in effect, judgement to go by default against her. Acting, it must be borne in mind, under the pressure of legal advice, Sir Charles Dilke did not go into the witness box to deny any of the statements which so gravely affected his character . . . . He was not called to repeat in Court and under oath the denial which . . . he gave to the charges in a statement addressed to his constituents . . . . Accordingly MR JUSTICE BUTT decided that MRS CRAWFORD had committed adultery, but that the petition against SIR CHARLES DILKE must be dismissed with costs . . .
>
> The manner in which the case proceeded – the responsibility for which rests solely with the co-respondent's legal advisors – and the nature of some of the Judge's remarks must almost irresistibly raise in simple minds the question with whom was MRS CRAWFORD guilty.[178]

The Times had put its finger on the contradiction which was to haunt Dilke. The popular view of the trial was that the judge ruled that Mrs Crawford had committed adultery with Dilke, but that Dilke had not committed adultery with her. As the implications of this dawned on the public, it became clear that Dilke had not been exonerated. In the climate of the time, it was unlikely that any politician could have survived with such a major question mark against his character; respectable opinion demanded stainless conduct. But any chance that Dilke could ride out the storm was destroyed by the puritan faction within his own party, which now began a relentless campaign against him.

The crucial note was struck by W.T. Stead in the *Pall Mall Gazette* that evening. Stead rejected the notion that Dilke had been vindicated. He expressed horrified disappointment at the result of the trial, arguing

> We had hoped that we might have been spared the unpleasant necessity of saying a single world upon the case . . . but the remarks of the *Daily News* and the *Daily Telegraph* this morning leave us no option . . . when the *Daily News* tells us that Sir Charles Dilke's character has now been vindicated after full and open trial . . . we are most reluctantly compelled to point out that such a statement is almost

exactly the reverse of the truth . . . . the grave imputations were stated publicly in open court, but there was no detailed reply . . . far from having been disproved, they have not even been denied in the witness box . . . [179]

By sounding this note, Stead had declared Dilke *persona non grata* to the moral purity lobby. Dilke himself was in no doubt as to the implications of Stead's editorial. In his diary for 13 February, Dilke noted, 'Renewed attempt by the *Pall Mall* to drive me out of public life. But I won't go now. In July I said to Emilia and Chamberlain: "Here is the whole truth – and I am an innocent man; but let me go out quietly, and some day people will be sorry and I shall recover a different sort of usefulness." They would not let me go. Now I won't go.'[180]

If Dilke was under any illusions about the difficulty of saving his career, they were dispelled on the following Monday. The *Manchester Guardian* condemned Dilke's behaviour at the trial, and commented, 'to ask us on the strength of this evasion to welcome him back as a leader of the Liberal Party is too strong a draft on our credulity or good nature'. The *Statesman* commented in similar terms, while it was reported that in Glasgow one of the Liberal associations had passed a resolution against including Dilke in a Liberal Cabinet as such would be condoning 'unrighteousness and wrong'.[181]

Dilke's main enemy, however, was the fanatical purity lobby within his own party which was now surging ahead on a relentless moral crusade. After the events of 1885 it was convinced of its own righteousness. It was soon to define its ideology as 'the nonconformist conscience'. And for the nonconformist conscience, absolute, spotless and above all demonstrable adherence to the dictates of Old Testament morality was demanded of all public figures as the condition of their being in public life.

Hugh Price Hughes had thundered in the influential Wesleyan journal the *Methodist Times* in September 1885 that 'all impure men must be hounded from public life, expelled by the Supreme Court of the Public Conscience of the Nation'.[182] Hughes had reiterated this principle in his speech welcoming Stead back from jail, asserting to loud cheers that, 'Hitherto it had been held that a man's public life had no connection with his private life, though the latter might be that of the fornicator . . . . In this reform they must begin at the fountain head. They must begin by cleansing the House of Commons.' Dilke was the first man to be the subject of this cleansing process.

The purity lobby backed Stead in condemning Dilke. General Booth, writing to Stead on 24 February 1886, dismissed Dilke with a summary judgement: 'I congratulate you on your lead in the Dilke business. What a shameful combination of lust, fraud and falsehood there seems to be. He will have to go.'[183] Booth was endorsing an onslaught which had now become hysterical. In his editorial of 16 February Stead had called on Dilke to resign as member for Chelsea, and went completely over the top by stating that 'We are willing to believe that the more terrible part of the charge brought against him is exaggerated [but] if that charge in its entirety were true, we should not exaggerate the universal sentiment that the man against whom so frightful an accusation could lie is a worse criminal than most of the murderers who swing at Newgate'.

THE IMPACT OF VIGILANCE

With this statement the note of hysteria which had long threatened to break through in Stead's writings finally emerged. Stead now seemed unable to distinguish between murder and immorality.

Stead's lead was followed by the Dyer brothers. The *Sentinel* excoriated Dilke's return to Parliament vitriolically:

> Only a strong sense of duty induces us to allude again to the conduct of Sir Charles Dilke. The charges against him are horrible in the extreme – the seduction of a girl-wife, the initiation of her into unnatural vices, and incidentally the degradation of other women, the keeping of mistresses, while holding one of the highest offices in the State. He had an opportunity of refuting those charges, if able to do so, in a Court of Law. That opportunity was not taken . . . .
>
> We are informed that on entering the House of Commons for the first time after the Divorce Court proceedings, Mr Chamberlain immediately joined Sir Charles Dilke, with whom he remained nearly an hour . . . possibly the cause of Mr Chamberlain's good humour was that his friend had steered clear of the witness box, of liability to a subsequent charge of perjury, and of compromising under cross examination in the witness box, others of equal official position.
>
> We have watched with care the course that Sir Charles Dilke has followed since the first public intimation last August of the charges against him . . . we have enquired, and we have weighed the reasons that have been given why he did not rebut the charges on oath. The result is a deliberate conviction that he never intended to enter the witness box, and that Mr Chamberlain never intended that he should do so; and that the extraordinary and ignominious shuffling that has been witnessed by the public has been the result of a detestable plot to restore a guilty man to power, and to screen others perhaps not less guilty than himself . . . . We unite in the protest of the *Pall Mall Gazette*, which speaks of Sir Charles Dilke's return to the House of Commons, with the criminal charges unrefuted, as 'an outrage upon the moral sense of the community' – a protest in which the Christian press also has joined.[184]

This extraordinary piece of witch-hunting libelled both Dilke and Chamberlain, flinging allegations without a shred of evidence, and showing a startling indifference to the actual legal situation. Dilke did not face criminal charges; divorce was a civil action. But by the time this piece appeared, the actual issues of the divorce hardly mattered. The baying puritan mob which W.T. Stead had unleashed was largely indifferent to niceties of law and evidence. If Dilke was to continue in public life, he had to attempt the almost impossible task of proving himself innocent of the charges made by Mrs Crawford. This he was forced to do.

Chamberlain suggested two courses of action in a letter of 22 February, both designed to let Dilke give evidence on oath. The first was to sue for libel. The second was to invoke the Queen's Proctor. Chamberlain wrote, 'Of course if you were quite clear that you wished to go into the box, it is possible to do so – either by action for libel or . . . by intervention of Queen's Proctor'.[185] The latter idea had been put forward by Stead in the *Pall Mall Gazette*, and the coincidence of the same idea coming from his main ally and his main opponent seems to have decided Dilke to invoke the Queen's Proctor.

The Queen's Proctor was a court official whose job was to intervene in the period between a decree nisi and a decree absolute to overturn the interim decree if cause could be shown that the court was deceived or that relevant facts were concealed from the court. By invoking the Queen's Proctor, Dilke put himself in the hands of another. Yet a libel action, in which Dilke would be the prosecutor and Stead would have to prove his statement, ran the risk of providing Stead with a ready-made platform. Given Stead's taste for martyrdom and self-publicity, this was a course of action fraught with risks.

Dilke had a third course of action, which was to do nothing. Cardinal Manning, to whom Dilke had confessed all, advised inactivity. On 2 March he wrote to Dilke arguing, 'All active attempts, such as Mr Stead seems to propose, would only more widely spread and keep alive the excitement . . . which will lose its intensity if met by silence . . . . In trials so great all human efforts fall short.'[186] Dilke, however, felt he had to take action. He was aware that the Queen's Proctor was already investigating the case, and felt he had to be seen to be supporting this move. Towards the end of March, he wrote offering to help the investigation. In consequence he was able to inform a meeting of two thousand of his constituents at the beginning of May that he had induced the Queen's Proctor to intervene to show that the divorce had been granted on the basis of an adultery which had never taken place. The die had been cast.

Dilke looked forward to the second trial with optimism. In the spring, preparations appeared to be going well. Dilke's special solicitor had discovered the mysterious Fanny, a former servant, Fanny Stock, and taken a statement from her. Dilke also now had evidence that Mrs Crawford had committed adultery with Captain Forster, which she had denied to her husband. Dilke's hopes therefore rose, despite recognizing that he was in for a hard fight. Crawford, defending his hard-won divorce, briefed Henry Matthews QC, who had not appeared in the first trial. Matthews was a Tory who had no sympathy for Dilke, and was one of the most powerful and aggressive cross-examiners at the Bar. But Russell was his equal, and Dilke looked forward to the action.

Before it had begun, however, Dilke suffered a serious blow. Dilke and his lawyers, James and Russell, assumed that he would still be a party to the action. This was mistaken; he had been dismissed from the case by Justice Butt and could now appear only as a witness. His attorneys would not have the power of cross-examination, which was limited to the lawyers appearing for Crawford, as the defender of the action, and the Queen's Proctor, seeking to have it overturned. When Dilke realized this, it was a crushing blow. 'If I had known that I should not be allowed to be represented [at] the intervention', he later wrote, 'I could not have faced it – the hardships of the course taken proved too great. But no one, of all these great lawyers, foresaw this.'[187]

His position was then as unfavourable as could be imagined. His fate was to hang on whether the Queen's Proctor could prove that he had not committed adultery with Mrs Crawford while Mrs Crawford was to testify that he had. Neither the Queen's Proctor, Sir Augustus Stephenson, nor the counsel briefed by the proctor, Sir Walter Phillimore, saw themselves as representing Dilke. Stephenson passed all relevant information to Crawford speedily, as a party to the suit, but barely acknowledged Dilke's existence. Phillimore refused to see Dilke at all. Dilke's state of mind was further clouded by losing his seat in the general election of 1886. Dilke had supported Gladstone over Irish Home Rule, and when Gladstone went to the country and lost, he suffered by losing his seat. Eleven days later, he went into the court in an attempt to save his political career.

Dilke's slender chance of victory was diminished still further as soon as the court began by a curious ruling of the judge, Sir James Hannen. He ruled that the Queen's Proctor had to make out his case that no adultery had taken place before the court heard Mrs Crawford's case that it had. This decision meant that Dilke had to argue that he had not committed adultery with Mrs Crawford before hearing in full the evidence claiming that he had. This put Mrs Crawford in the comfortable position of hearing Dilke's reply to her allegations before she had made them – which allowed her to shape her case to her own advantage.

Dilke proved a bad witness. He was unable to answer questions succinctly. He was able to respond reasonably well to questions about the days on which he was supposed to have slept with Mrs Crawford (23 February 1882 and 13 and 14 February 1883), and in denying adultery with his maidservant Sarah Gray, the woman Fanny Stock, who turned out to be a former nursery maid, and above all with Mrs Crawford. But on other issues he rambled and had to be directed by the judge not to include extraneous detail. Above all, he failed to cope with ruthless cross-examination by Matthews. Matthews induced Dilke to suggest that Mrs Crawford had invented the story of his adultery to cover her own adultery with Captain Forster. In making this statement he implied that the author of the anonymous letters to Crawford was Mrs Crawford's mother.

Matthews immediately attempted to bring in Dilke's relationship with this woman, Mrs Eustace Smith. Dilke refused to answer the question, arguing correctly that it was irrelevant. The judge ordered him to answer the question put by Matthews, stating that 'if any improper questions are put to you your Counsel will protect you.' Hannen had clearly forgotten that he had denied Dilke the right to be represented by counsel. Matthews then asked, 'Is it true or untrue that there are acts of indiscretion in your life which you desired not to disclose on cross-examination?' Dilke answered: 'Acts which came to an end eleven and a half years ago.' And Matthews said, 'Then it is true?' And Dilke replied, 'Yes.' The following day Matthews taxed him directly on the subject, asking whether it was true that he had been Mrs Crawford's mother's lover? Dilke replied: 'I was yesterday asked a question of a somewhat similar kind, and I replied to it. I must decline to answer that question.'[188]

While this was totally irrelevant to the question of Dilke's alleged adultery with Mrs Crawford, the point at issue, Dilke's admission that he had been 'indiscreet' with Mrs Crawford's mother, seriously damaged his reputation in the eyes of the jury.

Matthews' cross-examination of Mrs Crawford was very different from that directed to Dilke. The key issue before the court was Dilke's denial that he had committed adultery with Mrs Crawford, against her statement that he had.

Matthews' strategy was to destroy Dilke's credibility, while establishing that of Mrs Crawford. In so doing, he was assisted by her ability as a witness. Then aged twenty-three, she was attractive and highly intelligent. She was an articulate woman who made pointed and succinct answers to questions. She had a clear grasp of what she wanted to say, and appeared a truthful and straightforward witness.

The judge made her state on oath that she had committed adultery with Dilke. Following this crucial formality, Matthews took her through her story on oath. She claimed she had first committed adultery with Dilke on 23 February 1882 at an assignation house in Warren Street, off the Tottenham Court Road. In her diary she had written the entry CWD, standing for Charles Wentworth Dilke. She went again on 6 May, after which the couple met at Sydney Place or at Dilke's house in Sloane Street, usually in the morning. She described Dilke's bedroom in some detail, and claimed she was dressed by Sarah after the event. She spent the night at Sloane Street on 7 December 1882 and 13 February 1883. Later in 1883 the assignations were made at lodgings in Young Street or at Dilke's house. In 1883 she was introduced to 'Fanny'. She was shown a picture of Fanny Stock and identified her as the Fanny in Dilke's bedroom. During the summer of 1884 she had broken off the liaison at the instigation of Mrs Rogerson. She now suspected Mrs Rogerson of writing the 'Metropole' letter. She did not know who wrote the last letter, which precipitated her confession to her husband. She asserted she had not been unfaithful to her husband before meeting Dilke.

Phillimore then cross-examined. His first tactic was to force Mrs Crawford to admit she had committed adultery with Captain Forster. He did this most effectively. He secured the admission that she had committed adultery with Forster in 1884, and that she had lied to her husband about this. Phillimore established that at Easter 1885 she had gone to Dublin to see Forster, telling her husband that she was staying with Mrs Rogerson.

Phillimore cross-examined the CWD entry in her diary, establishing that other initials were written in the diary. They signified no more than that men came, completely innocently, to have tea. She admitted that she believed her mother to have written the letters to her husband, but now suspected some might have been written by Mrs Rogerson. She claimed Mrs Rogerson was also Dilke's mistress. She denied that she had written the final letter precipitating the confession, though a handwriting expert was called who claimed this was so. Crawford's lawyers then called a handwriting expert to argue that the letters were written by Mrs Rogerson.

Phillimore's central argument was that Mrs Crawford had made up the Dilke story to protect her real lover against the suspicions of her husband. He forced her to admit that she had been very much in love with Forster in the summer of 1885, and had aroused suspicions in her husband. She admitted that after making her confession she had specifically asked her husband not to put Forster's name in an action as co-respondent. Phillimore put it to her that when she made her confession she had hoped to marry Forster. Mrs Crawford denied this, saying, 'No, there never had been talk of marriage as Captain Forster was engaged at that time to be married to Miss Smith Barry. He told me, and I knew all along that he was engaged to her . . . .'[189] Before she left the witness box, after a request from the foreman of the jury, Mrs Crawford sketched a plan of the bedroom at the assignation house in Warren Street, showing the means of access to it and the shape of the staircase. This she did with apparent ease.

Phillimore then cross-examined Donald Crawford on his wife's confession. He elicited from Crawford the admission that he had suspected Forster but not Dilke, but was diverted away from Forster by the confession. The crucial exchange went thus:

Q. At the time of your getting the last anonymous letter, were you suspecting Sir Charles Dilke?
A. Not in the least.
Q. Were you suspecting Captain Forster?
A. I was . . . .
Q. . . . Did you – after your wife had made a statement to you with regard to Sir Charles Dilke – did you accept it? . . .
A. I did not doubt it at all in my mind from the time she said,'The man who ruined me was Sir Charles Dilke.' From the solemnity of her manner I had no doubt at all.
Q. Did you press her after that as to Captain Forster?
A. Yes.
Q. And she denied?
A. Yes.
Q. And with as much solemnity as she made her statement with regard to Sir Charles Dilke?
A. Yes, very earnestly; there were certain things which seemed a little suspicious. She asked me not to make him a co-respondent. She said, 'I do not want to ruin more men than one.' It seemed to me in one interpretation as if it were not quite true.[190]

Phillimore was arguing that Mrs Crawford had invented the Dilke adultery to defend her real lover, hoping to marry him. His case was strengthened when Phillimore cross-examined Forster, who had been called to give evidence against Dilke. Phillimore discovered that while Forster had indeed been engaged to Miss Smith Barry, he had broken off the engagement in January 1885. It was renewed at the beginning of July 1885, and he had married two months later.

This was circumstantial evidence for Phillimore's thesis, but by the time he cross-examined Forster, the point was almost irrelevant. Matthews had called several witnesses against Dilke discovered by Crawford's private detective, three of whom had given most damaging evidence against Dilke's character. These were the members of the Hillier family who lived on the ground floor of 65 Warren Street from April 1882 to July 1884. George Hillier testified that a man resembling Dilke used to visit the house quite frequently. His visit was usually preceded by a lady. He stayed for half an hour to an hour, and the lady left afterwards. Hillier was unable to describe the lady, but his wife and daughter stated that the woman was tall, fair, aged about twenty-eight, and certainly not

Mrs Crawford. This evidence was not proof of Dilke's adultery with Mrs Crawford, but it was profoundly damaging to what remained of his reputation. After it had been given, the judgment of the court in the Crawford case was not much in doubt. Dilke's character had been shot to pieces.

If there was any shred of credibility still clinging to Dilke, Henry Matthews cleverly removed it in his summing-up. In a bullying attack allowed remarkable licence by the judge, Matthews dismissed the first trial in the following terms:

> The judge who tried the case had rightly decided that there was no legal evidence against Sir Charles Dilke; but was there not moral evidence of the strongest kind against him? He was charged (by Mrs Crawford's confession) not merely with adultery, but with having committed adultery with the child of one friend and the wife of another . . . he was charged with having done with an English lady what any man of proper feeling would shrink from doing with a prostitute in a French brothel, and yet he was silent.[191]

Matthews had brutally, but cleverly, turned the issue away from whether Dilke had committed adultery with Mrs Crawford, on which the evidence was virtually non-existent, to the side issue of why Dilke had not given evidence in the first trial. Still worse for Dilke, the jury was now seriously misled by both counsel and judge. Matthews proceeded to argue that Dilke could not shelter behind his counsel. Did the jury not believe that they had not acted on instructions? At this point Russell rose to correct this slur, but was silenced by the judge, who ruled that Russell could not speak because his client was not party to the action. Matthews was allowed to continue, asking rhetorically what had made Dilke change his mind. Matthews claimed it was not a respect for the truth, but the fact that the press campaign had become politically inconvenient.

Matthews finished by denying the suggestion that Mrs Crawford had invented the story to protect Forster as 'most implausible'. If she was party to a conspiracy against Dilke, why had she not given her husband more help in his suit against him? He concluded that, 'The burden of proof was on the Queen's Proctor, who in order to be successful must show conclusively that Mrs Crawford had not committed adultery with Sir Charles Dilke. The jury could only give a verdict against his client if they believed that Mrs Crawford was a perjured witness and that a conspiracy existed to blast the life of a pure and innocent man . . . .'[192]

The task of proving conclusively that Dilke had not committed adultery with Mrs Crawford was all but impossible, and Phillimore in his closing address did not attempt to do so. He pointed to weaknesses in Mrs Crawford's statements, and to the refusal to admit to her adultery with Forster until she had been compelled to do so. For motive, there was the desire to shield Forster. At the time of her confession she was almost certainly unaware of the renewal of his engagement. The issue was not whether Mrs Crawford was guilty of adultery. This had now been established, and Crawford could have his divorce. The issue was whether she had committed one adultery or two.

Phillimore was sadly in error. The issue before the court was whether the decree nisi granted by the first court should stand, and this depended on whether adultery with Dilke had been committed. Thus the key issue was whether Dilke or Mrs Crawford were to be believed, and on this the judge summed up against Dilke. On the crucial issue of whether Dilke had instructed his counsel not to put him on the stand, the judge directed the jury as follows: 'Well, you must put yourself in his place. I may venture to suggest such an idea to you. If you were to hear such a statement made involving your honour, as it would do morally, whatever the legal view of the facts, would you accept the advice of your counsel to say nothing? Would you allow the court to be deceived and a tissue of falsehoods to be put forward as the truth?'[193]

Such a question asked of a jury of male Victorian ratepayers could only have one response. And given that slant, Sir James Hannen was inviting the jury to find against Dilke. This they duly did. They retired at 2.55 on the afternoon of Friday 23 July. They returned at 3.10. The clerk asked them, 'How do you find on the issue whether the decree nisi was pronounced contrary to the Justice of the case by reason of material facts not brought to the knowledge of the court?' The foreman replied, 'We find that it was not pronounced contrary to the Justice of the case'. Dilke had failed to get the decree nisi overturned.

There was still no real evidence that Dilke had committed adultery with Mrs Crawford. But the jury had preferred to believe Mrs Crawford was telling the truth rather than Dilke, and thus Dilke was held to be lying. His political career was irrevocably damaged. The outcome was what the Revd Price Hughes and the puritans wanted. Dilke could never become leader of the Liberal Party.

SEVEN

The Destruction of Parnell

THE 'UNCROWNED KING OF IRELAND'

The fate of Charles Dilke was a clear indication of the pitfalls awaiting politicians who fell short of the moral standards expected of politicians in late Victorian Britain. Absolute adherence to the marriage vows was demanded of those who had taken them, and celibacy was required of those who were not married. Anyone who was accused of indulging in sexual activity while unmarried, and with another man's wife, was placed utterly outside the pale. Fornication and adultery, as illicit sex was termed, was incompatible with high public office. Historians may doubt that Dilke was guilty of adultery with Mrs Crawford, but he failed to convince a jury of Victorian ratepayers of this, and paid a heavy price.

The activities of the purity lobby played a considerable role in bringing Dilke down, but it was clearly not a prime mover in the affair. Vigilance was characteristically more a reactive than a proactive force, and nowhere more so than in the Dilke case. Divorce and adultery had always been unrespectable activities, and the Divorce Act of 1857 had been passed only after long controversy. Where divorce was concerned, the moral purity lobby was pushing at an open door. It had, after all, been the editorial columns of *The Times* which had sounded the first note of dissent where the Dilke case was concerned, not the *Pall Mall Gazette*. Having accepted the legality of divorce, respectable opinion demanded it be used to bolster the sacrament of marriage by defining unacceptable behaviour. To have been declared a co-respondent in a divorce action was to become unrespectable. Until 1887, Queen Victoria would not allow even the innocent party to a divorce suit to attend her court.[194] The purity campaign was therefore reinforcing existing moral codes, albeit far more stringently.

Dilke regarded the *Pall Mall Gazette* as having led the attempt to drive him out of public life. This was only partly correct. He was right to see Stead and his colleagues as the most implacable element against him, and right to feel that they kept the controversy alive when otherwise it might have died down. Yet Dilke's fall was not merely due to the puritans. The fear of adultery and divorce was so

*Charles Stewart Parnell, the
'Uncrowned King of Ireland'*

deeply grounded in late Victorian Britain that it is exceedingly unlikely that
Dilke's career would have been undamaged even if the second trial had not taken
place. As he himself had noted in his diary, 'Such a charge . . . is fatal to supreme
usefulness in politics. In the case of a public man a charge is always believed by
many, even though disproved.'[195] Dilke did not even have the opportunity to test
his theory, for he was unable to prove the charge unfounded. His career was
damaged beyond repair, with enormous consequences for a Liberal Party bereft
of key leaders following the Home Rule crisis of 1886.

As a victim of the puritan attitude to marriage and divorce in late Victorian
Britain, however, Dilke pales into insignificance when compared to the
catastrophic fall of Charles Stewart Parnell. The controversy surrounding the
Crawford divorce case was completely overshadowed by the famous O'Shea
divorce action of 1890. If the first case had established the principle that to be
declared a co-respondent in a divorce action removed respectable status and
ended the prospect of high political office, the O'Shea action reinforced it with
the most tragic consequences for Britain and Ireland.

Parnell was a Protestant landowner who became known as 'the uncrowned
King of Ireland' through his militant leadership of the Irish Home Rule Party.
Parnell's career as leader of the party earned him a loyalty among the Catholic
population of Ireland unrivalled in the nineteenth century except by Daniel
O'Connell. His mastery of political tactics brought the Liberal Party under

Gladstone into *de facto* alliance in support of the Home Rule cause. Yet he threw away the loyalty of his Catholic supporters, the support of Gladstone's Liberals, and the chance to secure Home Rule, by a passionate, clandestine affair with the wife of one of his MPs.

The movement for Irish Home Rule had been founded by Isaac Butt, a Protestant Dublin lawyer who had defended Fenian insurrectionists after the failed uprising of 1867. Butt had come to the conclusion that the long tradition of armed insurrection by the Irish was doomed to failure. The best prospect of dealing with the appalling misrule of Ireland by the British was not through complete separation, but by a revival of the Irish parliament of the eighteenth century and its limited powers of local self-government. Butt therefore founded the Irish Home Rule Party in 1870, and was elected a Home Rule MP in 1871.

The ancient enmity between British and Irish had suffered a savage escalation in the potato famine of 1845–50. Rapid population growth and economic backwardness had, by the 1840s, reduced much of rural Ireland to total reliance on the easiest crop that primitive farming could grow – the potato. The potato was, however, subject to periodic attacks of blight. Official reports in the 1830s and early 1840s warned the authorities of the threat of serious famine if a widespread failure of the crop occurred. The authorities made little attempt to prepare contingency plans for such a disaster.[196]

When a partial failure of the potato crop took place in September 1845, the British prime minister, Sir Robert Peel, saw Free Trade as the answer, and he bent his efforts to repealing the corn laws restricting the import of cheap continental grain into Britain. This was relevant to industrial Britain; it was totally irrelevant to the potato-growing areas of Ireland, which had no money to buy in imported corn – or indeed, Irish-grown corn from their own country. The grain-growing areas of Ireland continued to export corn throughout the famine while the potato-growing areas starved. Thus when the potato blight returned with disastrous effect in 1846, the ensuing failure of the potato crop led to the worst famine in Western Europe in the nineteenth century. By the time the situation stabilized in 1850, the population of Ireland had declined by two million. Between half a million and a million of a total population of eight and a half million had died; an equal number had fled the country. The nationalist movement turned to insurrection. The immediate result was the Young Ireland rebellion of 1848. It was crushed. A further, hopeless rebellion took place in 1867, which was also crushed.

It was after defending the Fenian leaders of this rebellion that Isaac Butt concluded that complete separation from Britain was impossible, and that a limited measure of self-rule was all that could be hoped for. In 1871 he secured election as leader of an embryonic Home Rule Party. At the subsequent general election of 1874, fifty-nine Home Rule candidates were elected. The tradition of violence in Irish politics was far from abandoned, but a peaceful road forward appeared to open up.

It was Parnell, however, and not Butt, who was to reap the benefit. Butt relied on the reasonableness of the nationalist case to secure Home Rule. He failed to make any headway. In 1874, 1875, 1876 and 1877 he moved resolutions in the Commons in favour of Home Rule which were all heavily defeated. His motion of

April 1877 was defeated by 417 votes to 67. Only one non-Irish MP spoke for it, and only eight non-Irish MPs voted in favour. In 1878, Butt resigned as leader of the Home Rule Party, enabling a more militant leader to take over.

That leader was Parnell. Charles Parnell (1846–91), with estates in County Wicklow, was educated in part at Cambridge. He had, however, imbibed strongly anti-English feelings from his American mother and supported Home Rule. In April 1875 he took a Westminster seat at a by-election. He pondered Butt's failure and concluded that the rational argument in favour of Home Rule was doomed to failure. Only disruption would force the British to take Irish grievances seriously. Accordingly he led the Home Rule Party on a campaign of filibustering, twice keeping the House of Commons up all night. One session lasted an unprecedented twenty-six hours. It was the sensation of the hour. The horrified British saw Parnell as no better than a Fenian.

Parnell's parliamentary tactics were overshadowed by events in the Irish countryside which were to propel him to unchallenged leadership of the nationalist movement. By the late 1870s, European agriculture was suffering severe depression due to the flooding of the markets by cheap American grain. In Ireland, the depression threatened a repeat of the famine of 1845–50. Farmers were terrified that non-payment of rent would lead to a wave of evictions, and began to turn to violence. On 2 April 1878 Lord Leitram was murdered in Donegal and 'Captain Moonlight' – the mythical leader of the secret societies operating a policy of terrorism by night – began to rule much of Ireland. Parnell had no truck with violence, and moved to channel the protest in the countryside in ways he could control. He threw in his lot with the Land League formed by the Fenian, Michael Davitt, who had emerged from Dartmoor Gaol in 1877.

When Parnell threw in his lot with the Land League on 7 June 1879, he achieved an unprecedented hold over the Catholic population of Ireland. This was so manifest that he was widely believed to have complete control over all the players, which was not true. Parnell had no control over the reactions of individual peasants driven to desperation by events, and no control over the followers of 'Captain Moonlight'. But in the campaign to defend tenants' rights, Parnell was so dominant that the largely Catholic tenantry learnt to look instinctively to this Protestant landlord for leadership.

Gladstone's administration decided to deal with the land agitation by imprisoning Parnell and other leaders of the Land League. But when they did this in 1882 they found the violence escalated without his calming influence. Parnell was a force for moderation and constitutionalism, not murder and insurrection. The government of the most powerful empire in the world found itself negotiating with a prisoner in one of its own gaols for a compromise. In the Kilmainham Treaty (negotiated April–May 1882) the Liberals conceded financial compensation to evicted tenants in exchange for Parnell's promise to exert his influence against violence. This treaty was wrecked by the Phoenix Park murders of 6 May 1882. Yet though Gladstone was forced to bring in a coercion bill which imposed draconian police powers on Ireland for three years, Gladstone and the more intelligent of his colleagues had learned that Parnell was not an extremist but a statesman of stature. It was a lesson they took to heart.

THE IRISH DEVIL-FISH.

"The creature is formidable, but there is a way of resisting it. ✱ ✱ ✱ The Devil-fish, in fact, is only vulnerable through the head."
VICTOR HUGO's *Toilers of the Sea*, Book IV., Ch. iii.

Gladstone fighting the Land League, as seen by Punch, *18 June 1881*

While the coercion bill was in force, Parnell held that Parliament was irrelevant to Irish politics, and led a virtual boycott of the institution. From 1882 to 1885 Parnell virtually vanished. His colleagues rarely knew where he was or what he was doing. Yet such was his hold over his colleagues that his behaviour was unquestioned. When Parnell re-emerged in 1885, his hold over his party was undiminished. Parnell resumed his argument that Home Rule was the only replacement for coercion. Secretly, as we have seen, Gladstone came to agree. But Gladstone kept his counsel to himself hoping that the Conservatives would decide for Home Rule, thus solving Gladstone's problem of keeping Hartington and the Whigs in line.

Parnell also hoped for Conservative support. And in the autumn of 1885, while the Tories would not commit themselves, the noises they made seemed hopeful. In the absence of any pledges from the Liberals, Parnell decided to advise those Irishmen living in England to vote Conservative in the general election of 1885. It was a mistaken tactic. Parnell's intervention swung a number of English seats to the Tories, but not enough to deny the Liberals a majority. Parnell's eighty-six Irish Home Rule MPs held the balance. But by a fantastic freak of the poll, the majority of Liberals over Conservatives was exactly 86. If the Parnellites voted with the Conservatives, there would be a dead heat. But if they voted with the Liberals, who they had just opposed in the election, the Liberals would have an overwhelming majority.

As the public digested this remarkable outcome, Gladstone's son Herbert unofficially revealed his father's conversion to Home Rule to a number of pressmen. By 18 December the news was a front page sensation. Gladstone had been converted as early as August 1885 – well before the election. But to the public, the news appeared as an attempt to win Irish support and regain power. Gladstone had to win over aggrieved colleagues who had not been consulted or convinced over Home Rule. He failed. Hartington and Chamberlain led a group of dissident Liberal MPs to vote with the Tories and defeat the Home Rule Bill. Defeated in the Commons, Gladstone called for an immediate general election, only to lose heavily. A Conservative–Liberal Unionist coalition took office, pledged to oppose Home Rule.

Parnell's critics were muted despite the 1886 debacle because Parnell could not seriously be blamed for events – and because he had at least secured the support of a major British party for Home Rule. But the fortunes of the Home Rule Party were now tied to the fortunes of the Liberal Party. The Home Rulers faced the daunting prospect of a potential seven-year Parliament before the next general election was required. Parnell now led his party on a long march, aimed at convincing the Liberal Party, especially its Nonconformist wing, that the conversion forced upon it by Gladstone in 1886 was justifiable. The Irish had to prove they were thoroughly respectable and fit for self-government. Parnell's opponents, in reaction, were bent on proving the opposite. In particular, they wished to destroy Parnell's reputation as a respectable politician.

Parnell had long been dogged by his association with Fenians. A large body of anti-Home Rule opinion privately believed that Parnell was secretly in league with the men of violence, despite Parnell's vehement denials. The most serious allegation linked Parnell to the most brutal of all acts of violence in recent Irish history, the Phoenix Park murders. If true, Parnell was condemned as a liar and accomplice to an abominable crime. Parnell's opponents sought evidence linking Parnell with the murders, and were apparently vindicated when, on 18 April 1887, *The Times* published a facsimile of a letter apparently signed by Parnell justifying the murder of Burke, the under-secretary. Parnell denounced the letter as a forgery, but refused to take legal action. His hand was forced when one of his supporters sued *The Times* for libel, and fresh letters were produced. Parnell was forced to demand government action. The administration conceded a judicial inquiry in the form of a special commission, which began sitting in September 1888.

The inquiry produced sensations to rival any Victorian melodrama. In February 1889, *The Times* was forced to expose the original source of the alleged Parnell letters, one Richard Pigott, to cross-examination. Pigott was a disreputable Dublin journalist who had forged the alleged letters when suffering serious financial difficulties, and sold the results to the paper for £30,000. Parnell was represented by Sir Charles Russell, and Russell confronted Pigott in the witness box on 21 February 1889.

Russell conducted a cross-examination of exceptional brilliance, carefully constructed to prove Pigott guilty of systematic fraud. Pigott staunchly defended the authenticity of the letters until Russell cleverly induced him to write down a series of crucial words. The list contained spelling mistakes which also occurred in the facsimile letters. Russell then mercilessly exposed Pigott as a comprehensive liar and blackmailer, and when Pigott stepped down he was a broken man. Parnell turned to his solicitor, and remarked, 'That man will not come into the box again. Mr Lewis, let that man be watched. If you do not keep your eye on him you will find that he will leave the country.'[197] Parnell was right. When the commission reconvened on 26 February, Pigott was nowhere to be seen. The affair now reached a climax of pure Grand Guignol. On 28 February Pigott was seen in Madrid. The police were informed, and an inspector visited him in his hotel bedroom. As the inspector entered the room, Pigott drew a revolver, placed it to his head, and blew his brains out.

Parnell's reputation rose to new heights. It was widely believed that Parnell's opponents had deliberately forged the letters to discredit him. Though this was incorrect – the Conservatives and Liberal Unionists had hoped the letters were genuine, but were not directly involved – the belief reinforced the feeling in favour of Parnell and his cause. Support for Liberals and Home Rulers reached new heights on the mainland. In the summer and autumn of 1889, Parnell was the hero of the hour, and Gladstone's stand on Home Rule appeared completely vindicated. In December 1889 Gladstone marked his approval of Parnell by inviting him to his home at Hawarden to discuss the details of a Home Rule bill.

But just as Parnell's popularity reached its highest peak, fate intervened. In an extraordinary echo of the Dilke case, Parnell had reached the apogee only to be felled by a divorce action. Parnell left Hawarden on 19 December, having enjoyed a period of fruitful discussion. Exactly five days later, a long-maturing crisis over his private life burst into public view. On Christmas Eve 1889, Captain William O'Shea sued his wife for divorce. Charles Stewart Parnell was named as co-respondent.

THE SLIDE INTO THE ABYSS

The relationship between Parnell and Mrs Katherine O'Shea had been the subject of speculation in the upper levels of the Liberal Party since 1882. Mrs O'Shea was the wife of a Home Rule MP, Captain William O'Shea. Parnell used the captain and his wife to communicate with Chamberlain and Gladstone at the time of the negotiations for a peace treaty in 1882, and the relationship between the Irish leader and the O'Shea family was surrounded by rumours.

Gladstone himself certainly knew of the rumours. The home secretary, Sir William Harcourt, was said to have told the Cabinet on 17 May that the Kilmainham Treaty would not be popular 'when the public discovered that it had been negotiated by Captain O'Shea, the husband of Parnell's mistress'.[198] On 20 June, Gladstone's secretary, Edward Hamilton, commented in his diary regarding Katherine O'Shea that 'She seems to be on very intimate terms with Parnell; some say his mistress. It would have been far better for Mr Gladstone to decline point blank to see her or communicate with her; but he does not take the view of the "man of the world" in such matters . . . .'[199]

Indeed he did not. Gladstone simply refused to believe that Parnell would risk his cause by indulging in such an affair, knowing of the likely consequences of an adulterous relationship. When Gladstone's nephew, George Leveson Gower, referred to the rumours about this time, Gladstone snubbed him with the unanswerable comment that 'You do not ask me to believe that it is possible a man should be so lost to all sense of what is due to his public position, at a moment like the present, in the very crisis of his country's fortunes, as to indulge in an illicit connection with the wife of one of his very own political supporters'.[200]

Gladstone's sentiments were admirably liberal and principled, but mistaken. Parnell was indeed indulging in an affair with Mrs O'Shea. Although this was to be a well-guarded secret for another eight years, Parnell was gambling with his future and that of his party and cause.

Parnell had first met Katherine O'Shea in the summer of 1880. Parnell was then thirty-four years old, and a bachelor without any known attachments. Katherine was a married woman of thirty-five years, with three children. She came from an upper-class English family. Her father, a distinguished Anglican clergyman, was heir to a baronetcy, and her uncle, Lord Hatherley, was chancellor in Gladstone's first Cabinet. She had married Willie O'Shea at the age of twenty-one, when he was a dashing captain in the 18th Hussars. His position in the army overrode the fact that he was a Catholic Irishman, with an estate in County Clare.

The couple married for love, but after fourteen years of marriage the initial attraction had waned. Captain O'Shea had to spend much time abroad, notably in Madrid, where he had business interests. These were not lucrative, and the family came to rely on support from Katherine's wealthy widowed aunt, Mrs Benjamin Wood, known as Aunt Ben. She had bought a home at Eltham, Kent, for the

Katherine O'Shea, later Mrs Parnell.
This picture originated in the
Illustrevet Tidende, *1891–2*

family, where Katherine could bring up the children while nursing her. O'Shea rented a flat in London for business purposes, paid for by Aunt Ben. The relationship between Aunt Ben and the O'Sheas was so close that Aunt Ben had made a will leaving the greater part of her considerable fortune to Katherine. The O'Sheas were dangerously dependent on Aunt Ben's approval, and she demanded spotless respectability.

By 1880, these arrangements had existed for five years. O'Shea was frequently away from his wife, but Aunt Ben accepted that this was due to his Iberian business interests. To outward eyes the marriage was irreproachable. O'Shea may have been aware that his wife's feelings for him had cooled, but Katherine was certainly not estranged from her husband in 1880, and supported his attempts to build a political career. When O'Shea was elected MP for Clare as a Home Rule candidate in the election of 1880, she was hostess at a celebration dinner for her husband and his fellow Clare MP, the O'Gorman Mahon. In this way she became involved in Home Rule politics, and in the course of her husband's activities met Charles Stewart Parnell.

The first fateful meeting took place in the summer of 1880. Parnell took an immediate interest in Katie O'Shea, driving out with her when he should have been in Parliament, but Katherine was at first concerned only to advance her husband's precarious political career. O'Shea, more Whig than nationalist, had abandoned his Home Rule promises on arriving at Westminster and was supporting the Liberals. However Katherine must have responded sufficiently that summer to encourage Parnell. When Parnell returned to Ireland in September, Mrs O'Shea was uppermost in his mind. He seems to have been uppermost in hers. She wrote him two letters. He replied significantly: 'I received your two letters quite safely, and you may write me even nicer ones with perfect confidence . . . . I trust to see you in London on Tuesday next. Is it true that Captain O'Shea is in Paris, and if so when do you expect his return?'[201]

This was ambiguous. The ambiguity was soon removed. Parnell was not a man to let convention stand in his way when moved by great emotion, and Katherine moved him with intense passion. He visited England in October and when he returned to Dublin[202] wrote to Katherine in terms which suggest a Rubicon had been crossed. 'My own love', he wrote, 'you cannot imagine how much you have occupied my thoughts all day and how very greatly the prospect of seeing you again very soon comforts me.'[203] The relationship was now more than friendship.

O'Shea initially welcomed the close relationship between his wife and his leader, and Katherine later claimed he encouraged it deliberately for personal gain. But O'Shea cannot have expected the grand passion which developed. Indeed, in 1881 he discovered an unacceptable state of affairs, and there was an explosion. O'Shea arrived unexpectedly at Eltham and discovered evidence of an unannounced Parnell visit in the form of Parnell's portmanteau. Flying into a rage, O'Shea demanded Parnell fight him in a duel. Katherine and her sister smoothed down ruffled feathers and O'Shea accepted a promise that Parnell would not stay at Eltham in his absence. The status of the promise was later disputed. O'Shea claimed he accepted the promise made to him at face value, while for Katherine and Parnell the row marked the final end of the O'Shea marriage. Katherine recorded in her memoir of the affair later that 'from the date of this bitter quarrel Parnell and I were one, without further scruple, without fear and without remorse'.[204]

This may have been how Parnell and Katherine viewed matters. It was far from the full picture. For the next nine years Parnell and Katherine conducted their affair with such furtiveness that O'Shea was plausibly able to argue in the divorce court that he knew nothing of it, and believed his marriage to be a reality for at least five years. In January and February 1886 Parnell faced the famous Galway Mutiny, in which he had to intervene personally to impose an unpopular candidate on the Home Rule Association in Galway. The candidate was Captain William O'Shea. Yet informed observers noted that in the debate on the Home Rule bill that summer, Captain O'Shea did not vote. Within the Home Rule Party MPs speculated on the relationship between Parnell and the captain. Whatever the relationship was at that time, the crisis did not break till the end of 1889.

The divorce petition stated adultery to have taken place between April 1886 and the present. The allegations posed a terminal threat to Parnell's political career. Home Rulers in both Catholic Ireland and the British Liberal Party looked to the divorce court to exonerate Parnell from the charge of adultery, and thus the divorce court was the focus of intense interest when the trial opened on 16 November 1890.[205] O'Shea was represented by the solicitor general, Sir Edward Clarke. Mrs O'Shea was represented by Mr Lockwood QC and Mr Pritchard who had been briefed to deny adultery, but also contend on Mrs O'Shea's behalf that the petitioner 'had been guilty of connivance in the adultery'.[206] She also alleged he had wilfully separated himself from the respondent; that he himself had been guilty of adultery; that he had unreasonably delayed instituting the suit; and that he had had been guilty of cruelty towards the respondent.

Mrs O'Shea's allegations were bizarre. To deny adultery while simultaneously alleging collusion in the very same adultery is extraordinary conduct, provoking intense speculation on how the charges would be defended. The question is still open; Parnell and Mrs O'Shea did not turn up to defend the claims. When the trial opened, Mrs O'Shea's counsel announced that the action would not be defended, causing a sensation of the first order. Parnell's supporters were stunned that he did not defend the action, which he had all along claimed would vindicate him.

There were more sensations to come. O'Shea's action rested on the proposition that for many years he had been systematically deceived by Parnell and Katherine, who had consistently denied rumours that they were having an affair while pursuing a carefully planned clandestine relationship. O'Shea argued that after the portmanteau incident of 1881, he had been assured by his wife (Parnell made no promises) that she would not see Parnell again without O'Shea being present. In the formal language of the court, 'the incident terminated, and the affectionate relations which had always existed between Captain O'Shea and his wife were resumed'.[207]

O'Shea's counsel argued that despite this promise, Parnell continued to visit Katherine in the absence of her husband, sleeping at Eltham when O'Shea was away from home. The implication was that Katherine was conducting sexual relations with both O'Shea and Parnell simultaneously, a particularly damaging allegation since Mrs O'Shea had borne three children in that period. O'Shea argued that his suspicions were not raised till the summer of 1884, when rumours of the relationship reached his ears. He wrote to Parnell on 4 August threatening to take the Chiltern Hundreds and remove his family abroad rather than allow further scandal to attach to his name. Parnell wrote back a blunt denial on 7 August saying that 'I do not know of any scandal, or any ground for one, and can only suppose that you have misunderstood the drift of some statements that have been made to you'. The same day O'Shea received an affectionate letter from his wife, the full draft of which reads:

My dear Willie – I am very sorry that you should have waited in on my account, but after our conversation on Tuesday I could not imagine that you would expect me – in any case, I was feeling scarcely strong enough to travel again in the heat yesterday, and for the children's sake I should not like to die yet, as they would lose all chance of aunt's money, and, however good your appointment, they will scarcely have too much, I would imagine, and certainly we have a better right to all she has to leave than anyone else. I am going up to town early to-morrow, and should like to see you before you leave, but not to continue the conversation we had on Tuesday. I will call about 4 o'clock, if that will suit you, yours, K. O'Shea.

Edward Clarke suggested that this was a denial of the rumours, but a careful reading shows that this was not so. In this letter, the first from Mrs O'Shea cited in court, she did not mention the rumours, but was very careful to remind O'Shea of the money his children could inherit if Aunt Ben willed Katherine her money. O'Shea was being warned not to rock a lucrative boat. None of the letters produced by O'Shea during the court action was subject to cross-examination so the charge of collusion was never examined. It is, however, worth noting that these letters can be read in two ways. The court read them as innocent indignation by O'Shea and conscious deceit by Katherine and Parnell. But they can equally be read as a protest for the record, and a denial for the record, with a warning by Katherine not to jeopardize financial arrangements of importance to O'Shea. This alternative explanation was never aired in court.

The 1884 letters seemed to show a pattern of innocence compounded by deceit. O'Shea's counsel reinforced this in the minds of the court by producing further letters to the captain denying impropriety, while proving beyond doubt that Parnell and Katherine were conducting an affair. Indeed, in February 1885 two of Parnell's horses were brought to Eltham and lodged in Mrs O'Shea's stables. O'Shea claimed to be unaware of this, and of the arrival of a third horse in the early part of 1886.

O'Shea argued that he suspected nothing of this until the appearance of a paragraph in the *Pall Mall Gazette* of 24 May 1886, entitled 'Mr Parnell's Suburban Retreat'. This noted that Parnell had been involved in a riding accident while driving from Eltham station to Wonersh Lodge, Mrs O'Shea's home. O'Shea immediately demanded to know why Parnell was staying at his home in defiance of the agreement made in 1881. Katherine replied sweetly that: 'I have not the slightest idea of what it means, unless, indeed, it is meant to get a rise out of you.' Parnell then wrote to Katherine O'Shea, to wit: 'My Dear Mrs O'Shea – your telegraph in reference to the paragraph duly reached me. I had a couple of horses at a place in the neighbourhood of Bexleyheath, but as I am now unable to be much away from London, I have turned them out to grass for the summer. I am very sorry that you should have any annoyance about the matter . . . .' Mrs

---

MR. PARNELL'S SUBURBAN RETREAT.

Shortly after midnight on Friday evening, Mr. Parnell, while driving home, came into collision with a market gardener's cart. During the sitting of Parliament the hon. member for Cork usually takes up his residence at Eltham, a suburban village in the south-east of London. From here he can often be seen taking riding exercise round by Chiselhurst and Sidcup. On Friday night as usual his carriage met him at the railway station by the train which leaves Charing-cross at 11.45. As he was driving homeward a heavy van was returning from Covent-garden market, and this came into collision with Mr. Parnell's conveyance, damaging it, but fortunately causing no serious injury to its owner, who after a short pause continued his journey.

The fatal paragraph in the Pall Mall Gazette, *24 May 1886*

O'Shea showed the letter to her husband, but if she hoped this would maintain the status quo, she was wrong.

This news was the breaking-point in relations between the captain and his wife. On 2 July 1886 O'Shea wrote from Carlsbad with a story that an American lady, Mrs Pell, had been reading an American paper in his company when she had suddenly said:

> 'Here is your name in the Press, Mr O'Shea.' She read about a paragraph or two, then suddenly stammered, being as red as a peony, and exclaimed, 'Oh, I am so sorry, I can't go on', and tried to turn it off. Of course we were more than ever interested. I knew what it was well enough; swore I didn't &c. There it all was about Mr P's Asphasia at Eltham, Mr P's suburban retreat during the absence of the husband . . . . I merely said . . . the worse features of American politics had been introduced into our country by filthy swine like Parnell and his crew. You may, perhaps, understand some day the terrible curse there is on the family.[208]

Edward Clarke read this correspondence as proof positive that O'Shea had not known of what was going on behind his back until spring 1886. The evidence can be read in a different sense. The appearance of the *Pall Mall Gazette* and American paragraphs signalled that the secret could no longer be kept. Coming on top of the famous Galway Mutiny of February 1886, which revealed that members of the Irish parliamentary party were talking of the relationship, it is quite feasible that O'Shea realized that his career as a complaisant husband was now coming to an end and that he would have to change tack. However, this was not a view put in public in November 1890.

O'Shea argued that from this point onward his relationship with his wife deteriorated, as she continually insisted on seeing Parnell. On 9 October 1886 a paragraph appeared in the *Sussex Daily News* stating that Parnell had been staying at Eastbourne with Mrs O'Shea, with Captain O'Shea's knowledge. O'Shea wrote to his wife but she denied any knowledge of Parnell being in Eastbourne. On 18 December he saw a paragraph in a newspaper suggesting that Parnell was at Eltham. He asked his son, Gerard, about it, but the son, defending the mother, denied the story was true. Gerard, however, feeling his father was being badly treated, entreated his mother to give up Parnell. Accordingly on 27 June 1887 she wrote a letter to Gerard stating, 'I am willing to meet your wishes with regard to Mr Parnell. I agree that there shall be no further communication, direct or indirect.'[209]

O'Shea claimed that he again believed that the affair was over, but that at the end of 1889, 'I received information that Mr Parnell was living in the house at Brighton with Mrs O'Shea. I then consulted my solicitors and filed this petition. I obtained the information on the 20th of December and the petition was filed on the 24th.' The immediate point was certainly true. On 20 December Gerard had visited his mother in Brighton, and discovered Parnell's clothes in the house. There was, O'Shea later reported, 'a dreadful scene' in which Katherine admitted her continuing affair. Three weeks later O'Shea told W.T. Stead, 'Mr Parnell is a goner, and the first witness against Mrs O'Shea will be her own son'.[210]

Given the facts of the matter, and the overwhelming weight of evidence in Captain O'Shea's hands, it is deeply surprising that Parnell had taken a sanguine view of the case; and still more surprising that he allowed Katherine O'Shea to make her muddled and offensive allegations in response. But behave like this he did. In public the couple behaved as if preparing for a triumphal counter to O'Shea's attack. Parnell himself responded to the divorce suit by absolute denial. He convinced his supporters of his innocence by the vehemence of his denials. In the eleven months before the hearing, Parnell displayed total confidence in being cleared of O'Shea's accusations. Parnell told a leading Liberal politician, John Morley, only five days before the action was due to be heard, that there was no prospect of his going into retirement: 'No chance of it. Nothing in the least leading to disappearance . . . . The other side don't know what a broken-kneed horse they are riding.'[211]

What led Parnell to have such confidence? The most plausible explanation is that he believed O'Shea could be bought off. Katie later claimed that O'Shea was offered sums of between £20,000 and £60,000, and O'Shea's own counsel, Edward Clarke, believed that he would not appear on the day of the trial. O'Shea wrote to Chamberlain shortly after the trial stating, 'No-body except myself knows what a fight it was or the influences, religious, social and pecuniary, that were brought to bear in the hope of "squaring" me. The last offer was made to me through my son the evening before the trial and was equivalent to over £60,000.'[212] Presumably if the divorce action collapsed, Katie O'Shea could counter-sue for divorce on the grounds of adultery and cruelty, gain a divorce with her character intact, and then secure the goal which she and Parnell had longed for, their own marriage. They may even have believed that under these circumstances, Catholic Ireland would tolerate Parnell's continued leadership of the Home Rule Party.

If these were indeed Parnell's plans, they were an illusion, because the money was never likely to be forthcoming. Parnell was notoriously short of money. Katherine O'Shea was nominally wealthy, having at last inherited her aunt's fortune when the aunt died in May 1889, but she could not touch her legacy because other members of the family contested the legality of the will; £60,000 was beyond either Parnell or Katherine O'Shea to find. They believed they could buy the captain's complaisance, but they wholly lacked the means to do so. Katherine later told Henry Harrison that it was not O'Shea's high-minded principles which prevented him taking the money, but her inability to produce hard cash.[213]

This explanation is plausible and explains much that would otherwise be perverse. If Parnell and Katherine O'Shea believed that the captain would withdraw rather than enter the courtroom, then the muddled counter-charges could become an effective weapon against him. But once the captain had decided to proceed with the action, the case advanced by Katherine immediately became indefensible. Katherine and Parnell dared not appear in the courtroom to argue their case without risk of being charged with perjury. Edward Clarke triumphantly argued: 'It is perhaps not to be wondered at that Mr Parnell did not venture to add a criminal offence to that course of faithlessness and falsehood by which during these years he had betrayed the wife of the friend who had trusted him.'[214]

This was a crushing attack on Parnell. Historians have debated at length its justification, largely concluding that it was not the whole truth, and probably not even part of the truth. But in November 1890, it was almost universally believed. Parnell was successfully accused of adultery and systematic falsehood. The undefended action carried its own message. To the Victorian public in both Britain and Ireland, Parnell was an adulterer and a liar. Unlike the Dilke case, where there was legitimate room to doubt whether the co-respondent was guilty as charged, Parnell had undoubtedly been Katherine O'Shea's lover, and appeared to have consciously concealed the fact. In the climate of late Victorian Britain, this meant his political career was over. Alas, this lesson was obvious to all but the one man to whom it applied. Charles Stewart Parnell decided to ignore the political implications of the verdict of the court.

PARNELL'S LAST STAND

When the court granted Captain O'Shea his divorce, it plunged the Home Rule Party into crisis. Parnell's enemies took full advantage of the situation. *The Times* took particular pleasure in exploiting the allegation that Parnell had used a fire escape to avoid Captain O'Shea when disturbed visiting Katherine. It argued in a leader on 18 November that the trial showed:

> domestic treachery, systematic and long continued deception, the whole squalid apparatus of letters written with the intent of misleading, houses taken under false names, disguises and aliases, secret visits and sudden flights . . . . If Captain O'Shea had been a consenting party to the intrigue, . . . what was the need for MR PARNELL's aliases, disguises and deceiving letters? Why should he have escaped from MRS O'SHEA's house at Brighton by climbing down the fire escape. . . ?

The truth of this fire escape allegation was later strongly denied by Mrs O'Shea, but her denials were useless. The 'fire escape' incident vividly illustrated the 'deceit' theory and was endlessly recycled as the symbol of Parnell's perfidy.

The Times ruthlessly exposed the dilemma O'Shea's decree nisi posed for the supporters of Home Rule. The paper contended:

> . . . if Mr Parnell intends to remain at the head of the Irish parliamentary party, as appears to be suggested by his issue of a circular to his following on the very day on which he withdrew from his defence in the Divorce Court, he will place the Gladstonians in a grievous dilemma. To part company with the master of 86 votes [i.e. the 86 Home Rule MPs] or to stand shoulder to shoulder with the person described by Mr Justice Butt as 'the man who takes advantage of the hospitality offered him by the husband to debauch the wife' are courses equally uncomfortable to an Opposition professing to be peculiarly the party of moral purity.[215]

The Times was right. Whether *any* politician in late Victorian Britain could survive involvement in a divorce action is open to doubt. For a politician linked closely with a Liberal Party containing a powerful moral purity lobby, the chances were distinctly remote. The only possibility of continuing the alliance lay in the fact that Parnell was an Irish, not a Liberal, politician, and not directly subject to Liberal morality. Gladstone initially took the view that the matter was for the Irish party to resolve, and he remained silent in the crucial week following the court decision. On 19 November he wrote to John Morley to argue, 'that we the Liberal party as a whole, and especially its leaders, have for the moment nothing to say to it, that we must be passive, must wait and watch. But I again and again say to myself the words I have already quoted, say them I mean in the interior and silent forum, "It'll nae dae . . . ".'[216]

Gladstone privately hoped that Parnell would see that his position was untenable and resign, at least temporarily. This was also the private hope of the Irish Catholic hierarchy, which was also silent in the week following the divorce. Parnell, however, had no such intention. He had made his decision on the night before the case. Katherine O'Shea recalled later that he told her

> I have given, and will give, Ireland what is in me to give. That I have vowed to her, but my private life shall never belong to any country, but to one woman. There will be a howl, but it will be the howling of hypocrites; not altogether, for some of these Irish fools are genuine in their belief that forms and creeds can govern life and men . . . . But I am not as they, for they are among the world's children . . . if they turn from me, my Queen, it matters not at all in the end.[217]

Such an attitude may appear fatalistic, but Parnell was anything but fatalistic. He chose initially to ignore the 'howling' which he knew would arise from the divorce, and called a meeting of the parliamentary party for 25 November with this aim in view. But if the howling continued, he was prepared to fight for his political life. And in the week leading up to the meeting, Parnell's supporters in the party rallied support for what was to prove a Pyrrhic victory.

Superficially, it appeared that Irish Home Rulers backed Parnell completely. On 18 November a meeting of the central branch of the Irish National League was assembled, presided over by Parnell's supporter John Redmond. It endorsed a pledge of loyalty to Parnell. Two days later a meeting at Leinster Hall, Dublin, passed a resolution of support for Parnell proposed by Justin McCarthy, vice-chair of the party. The resolution was penned and seconded by T.M. Healy, one of Parnell's bitterest opponents within the Home Rule Party, who had been shocked by an editorial written by the Revd Price Hughes the previous day. Healy's support for Parnell was based on the implication, clearly set out in his speech, that by supporting Parnell publicly, the leader would listen to private advice to go quietly. Parnell missed the implication. He may also have been misled by the silence of the Roman Catholic hierarchy.

While the Home Rule Party was rallying behind its leader, however, the Liberals were moving in the opposite direction. Liberal papers were initially divided on the issue. The most influential, the *Daily News*, managed to remain silent for a whole week. The *Star* and the weekly *Speaker* argued that the decision concerning Parnell was an Irish one. Labouchere in *Truth* advised him to continue. The *Manchester Guardian* failed to see why Parnell should be drummed out of public life.

These papers were swimming against a swelling tide. As might be expected, the *Pall Mall Gazette* was in the van, coming out against Parnell on 18 November. W.T. Stead no longer edited the paper, but his successor E.T. Cook continued its moral purity stand. Cook argued: 'Can any sane man believe that the home rule cause will benefit during the next six months by the hero of the many aliases being retained as one of the twin commander in chiefs, or that the fire escape will be the golden bridge to conduct the waverers back to the liberal party?'[218] Michael Davitt, the left-wing Irish leader, called for Parnell to withdraw in the *Labour World* on 20 November. But it was the growing chorus from the Nonconformists which was decisive.

On 19 November the popular Baptist leader, Dr Clifford, stated the purity position in a letter to the *Star*. He wrote, 'If the members of the Irish parliamentary party do not wish to . . . indefinitely postpone the victory of a policy based on justice and right, they must insist on Mr Parnell's immediate retirement. HE MUST GO. British politics are not what they were. The conscience of the nation is aroused. Men legally convicted of immorality will not be permitted to lead in the legislation of the kingdom.'

So clear a statement placed Gladstone firmly on the horns of his dilemma. Price Hughes temporarily clouded the issue by a sadly hysterical piece in the *Methodist Times* of 20 November, which concluded a denunciation of Parnell with the near-racist comment that 'We do not hesitate to say that if the Irish race deliberately select as their recognised representative an adulterer of Mr Parnell's type they are as incapable of self-government as their bitterest enemies have asserted. So obscene a race as in those circumstances they would prove themselves to be would obviously be unfit for anything except a military despotism.'[219]

It was reading this which prompted Healy in Dublin, grunting that it was time to 'teach these damned nonconformists to mind their own business',[220] to pen the motion supporting Parnell.

Gladstone could ignore hysteria of the Hughes type. He ignored W.T. Stead's three letters in the week following the trial, and even two letters from Cardinal Manning. But he could not ignore evidence from his sober and conscientious lieutenants. On 20 November J.J. Coleman, the mustard manufacturer and Gladstone's close friend, wrote warning of the broad effect on Nonconformist opinion. 'They will say, "We will not trust the Irish Nation to Mr Parnell, and by his remaining as leader we see he is the dictator of Irish opinion, and the Irish members who support him and speak of his honour etc are no more worthy of support than he is".'[221]

That Coleman had judged correctly was shown by the meeting of the National Liberal Federation which, by pure chance, was held at Sheffield on 20 and 21 November. John Morley was due to attend, taking with him Harcourt. He asked Gladstone for the official line and was awarded the delphic pronouncement of 19 November. Morley and Harcourt therefore spent two uncomfortable days in

Sheffield warding off rank and file anger. When he received the reports of the meeting, Gladstone was left in no doubt that continued support for Parnell would lead to disaster for the Liberals. H.J. Wilson wrote saying,

> There are differences of opinion as to whether Mr Parnell's withdrawal should be permanent or temporary. . . . But alike from members of parliament, candidates, chairmen of Liberal Associations, and political agents, there is an all but unanimous concensus [sic] of opinion that the practical result of his appearance at the present time as leader will have a disastrous effect on the by-elections of Great Britain.

Morley reported in the same vein. He wrote in his diary that it was not just the devout who were anti-Parnell, but 'the secular caucus man was quite as strong . . . . The breach of the moral law . . . was not all. It was accompanied by small incidents that lent themselves to ridicule and a sense of squalor. How could candidate or voter fight elections under a banner so peculiarly tainted?' Harcourt was equally emphatic. The opinions expressed in Sheffield were not just those of 'screamers' like Stead, but were 'absolutely unanimous and extremely strong' against Parnell remaining as leader of the Irish Home Rule Party, and the Liberals had to say so. 'Whether it means a severance from the Irish Party I know not, but any other course will certainly involve the alienation of the greater and better portion of the Liberal Party of Great Britain – which after all is that which we have mainly to consider.'[222]

Gladstone could no longer sit on the sidelines. He wrote to Arnold Morley that 'I conceive the time for action has now come', and decided to move from Hawarden to London. He wrote to Harcourt asking him to tell Justin McCarthy that 'the continuance of Mr Parnell in the leadership of the Irish Party at the present moment would be, notwithstanding his splendid services to his country, so to act upon British sentiment as to produce the gravest mischief to the cause of Ireland . . . and to make the further maintenance of my own leadership for the purposes of that cause little better than a nullity'.[223]

Gladstone could hardly have hinted more pointedly that he would resign if Parnell remained leader, but Parnell was not to receive the hint. He had vanished once more. Morley contacted Parnell's secretary, Henry Campbell, to arrange to meet Parnell at eleven o'clock on Tuesday 25 November – the day appointed for Parnell to meet the Home Rule MPs. Meanwhile Justin McCarthy was summoned to meet Gladstone.

The following day, 24 November, Gladstone arrived in London and met with Lord Granville, Harcourt and the two Morleys. Harcourt was for telling Parnell bluntly that he had to go because of his immorality. Gladstone was appalled by this stark intrusion of morality into politics, and declined to become arbiter of morals in this way. 'What', he cried, 'because a man is what is called leader of a party, does that constitute him a judge and accuser of faith and morals? I will not accept it. It would make life impossible.'[224] Whatever Gladstone's private view of the moral issues, he considered the Parnell question purely as an issue of political strategy.

At this point Justin McCarthy arrived, and Gladstone went into private interview with him. McCarthy was shocked by Gladstone's attitude, so shocked that he did not understand what Gladstone was saying to him. Gladstone may have realized this, because after McCarthy had left he wrote a letter making his intentions plain and gave it to Morley to show to Parnell when Morley met him the next morning.

But Morley did not meet Parnell before the fateful meeting, Henry Campbell having failed to find Parnell to arrange a meeting. McCarthy had met his chief, but failed to convey even such of Gladstone's message as he understood. Thus Parnell did not know of Gladstone's intended resignation when he attended the meeting of Irish MPs. But Parnell could hardly have misunderstood the growing storm within the Liberal press. That very morning the major Liberal paper, the *Daily News*, had carried the warning that Parnell 'ought to know that for thousands of his English supporters there are higher considerations than party politics, and that neither for him nor for any other man will they condone a distinct violation of the moral law'.[225]

Parnell was immovable. When the motion to re-elect him as leader was put to the meeting, Jeremiah Jordan, Captain O'Shea's successor as a member for Clare, appealed to Parnell to retire, if only for one month. Parnell refused to countenance it, and rising among cheers defended his position vis-a-vis O'Shea. The assembled MPs then re-elected Parnell unanimously as chair for the coming session. McCarthy made no attempt to warn his fellow MPs of the consequences. Some of the MPs may have voted for Parnell misled by a statement in the morning's *Standard* that Parnell would retire if re-elected. There was no basis for this statement.

Immediately after the meeting, Morley finally made contact with Parnell and gave him Gladstone's letter. Parnell read the letter and politely declined Gladstone's advice. Gladstone was informed, and made the precipitate decision to publish his letter. The letter was published the same day and shocked Home Rule MPs. Thirty signatures of Irish MPs were immediately collected demanding a recall meeting to consider the situation, half the number of MPs who had voted for Parnell's re-election. The meeting was held, but Parnell was adamant. He had been elected and he would not resign. The MPs then began to split on what became familiar lines. Parnell's supporters argued it was against everything the Irish party stood for to accept dictation from the British. Parnell's opponents argued that to allow Gladstone to resign over Parnell's leadership would lose Home Rule for a generation. The meeting adjourned amid deepening divisions. It had received a telegram from Tim Healy in Dublin asserting that Gladstone's continued leadership of the Liberal Party was all-important to the Irish cause. The rending of the Home Rule Party had begun.

In the catastrophe which was about to overwhelm Parnell, all the cards were in the hands of the growing opposition. But immediately it appeared that an anti-British card might save the day. On 29 November Parnell issued a manifesto accusing Gladstone of wishing to backtrack on Home Rule. This implausible document convinced many Irish that Parnell was now impossible. And on 30 November the Irish primate, Archbishop Walsh, finally spoke. 'If the Irish

Parnell campaigning in Cork, from the Illustrated London News, *20 December 1890*

leader', he said, 'would not or could not give a public assurance that his honour was unsullied, the party that takes him or retains him as its leader can no longer count on the support of the bishops of Ireland.'[226] Parnell should have read this as proof that his position in Ireland was crumbling. He chose not to do so, and appealed to the Irish MPs for continued backing as leader.

The crucial meeting of Irish MPs opened on 1 December in Committee Room 15 of the House of Commons. Parnell offered to resign if Gladstone gave acceptable guarantees as to the future provisions of a Home Rule bill. This appeared a skilful tactical move. But the issue was not Gladstone, it was whether Parnell could be trusted, and after the evidence given in the divorce case, Parnell had lost the confidence of his MPs. At the end of the second day a motion was moved that the debate should move to Dublin and the Irish people be consulted. It was lost by 44 votes to 29, and the threatened split in the parliamentary party finally occurred. The party spent the rest of the week in agonized and fractious debate, but the two camps revealed in this vote did not shift. On 6 December Justin McCarthy led 44 Irish MPs from Committee Room 15, leaving Parnell with just 26 loyal supporters.

The battle now shifted to Ireland. On 9 December the House rose for the Christmas recess, and that evening Parnell told a journalist, Alfred Robbins of the *Birmingham Post*, that he 'had not the slightest fear of carrying with him the Irish people'. He was to be tragically enlightened. Almost immediately a by-election in

Kilkenny enabled him to put his hopes to the test, but despite having a good candidate he was beaten by two to one. Only in one district was the parish priest on his side, and only in that one district had the Parnellites a majority. The local Bishop of Ossory claimed after the election on 22 December that 'his followers are like spaniels at the feet of the priests, watching for a token of forgiveness.'[227]

The ruthless use of clerical power was the turning point of the campaign, underlining – as Parnell should have known – the power of the Catholic Church. Parnell should have had no illusions about the consequences in Ireland of his affair with Mrs O'Shea; and if he did, he paid the heaviest of prices. Two more by-elections were held, North Sligo in April, Carlow in July 1891. In both the Parnellite candidate was beaten. In June Parnell married Mrs O'Shea, thus deepening the hostility of the bishops and priests. His health was seriously affected by the campaign, and on 27 September, campaigning in a rainstorm while suffering from rheumatism, he caught a severe chill. He returned home to Brighton seriously ill and was put to bed by his wife. His condition steadily deteriorated. Late in the evening of 6 October he kissed his wife, then fell into a coma. He died the same night.

EIGHT

Oscar Wilde and the Fear of Decadence

MORAL CODES AND MORAL PANICS

The death of Parnell brought an unexpected and tragic end to a conflict which could only end in his defeat. Parnell had successfully challenged the might of the British empire and defied its politicians. He could not defy puritan morality. It is surprising that he managed to sustain his clandestine relationship as long as he did, but once Captain O'Shea had decided to force through his divorce, his ultimate defeat was inevitable. Lawrence Stone has contended that late Victorian society saw a more permissive morality. The fate of Parnell is a bleak reminder of how little this was so, where public figures were concerned. 'British politics are not what they were', the Baptist preacher Dr Clifford had thundered in the *Star* after the storm broke, 'the conscience of the nation has been aroused.' And so it had. Or more precisely, the conscience of the Nonconformists had been aroused, and forged into an implacable instrument for moral purity by the events described in this book.

Indeed, Nonconformity played so great a role in the fall of Parnell that for many observers, at the time and later, the rebellion of the Nonconformists was seen as the prime cause of Parnell's demise. Hugh Price Hughes exulted at the role played by Nonconformity in the affair, and contrasted the aggressive attitude of the Nonconformist preachers with that of the Church of England, 'although it was established and profusely endowed for the express purpose of maintaining national righteousness, it had not spoken yet'.[228] The role of the Nonconformist conscience can be overstated. Hughes may have been correct to stress Anglican silence where the Parnell divorce case was concerned, but it is certainly not true to think that Anglicans, or other Christian groups, were indifferent to the development of Victorian morality. Josephine Butler and Ellice Hopkins were not isolated figures in the Anglican Church, and there was growing activity by the Anglicans in purity work during the episcopate of Archbishop Benson. Nor can the role of the Catholic Church under Cardinal Manning, in both England and Ireland, be ignored. The *coup de grâce* to Parnell was delivered in Catholic Ireland, and the firmness of Catholicism for hard-line Christian morality was never in doubt.

The visibility of the Nonconformists in the purity movement did, however, add a new militancy to Christian morality. The single-mindedness they provided was driven by sharp class consciousness, particularly of those elements of the rising middle classes who felt themselves to be outsiders in Victorian society. The perspective of Nonconformists like Stead and Hughes was that of the chapel-worshipping elements of the professional and commercial middle classes. The most vital aspect of this perspective was the deeply rooted suspicion that there was corruption in high places. The self-made men and women who worshipped in chapel and lived by the gospel of salvation through work, believed that the traditional aristocratic ruling classes who still dominated Parliament and the legal system were morally flawed. It was this distinctive perspective which gave social purity much of its cutting edge in Victoria's last two decades.

This sense of class prejudice was expressed with great clarity by Hugh Price Hughes in 1891 when he argued that the purity movement was aimed at curbing aristocratic vice: 'It never reached the aristocracy and it has not reached them yet. Their ideals, their notions of morality, their conceptions of the Christian religion are strangely different from those which saturate every other section of English society . . . . No class of society suffers more from spiritual ignorance and sin.'[229]

That this is debatable is not the point. Hughes was expressing in characteristically extreme form an attitude widespread in Nonconformist circles, particularly those involved in vigilance activities. It was an article of faith within the purity lobby that innocent lower-class virgins were being sacrificed to satisfy plutocratic lust. The great achievement of the Congregationalist Stead was to take this view out of the narrow circles of active Nonconformity and sensationalize it, and by doing so provide a distinctively Nonconformist dimension to the purity lobby. The phrase 'corruption in high places' summed up this ultra-critical attitude to the life of the plutocracy. It struck a chord in the wider culture and echoed far beyond the confines of the purity movement.

It was in making such connections with the wider culture that the purity movement had the greatest impact on the morality of its society. The direct impact of social purity was in the defeat of the Contagious Diseases Acts, and the campaign for the 1885 Criminal Law Amendment Act. But beyond that it had a pervasive impact on attitudes and behaviour which had less to do with political campaigning than the reinforcement of existing trends within the wider culture of respectable society. This is clearly so where the development of respectable attitudes to marriage and heterosexual behaviour is concerned. The 1880s and 1890s were not permissive where these were concerned.

In the period following the passing of the 1885 act, however, social purity and the Nonconformist conscience vied with newer concerns to shape the politics of morality. The decade following Stead's triumph witnessed a growing moral panic over national decline and social decadence, to which the vigilance lobby and its associates were marginal at best. This moral panic came to overshadow concerns about marriage and heterosexuality as the focus of debate over the politics of sexuality. Nothing illustrates this better than the moral panic over homosexuality and decadence which developed in the last decade and a half of the nineteenth century, and whose high point was the trial and imprisonment of Oscar Wilde.

The pipe dreams of Henry Labouchere, Punch's '*Fancy Portrait*', *2 April 1881*

The developments which led to the prosecution of Oscar Wilde were not a simple expression of Victorian homophobia, and certainly not an unproblematic outcome of the Maiden Tribute campaign. The relationship between moral purity and late Victorian homophobia is particularly difficult to establish. It is well known that Wilde was prosecuted under Liberal MP Henry Labouchere's notorious amendment 11 to the Criminal Law Amendment Act (1885). Because the clause is embedded in the 1885 act, it is often assumed that the amendment and Wilde's subsequent prosecution were the product of one seamless web of puritanism. It would be a great deal easier for historians of sexual politics if this were true. There is, however, no simple link between Labouchere's amendment and the purity crusade. It is undeniable that Labouchere's amendment was part of the Criminal Law Amendment Act. We have already seen that this was forced through Parliament by Stead's Maiden Tribute campaign; and Labouchere later claimed that his move was part of the wider purity movement and was directly instigated by Stead. Yet there is much that is puzzling about this claim, and evidence that Labouchere was being economical with the truth when he made it.

Henry Labouchere's amendment to the Criminal Law Amendment Act made gross indecency by male persons a misdemeanour punishable by a maximum of two years' imprisonment with hard labour. The clause reads:

Any male person who, in public or private, commits, or is a party to the commission of, or procures or attempts to procure the commission by any male person of, any act of gross indecency with another male person, shall be guilty of a misdemeanour, and being convicted thereof shall be liable at the discretion of the court to be imprisoned for any term not exceeding two years, with or without hard labour.[230]

This amendment is often believed to have been the decisive moment when homosexuality was outlawed in Britain. This is not so. Male homosexuality had been illegal in England since an act of 1533, which made buggery a felony punishable by death. This act was enforced with increased reluctance in the Victorian period. The death penalty was abolished and replaced with life imprisonment in 1861, but so draconian a punishment made the enlightened uneasy.

What Labouchere's amendment did was to provide a less draconian, and hence more easily enforceable, punishment for homosexual acts. F.B. Smith, whose study of Labouchere's amendment is an admirable piece of historical research, comments that

> The old act appears to have been invoked rarely, and successful prosecutions under it seem to have been infrequent. Now, by contrast with the severe punishments the 1861 Act inherited from its 16th century precursors, a more lenient 'acceptable' penalty was created. But within the decade there developed in the British public a rabid detestation of male homosexuality. In this context Labouchere's amendment, with its weak provisions about evidence, and exposure of 'consent' and 'procuring' to expansive judicial interpretation, became a terrible instrument.[231]

Smith's judgement is sound. Labouchere may have been attempting to provide a less severe sentence than life imprisonment for the offence. But as British attitudes to male homosexuality became rabid in the decade after the amendment became law, it became the weapon of persecution for Oscar Wilde and many others.

It would therefore be logical to imagine that Labouchere's clause was part of the developing moral crusade which had brought the government to rush through the Criminal Law Amendment Act in the summer of 1885. Yet a close reading of the evidence casts doubt on this view. Labouchere was not part of the social purity movement, and while deeply concerned with the class injustice of the Jeffries trial[232] played no part in the Maiden Tribute affair. He was extremely cool about Stead's articles in the *Pall Mall Gazette*, and was scathing about the Criminal Law Amendment Act in his journal, *Truth*. He was deeply hostile to Stead, a rival but more successful newspaper editor, and supported Stead's imprisonment.[233] Labouchere was not obviously a supporter of social purity. Nor was social purity keen on Labouchere's amendment. Stead noted the clause briefly and without comment in the *Pall Mall Gazette*. Stead showed no dislike of male homosexuality, and was brave enough in 1895 to show public compassion for Oscar Wilde. While Labouchere later claimed that he acted after receiving a dossier of homosexual scandals from Stead, Stead left no evidence of this, and no such dossier has come to light. There seems little basis for Labouchere's later claim that he was acting on Stead's behalf in moving the amendment.

There is even less basis for assuming that Labouchere was supported by the broader social purity movement. Social purity displayed no interest in male homosexuality at all in the agitation for the Criminal Law Amendment Act. As we have already seen, its concern was white slavery, prostitution and the age of consent. Homosexuality is conspicuously not mentioned in the agitation, and it is notable that among the public votes of thanks moved at social purity meetings after the passing of the Criminal Law Amendment Act, Labouchere's name does not appear. Whatever he subsequently claimed about his amendment being part of the broader agitation, it seems certain he was acting out of a private agenda.

Indeed, it is surprising that Labouchere's amendment was taken at all. The Criminal Law Amendment Act was, as its title says, 'An Act to make further provision for the Protection of Women and Girls, the suppression of brothels, and other purposes', and the catch-all 'other purposes' stipulation cannot conceal the fact that it was clearly designed to defend women and girls. Male homosexuality had been mentioned by no-one until, late in the evening of 6 August, Henry Labouchere rose to address the House of Commons.

What followed was a travesty of a debate. Labouchere rose to move his amendment, and immediately had to give way to a Mr Wharton, who raised a point of order. He wanted to know whether the clause Labouchere was about to move was within the scope of the bill, as it 'dealt with a totally different class of offence to that with which the bill was directed'. The Speaker gave the remarkable ruling that 'At this stage of the Bill, anything can be introduced into it by leave of the House'.[234] Labouchere then moved his amendment, which initially provided a penalty of one year in prison, with or without hard labour.

Labouchere made the extraordinary statement:

> This is my amendment, and the meaning of it is that at present any person on whom an assault of the kind here dealt with is committed must be under the age of 13, and the object with which I have brought forward this clause is to make the law applicable to any person, whether under the age of 13 or over that age. I do not think it necessary to discuss the proposal at any length, as I understand Her Majesty's government are willing to accept it. I therefore leave it for the House and the Government to deal with as may be thought best.

Labouchere therefore offered no argument for his amendment. The House proceeded to nod the amendment through. Only Mr Hopwood spoke from the back benches, and he explicitly stated that he did not wish to say anything against the clause. Sir Henry James (former Liberal attorney-general) then moved that the punishment be doubled to two years' imprisonment, again without explanation. This was accepted by Labouchere, and the clause as amended was agreed to and added to the bill. *Hansard* does not record a vote. The entire proceeding takes up precisely 472 words in *Hansard*.

This debate was scandalously inadequate. The House of Commons had been debating the Criminal Law Amendment bill for nearly a month, against the background of the intense agitation organized by W.T. Stead described above. It may well have been throughly tired of the whole subject, as F.B. Smith has argued.[231] The amendment was taken late on a hot summer's night in a thin house which may simply have wanted to go home and have done with the final details of the bill. Be that as it may, the haste with which the clause was passed prevented serious debate. H. Montgomery Hyde suggests[235] that only Sir Henry James realized the implications of the bill. Wharton and Hopwood, both of whom opposed the bill in principle on civil liberties grounds (they believed it to be a blackmailer's charter), may also have realized the potential threat of making private acts subject to a charge of gross indecency. But they remained silent. Thus the amendment passed almost undebated, and on the following day, 7 August, the bill was rushed through the third reading in the Commons and sent on to be rubber-stamped by the Lords.

The deeply inadequate nature of the debate leaves much about the motives behind Labouchere's clause obscure. Frank Harris, the contemporary journalist, later claimed that Labouchere, the Liberal man of the world, intended the clause to sabotage the bill. He argued: 'Mr Labouchere, the Radical member, inflamed, it is said, with a desire to make the law ridiculous, gravely proposed that the section be extended so as to apply to people of the same sex who indulged in familiarities or indecencies. The Puritan faction had no logical objection to the extension and it became the law of the land.'[236]

Harris is notoriously unreliable, and the looseness of this comment invites caution ('people' rather than 'male persons', 'Puritan faction' rather than government, for example). Historians have tended to dismiss his view, arguing that Labouchere meant his amendment seriously, and expected the consequences. For once, however, Harris may have been right. Labouchere may well have been intending to make the passage of the bill ridiculous by his amendment, expecting it to be ruled out of order or subject to serious and critical debate, possibly leading to its withdrawal. But this is speculation. Labouchere later gave contradictory accounts of his motives, possibly coloured by the homophobic upsurge of feeling of the subsequent decade.[237]

The reasons for Labouchere's amendment therefore remain shrouded in mystery. It is clear, however, that the amendment cannot be taken to be part of the purity campaign as such, however much it contributed to tightening the moral code. More importantly, once it had been passed, it took on a life of its own. Whether or not Labouchere intended the consequences which now ensued, his action was one of the triggers of a homophobic moral panic which was to gather momentum until, ten years later, it gained its most prominent victim in the person of Oscar Wilde.

THE EMERGENCE OF HOMOPHOBIA

Whatever Labouchere's motives in moving his amendment, there is no doubt that it served to focus the latent homophobia in late Victorian Britain. In the mid-Victorian period, homosexuality had not been a major public controversy. But by the 1880s, the existence of a homosexual underworld of unknown size had become a significant public issue. The next decade saw homophobia become endemic.

The roots of this moral panic lay in the growing awareness by the Victorians of a homosexual subculture in their midst. Montgomery Hyde argues that 'There is abundant evidence to show there was a flourishing trade in male prostitution in London from the 1860s onwards',[238] and quotes a piece of Holywell Street pornography of the period as saying, 'The increase of these monsters in the shape of men, commonly designated margeries, poofs etc, of late years, in the great Metropolis, renders it necessary for the safety of the public that they should be made known . . . the Quadrant, Fleet Street, Holborn, the Strand etc are actually thronged with them!'[239] It may be significant that according to the *Oxford English Dictionary* the word 'poof' for homosexual was first used in the 1850s–60s.[240]

Yet the existence of a homosexual underworld did not become widely known till the Boulton and Park trial of 1871. Boulton and Park were transvestites who were arrested in April 1870 as they were leaving the Strand Theatre dressed as women. Ernest Boulton, aged twenty-two, and his inseparable companion, Frederick Park, aged twenty-three, were charged with intent to commit a felony. Letters found in their lodgings appeared to implicate Lord Arthur Clinton, thirty-year-old son of the Duke of Newcastle, as well as two men living in Edinburgh, Louis Charles Hurt and an American, John Safford Fiske. Boulton, familiarly known as 'Stella', was intimate with Lord Arthur, who had had visiting cards printed for Boulton in the name of 'Lady Arthur Clinton'. All five men were indicted but Lord Arthur died before the trial opened. Two doctors obligingly stated that he died from exhaustion resulting from scarlet fever. Sceptics believe he killed himself to avoid the shame of a court appearance.[241]

The four remaining defendants had to endure six magistrates' hearings before they were committed to trial. They eventually arrived before Lord Chief Justice Cockburn on 9 May 1871 amid intense but good-natured public interest. It is clear that the authorities were markedly unsure how to proceed. The police surgeon, Dr Paul, who examined Boulton and Park for evidence of sodomy after they were taken into custody, claimed never before to have encountered a similar case. His only knowledge was from an article in a case history published in *Medical Jurisprudence* dealing with a dead body discovered in 1833. The other doctors called to give evidence could not agree what the signs of sodomy were. When an anonymous letter writer informed Dr Paul about the work of the French investigator Tardieu, one of the defence lawyers attacked him for relying on 'the newfound treasures of French literature on the subject – which thank God is still foreign to the libraries of British surgeons'.[242]

Although there was strong suspicion that all the defendants were homosexuals, the prosecution had no actual evidence that this was so. It was not illegal to be a transvestite, and Hurt and Fiske could not even be accused of this. Boulton and Park, who did habitually go about dressed as women, did so with such open flamboyance that they could not be seen as sinister figures. The defence argued that dressing up as women was simply a part of play acting which the two men indulged in as part of amateur theatricals, and both the judge and the jury accepted this argument. Cockburn summed up so strongly in their favour that the jury took only 53 minutes to find all four defendants not guilty. The verdict was greeted with loud cheers and shouts of 'Bravo!' *The Times* welcomed this decision with the comment:

> THE QUEEN V BOULTON AND OTHERS is a case in which a verdict for the Crown would have been felt at home, and received abroad, as a reflection on our national morals, yet which, for that very reason, could not be hushed up after popular rumour had once invested it with so grave a complexion . . . . Now that justice has been satisfied and the whole story thoroughly sifted, the verdict of the jury should be accepted as clearing all the defendants of the odious guilt imputed to them.[243]

Given that *The Times* and others considered that the national reputation was at stake, Boulton and his fellow-defendants were extremely fortunate that the court accepted their defence. The popular view of what they had been up to was expressed in the limerick:

> There was an old person of Sark,
> Who buggered a pig in the dark,
> The swine in surprise,
> Murmured 'God blast your eyes,
> Do you take me for Boulton or Park?'[244]

Twenty years later, it is unlikely Boulton and Park would have received so indulgent a hearing.

Boulton and his circle could be put down as harmless eccentrics, but the police and the well-informed became increasingly aware of an active homosexual subculture in London and other cities. In 1881 a semi-fictional account of a London homosexual prostitute named Jack Saul appeared under the title *The Sins of the Cities of the Plain: or the Recollections of a Mary Ann* (2 vols). Jack Saul was a real individual, who was to give evidence in court during the Cleveland Street scandal (he had lived with Hammond, who ran the Cleveland Street brothel).

Saul's autobiography of his life as a male prostitute asserted that there was a substantial subculture of homosexual brothels in London where gentlemen could sleep with lower-class boys, often soldiers, and for high prices. He quotes an ex-soldier, Fred Jones, as saying: 'There are lots of houses in London where only soldiers are received, and where gentlemen can sleep with them. The best known is now closed. It was the tobacconist's shop next to Albany Street barracks in Regent's Park, and was kept by a Mrs Truman. The old lady would receive gentlemen and let us know. That is all over now, but there are still six houses in London that I know of.'

Jack discusses his work in a brothel run by a man with the curious name of Inslip, and comments: 'I afterwards found that no gentleman was admitted to the freedom of this establishment unless he first paid an admission fee of one hundred guineas, besides a handsome annual subscription and liberal payments for refreshments and the procuration of boys or youths like myself.'[245]

Given these sums of money, very considerable indeed in Victorian terms, it is no wonder that puritans like Hugh Price Hughes considered the upper classes riddled with depravity. Financially and socially, such institutions could cater only for members of the plutocracy.

Suspicions of widespread homosexuality among the aristocracy were massively reinforced by the Dublin Castle scandal of 1884, the first major homosexual scandal of the period under discussion. Dublin Castle was the centre of British administration in Ireland, and was deeply detested by Irish Home Rulers. The Irish Home Rule MPs William O'Brien and Tim Healy were therefore extremely interested when they heard rumours of a homosexual ring active in the castle. The informant named specifically County Police Inspector James Ellis French as a key element of the ring. Healy then wrote a leading article in the Home Rule journal *United Ireland* hinting at scandals involving various Crown employees in Ireland, notably Inspector French. French then issued a writ for libel, naming the editor of *United Ireland*, William O'Brien.

O'Brien found that detectives in the RIC would not testify on his behalf, understandably fearful for their jobs. O'Brien went to see Sir George Lewis, the most famous scandal lawyer in London, and on his recommendation employed a private detective called Meiklejohn. Meiklejohn had been in Dublin for less than a fortnight when he discovered an extensive homosexual network, at the apex of which were two leading members of the gentry. These were Mr Gustavus Charles Cornwall, secretary of the General Post Office and brother-in-law of the Scottish baronet Sir Robert Dalyell, and Captain Martin Kirwan of the Royal Dublin Fusiliers, who was a cousin of Lord Oranmore. As a result of Meiklejohn's investigations, four men came forward to give evidence of their relations with these two men, though they were clearly running the risk of incriminating themselves.

French dropped his libel action due to lack of funds, but the action was taken up by Cornwall, who had been named in *United Ireland*. The case of Cornwall v. O'Brien was tried in Dublin in July 1884, and caused an immense sensation.

The libel action was one of high drama. The defence found their witnesses had developed cold feet. One, an army officer, had already fled to France. The other three refused to testify. Only at the eleventh hour did the witnesses agree to take the stand; and from that point the issue was not in doubt. All three gave detailed and comprehensive evidence of sexual misconduct with them by Cornwall. The jury took only an hour to find in favour of the defendant.

Following the verdict, it was inevitable that criminal prosecutions would ensue. Cornwall, French, Kirwan and seven other defendants were arrested and brought to trial before a senior judge, Baron Dowse. Cornwall and Kirwan were tried jointly on several counts, charging them with conspiracy to commit homosexual acts. But though the evidence of the witnesses in O'Brien's libel case was repeated, the jury was not satisfied beyond reasonable doubt and the trial ended in a disagreement. Immediately afterwards another of the prisoners named James Pilar pleaded guilty and was sentenced by Baron Dowse to the extraordinarily punitive sentence of twenty years' penal servitude. French was then put on trial separately, but this jury also disagreed.

Cornwall and Kirwan were tried again at the next sessions, when according to Montgomery Hyde the evidence included the remarkable fact that Meiklejohn had told one of the witnesses for the Crown, a man called Taylor, that Taylor 'was liable to penal servitude for life, but that it would be his salvation if he could give evidence that would implicate Cornwall'.[246] This may have been a material factor in the jury's acquittal of the defendants, the jurymen adding the rider that the evidence produced by the Crown 'was not considered sufficient'. There was some doubt as to whether French could stand trial a second time, as he had suffered a complete mental breakdown, but he was eventually put in the dock, only for the jury to disagree again. Dublin Castle insisted the unfortunate man be put on trial a third time, and on this occasion he was convicted and sentenced to two years' imprisonment.

Politicians quickly realized the immense political dangers implicit in a homosexual scandal such as this. Gladstone had moved to show his confidence in the Dublin administration by promoting G.O. Trevelyan from chief secretary for Ireland – a post outside the Cabinet – to chancellor of the Duchy of Lancaster, a Cabinet post. But neither the vindictive prosecutions of French and his associates nor Gladstone's show of confidence could dissociate the Liberals from the taint of the Dublin scandal. Earl Spencer soldiered on as lord lieutenant for Ireland till the Liberals were defeated in the 1886 election. On his resignation, a Dublin wit suggested that he be given a couple of steps up the peerage by Queen Victoria with a new title – Duke of Sodom and Gomorrah.[247] The Victorians were now conscious of the existence of homosexuality in high places. This consciousness was to be reinforced five years later by a still more sensational scandal.

In July 1889, the police were alerted by the Post Office authorities to a homosexual vice ring operating in central London. A number of telegraph messenger boys had become involved in a male brothel situated in Cleveland Street, near the Tottenham Court Road. Newlove, a clerk at the GPO, had acted as procurer, together with an ex-GPO employee named Veck. The brothel was run by one Charles Hammond. Newlove was arrested, and made the startling allegation that among the habitués of the brothel were Lord Arthur Somerset, the Earl of Euston, and Colonel Jervois. Scotland Yard immediately ordered the house to be put under observation. Hammond was found to have fled, but Lord Arthur Somerset was identified by the policeman on duty as visiting the now empty house.

The police realized they had uncovered a hornets' nest. Somerset was a major in the Royal Horse Guards (the Blues), the élite cavalry regiment. He, moreover, was a decorated veteran of the battle of Abu Klea in 1885. Still worse from the police viewpoint, he was an intimate of the Prince of Wales, who had appointed him equerry and superintendent of his stables. The police decided that the case was becoming a very hot potato, and consulted the director for public prosecutions. The DPP was extremely reluctant to take up the issue, and his office referred the matter to the home secretary, the Conservative Henry Matthews. Only after a direct instruction from the home secretary did the DPP proceed to evaluate the evidence with a view to a prosecution.

The proximity of this scandal to the heir to the throne induced extreme nervousness within Whitehall. Sir Augustus Stephenson, the DPP, consulted with attorney-general and solicitor-general, and all three of the government's law officers agreed that the evidence against Somerset was strong enough to justify prosecution. Matthews demurred and referred the matter to the prime minister, Lord Salisbury. Salisbury in turn referred the issue to Lord Halsbury, the lord chancellor. On 7 October, Halsbury advised that the evidence was insufficient to prosecute. Both Scotland Yard and the law officers disagreed, and a sharp dispute broke out within the corridors of power.

By mid-October, in fact, a major political scandal was brewing. The two minor characters, Newlove and Veck, had been prosecuted and convicted. Hammond fled through France to Belgium, and was preparing to escape to America, to avoid extradition. Lord Arthur Somerset's name was being bandied round the London clubs and he had become aware of the fact. Desperate to know his fate, on 18 October he induced Sir Dighton Probyn, comptroller of the Prince of Wales' household, to seek an interview with the prime minister. Probyn met Salisbury at 7.30 that night, and discussed with him whether a prosecution of Somerset was likely. Salisbury later claimed to have given no indication one way or the other, but critics believed that he told Probyn that a warrant was about to be issued for Somerset's arrest. Whether he did so or not, that very night Somerset escaped to France, from where he never returned. The warrant was delayed till 12 November, by which time Somerset had resigned from the Blues, avoiding the threat of being cashiered.

These events sparked a major political controversy, fanned by the Liberal newspapers and brought to a head by Henry Labouchere in the Commons on 28 February 1890. For Labouchere the scandal offered a perfect chance to justify his actions in 1885, and he seized the opportunity. He alleged that chief government officers, including the prime minister, had conspired to defeat the course of justice. He alleged that the Cabinet had attempted to hush up the affair. Specifically he alleged that the government had conspired to help Hammond to escape to the USA, that Newlove and Veck had received unusually light sentences to buy their silence, and that the authorities had made no attempt to follow people visiting the house while it was under surveillance. Most damagingly, he alleged that Salisbury had warned Probyn that a warrant was about to be issued, enabling Somerset to escape.

The attorney-general stoutly defended the government. He argued that it had been Somerset's lawyer, not the government, who had arranged for Hammond to escape to the USA. He further argued that the sentences had been a matter for the judge, and challenged Labouchere to name him as partner to conspiracy. He then asserted that the prime minister did not warn Probyn of an impending warrant. He did not take up the charge that the police had not followed visitors to the house. but he did not need to. Labouchere had been provoked into calling Salisbury a liar, he was suspended, and his amendment was defeated by 206 votes to 66.

Labouchere's complaints of a government conspiracy to conceal the ramifications of the Cleveland Street scandal were silenced by his suspension. His strident attacks had, however, given fresh weight to the potent belief that corruption existed in high places close to the government and the court. Cleveland Street fuelled the intense suspicion that decadence was rampant within the Establishment. In the 1880s, the suspicions were of heterosexual misbehaviour. By the early 1890s homosexuality had come to overshadow adultery as a source of moral panic. It was in this highly charged moral climate that Oscar Wilde conducted his affairs.

THE CROWN VERSUS OSCAR WILDE

The last decade of Victoria's reign is often portrayed as the 'naughty nineties' or the 'gay decade', as if Britain was experiencing a light-hearted era of superficial frivolity and permissiveness. This is a mistaken view. The public mood was prudish and strait-laced, and respectable behaviour continued to be tightly regulated and censorious. These were common features of nineteenth-century culture; what was new about the nineties was the fear of the future and the belief in social decline summed up in the phrase '*fin de siècle*'. The phrase indicated more than the obvious imminence of the end of the century. It expressed the belief that the best years had gone, and that a widespread decay was setting in. This fear of decadence was reinforced by the homosexual scandals of the 1880s, and by the work of the artists in the Aesthetic movement. Fear of the Aesthetics as the harbingers of weakness and decay at the heart of the empire became pronounced. In the heightened consciousness of moral issues produced by the moral purity crusade, these fears rose to unprecedented heights in the middle nineties. They found their outlet in the events which led to the downfall of Oscar Wilde.

The fall of Oscar Wilde is often seen as an inevitable consequence of the Labouchere amendment. This is not so. The image of a remorseless, homophobic moral lobby pursuing a hunted artist to his destruction is misplaced. Wilde was not hounded by a vengeful state seeking to enforce the Labouchere amendment. Wilde initiated the legal processes by which he was destroyed, by suing the Marquess of Queensberry for libel. Queensberry, in his famous challenge to Wilde, could do no more than accuse him of 'posing as a somdomite' [sic]. The insult was written on a card delivered to his club, which only three people knew about. The wisest of his friends urged him to ignore Queensberry's taunt, in which case the subsequent trials could not have taken place. The society solicitor Sir George Lewis later said that if he had been professionally consulted, he would have advised Wilde to tear up the card and ignore Queensberry. The unresolved issue of the fall of Oscar Wilde is not why it occurred, which his biographers have long since established, but why Wilde believed he could defy the moral lobby, its legal apparatus, and the massive hostility to decadence and homosexuality which were unmistakable by the early 1890s. Wilde chose to flout the morality of his time, and by doing so triggered his own downfall. He appeared to have no understanding that he was doing enormous damage to himself and the homosexual subculture to which he belonged.

The origins of Wilde's challenge to morality lie in the game of image-making which he had been playing since coming down from Oxford in 1879. Wilde

MAUDLE ON THE CHOICE OF A PROFESSION.

Maudle. "How CONSUMMATELY LOVELY YOUR SON IS, MRS. BROWN!"

Mrs. Brown (a Philistine from the country). "WHAT? HE'S A NICE, MANLY BOY, IF YOU MEAN THAT, MR. MAUDLE. HE HAS JUST LEFT SCHOOL, YOU KNOW, AND WISHES TO BE AN ARTIST."

Maudle. "WHY SHOULD HE BE AN ARTIST?"

Mrs. Brown. "WELL, HE MUST BE SOMETHING!"

Maudle. "WHY SHOULD HE BE ANYTHING? WHY NOT LET HIM REMAIN FOR EVER CONTENT TO EXIST BEAUTIFULLY?"

[*Mrs. Brown determines that at all events her Son shall not study Art under Maudle.*

George du Maurier caricaturing the aesthetic male, Punch, *12 February 1881*

Oscar Fingall O'Flahertie Wills Wilde
(1854–1900) photographed in 1894

arrived in London as a brilliant but unknown young man with a double first, the Newdigate Prize in poetry, and a talent for self-advertisement. He had no interest in a conventional career, but was determined to make a name for himself as a writer. 'We live in an age of inordinate personal ambition', he wrote in a letter of the time, 'and I am determined that the world shall understand me.'[248]

What was there to understand? Wilde was certainly committed to the Aesthetic movement. But while his commitment to 'art for art's sake' was sincere, he saw in it an opportunity to make his name. Aestheticism was the cult of the moment. George du Maurier satirized the trend for foppishness among artistic young men with his caricatures Poslethwaite and Maudle, and *Punch* criticized 'aestheticism' as 'an effeminate, invertebrate, sensuous-sentimentally Christian but thoroughly pagan taste in literature and art'.[249] This view of the movement was to echo down the years. A less pompous critique was that levelled by Gilbert and Sullivan in *Patience*, which opened in London on 23 April 1881. Satirizing the school of 'fleshly poets', the opera clearly aimed at the Pre-Raphaelites, especially Rossetti, rather than the largely unknown Wilde.

However D'Oyly Carte knew Wilde to be the most prominent young man in the Aesthetic movement in London, and when he took the production to New York he realized Wilde's potential for advertising purposes, and arranged for Wilde to make a lecture tour of the USA. Wilde duly arrived in New York in January 1882, dressed in suitably 'aesthetic' clothes.

From this point on, Wilde was firmly in the public eye, and he took pains to maintain his position. But while Wilde flirted with decadence, he did not at this early stage flirt openly with homosexuality. In November 1883 he became engaged to his future wife, Constance, and married her in May 1884. This was not a marriage of convenience – two children, Cyril and Vyvyan, were born in the next two years. And whether or not Wilde may have possessed homosexual traits, his sexual tastes were initially conventional. Hyde quotes an incident when, after a lecture on the beauties of English art in New York in 1882, a group of young men approached Wilde with the immortal line, 'And now, Oscar, after all that soulthrob, of course you feel like a bit of skirt', and whisked him off to a brothel. Wilde went with enthusiasm.[250]

Wilde's known heterosexuality provided the foundation of the myth that Wilde's flirting with homosexual gestures (such as wearing green lilies, the badge of the French homosexual) was merely a feature of his habitual desire to flout convention. The myth did not survive the trials. Sometime in the later 1880s, Wilde turned to homosexuality. It is likely that the year was 1886, and that the turn involved a flamboyantly homosexual youth called Robert Ross. Wilde met the precocious Ross in that year, when the latter was seventeen. Wilde was later accused of corrupting youth, but where Ross was concerned no corruption was necessary. Ross set out to seduce Wilde, and both privately claimed later he was successful.

The crucial encounter with Robert Ross was only a brief love affair. It was over by the time Ross went up to Cambridge in October 1888, but had lasting effects. Wilde wrote to Ross on hearing he was going up to King's, saying, 'I congratulate you . . . . University life will suit you admirably, though I shall miss you in town. . . . Do you know Oscar Browning? You will find him everything that is nice and pleasant.' He added significantly that he had just been to Stratford-upon-Avon, where he had proposed the toast to his old friend Lord Ronald Gower, the homosexual sculptor whose statue of Shakespeare had just been unveiled. Wilde concluded, 'My reception was semi-royal, and the volunteers played "God Save the Queen" in my honour'.[251] By 1888, Wilde had no illusions as to his sexuality.

But this did not mean inevitable disgrace, as the reference to Oscar Browning should remind us. Oscar Browning was notoriously suspected of being a homosexual throughout a long teaching career, but never confirmed the suspicions. He lost a lucrative post as housemaster at Eton because of too close a friendship with a boy, George Nathaniel Curzon, future viceroy of India. Yet Curzon's father supported Browning's association with his son, and they continued to meet and correspond for fifty years. Browning subsequently obtained a post at King's, where he spent most of a long life living up to an eccentric reputation. No-one seemed to mind that he associated almost exclusively with men, even when he entertained blue-coated sailors in his rooms singing boisterous songs and getting drunk. While this was hardly conduct becoming a Cambridge don, he eventually retired undisgraced and was awarded the Order of Merit. It is clear that mere outrageous behaviour was not enough to produce legal action. In order to trigger the growing homophobia of late Victorian Britain, an almost conscious effort was required. Tragically for Wilde and the homosexual subculture, Wilde's behaviour provided exactly such a trigger.

Wilde's first step along the road which led to the Old Bailey was the publication, in 1890, of his only novel, *The Portrait of Dorian Gray*. By 1890 he was outwardly a respectable married man with two children who had dabbled with journalism. Wilde had even edited a magazine from 1887 to 1889, the *Woman's World*. He threw all this away with a novel which smacked of both decadence and homosexuality. When it appeared as a story in *Lippincott's Monthly Magazine* in July 1890, it created a stir. The most serious criticism was in *The Scots Observer*, edited by an old acquaintance of Wilde's, W.E. Henly. The deeply damaging attack read in part:

> Mr Oscar Wilde has again been writing stuff that were better unwritten; and while *The Picture of Dorian Gray* . . . is ingenious, interesting, full of cleverness and plainly the work of a man of letters, it is false art – for its interest is medico-legal; it is false to human nature – for its hero is a devil; it is false to morality – for it is not made sufficiently clear that the writer does not prefer a course of un-natural iniquity to a life of cleanliness, health and sanity . . . . Mr Wilde has brains, and art, and style; but if he can write for none but outlawed noblemen and perverted telegraph boys, the sooner he takes to tailoring (or some other decent trade) the better for his own reputation and the public morals.[252]

The reference to Cleveland Street was unmistakable, and drew the reader's attention to an alleged homosexual bias in the book which was alluded to in the trials five years later. On the basis of this and other hostile reviews, W.H. Smith, the wholesalers, informed Ward Lock that as the story had 'been characterised by the press as a filthy one', they were withdrawing the July issue of *Lippincott's Magazine* from distribution. The matter went no further, and the story was published as a book with six additional chapters without legal consequence. Wilde could count himself lucky. The prosecution of the bookseller Vizetelly in 1888 for publishing Zola and other allegedly indecent French authors had resulted in three months' imprisonment with hard labour. But if Wilde suffered no immediate legal consequence from *Dorian Gray*, the episode placed him firmly in the public eye as a leader of the 'decadent' movement. It was not an unmixed blessing.

Wilde was astute enough, however, to recognize the dangers of too close an association with decadence, and switched his creative focus to writing sparkling light comedies. The first of his great successes, *Lady Windermere's Fan*, was premiered on 20 February 1892. Constance was present to witness her husband's triumph, and despite the whispers about Wilde which circulated around London, it would have been a bold figure who suggested the playwright was anything other than a happily married man with a brilliant career before him. The gaggle of young men who drank the night away with Wilde after Constance had gone home appeared little more than camp followers. Yet the group – which included Robbie Ross, More Adey, Edward Shelley, Reggie Turner, Maurice Schwabe, nephew by marriage of Frank Lockwood, who was to prosecute Wilde in 1895, and Lord Alfred Douglas – were all implicated in the homosexual subculture. And in Lord Alfred Douglas, fate had provided Wilde with a fatal fascination.

Punch's *'Fancy Portrait'* of the
aesthetic Oscar Wilde, 25 June 1881

Lord Alfred Douglas (1870–1945) was the third son of John Sholto Douglas, 9th Marquess of Queensberry (1844–1900), sponsor of the famous code of boxing rules. Lord Alfred was habitually known by his family nickname of Bosie. Wilde first met Bosie in 1891, as a far from innocent student at Oxford. Although his father was to claim in 1895 to be defending Bosie against the corrupting influence of Wilde, Bosie needed little corruption. Wilde claimed in the memoir written in his prison cell and called *De Profundis* that 'Our friendship really begins with your begging me in a most pathetic and charming letter to assist you in a position appalling to anyone, doubly so to a young man at Oxford; I do so, and ultimately through your using my name as your friend with Sir George Lewis I began to lose his esteem and friendship'.[253] The letter appears to have been written in 1892 and to relate to a scandal involving Bosie's interest in young boys. Sir George Lewis was a man only called in to resolve serious scandals for the rich and powerful.

Wilde was delighted to help Bosie. He was deeply attracted to the intensely pretty, poetic and self-willed young man, and Bosie reciprocated. The relationship was not primarily physical. Some sexual relations appear to have taken place between Wilde and Bosie, but they were not sustained. What held Wilde and Bosie together was a joint fascination with exploring the underworld of rent boys and rough trade of predominantly working-class youth. Wilde had considerable difficulty at his trials explaining why a man of his class and attitudes enjoyed entertaining uncultured lower-class boys. He only came up with a convincing explanation from his prison cell, in a famous passage: 'People thought it dreadful of me to have entertained at dinner the evil things of life, and to have found pleasure in their company. But then, from the point of view through which I, as an artist in life, approach them they were delightfully suggestive and stimulating. It was like feasting with panthers; the danger was half the excitement.'[254]

Wilde was thus not a hunted figure running from persecution. The frisson of danger implicit in challenging the law was a large part of his motivation for delving into the underworld. How long Wilde could have sustained his double life of glittering literary success and excursions into the underworld of rent boys and blackmailers is an open question. By 1894 even the trusting Constance was becoming deeply suspicious. But what triggered disaster was the frenetic opposition of Queensberry to Wilde's association with his son.

John Sholto Douglas was an arrogant, uncultured but extremely wealthy member of the Scottish aristocracy, whose character was marked by violent aggressiveness. At the age of twenty Queensberry met the beautiful and cultured Sybil Montgomery, fell madly in love with her, and married her. It was a disastrous mismatch. Queensberry was the archetype of the hunting and shooting aristocrat, addicted to pugilism, while his wife was an aesthete who immersed herself in literature, painting, music and poetry. After a year of marriage Francis, Viscount Drumlanrig, was born, a year later Percy, and two years later Alfred. Two other children were born, Sholto in 1872 and Edith in 1874. Shortly after the birth of Francis, Queensberry and his wife began to disagree violently. After Percy was born, Sybil became indifferent to her husband, and indifference turned to hatred. Queensberry displayed considerable cruelty to his wife. From 1875 the couple were estranged and living apart and in 1887 Sybil obtained a divorce. The children, who were naturally devoted to the mother who brought them up, came to hate their father, and none more than Bosie.

Bosie reacted against his father's sporting inclinations (except for a talent for running), and followed his mother's interest in the arts. This rejection of his father's lifestyle infuriated Queensberry. It also helped trigger a latent monomania over homosexuality. Queensberry believed that his father-in-law, Sir Alfred Montgomery, possessed homosexual traits, and became obsessed by fear that his sons would inherit them. His suspicions centred first on his eldest son, Drumlanrig. Drumlanrig was a pleasant but rather dim young man, who attempted a career as a soldier but after failing to rise above the rank of lieutenant left the army. His grandfather then introduced him to Lord Rosebery, then Gladstone's foreign secretary, who employed him as his private secretary.

It was a puzzling choice. Drumlanrig had few obvious political skills, and fewer still of the characteristics required of a private secretary. Queensberry came to regard the appointment as part of a homosexual conspiracy, and was further wounded when Drumlanrig was given an English peerage, enabling him to sit in the Lords. His father had been denied this privilege. Queensberry began writing offensive and violent letters to Rosebery, Gladstone and the queen. He did not stop at letters. When Rosebery fell ill that summer and went to Bad Homburg in Germany to take the waters, Queensberry followed him and prowled round Rosebery's hotel, threatening to thrash the foreign secretary with a dog whip.

Rosebery wrote to Queen Victoria observing that one of his less pleasant duties was 'to be pursued by a pugilist of unsound mind'. Queensberry was not a laughing matter, however. When the Prince of Wales, who was also at Bad Homburg, failed to mediate, the chief commissioner of police was called in. He reported to Rosebery that 'The Marquess of Queensberry, in consequence of the entertainment I had with him, found it advisable to part this morning with the 7 o'clock train to Paris'.[255]

This quarrel ended in tragedy. In October 1894, the shy and phlegmatic Drumlanrig was invited to a party at Quantock Lodge, near Bridgewater. Drumlanrig was still private secretary to Rosebery, now prime minister. A week earlier he had proposed to his hostess's niece, Alix Ellis, and been accepted. The party should have been a cheerful opportunity to announce the engagement. However, on 18 October, Drumlanrig detached himself from a shooting party to look for a winged bird. Having disappeared from view, the party was startled to hear a single shot from his gun. They found Drumlanrig dead, killed by single shot which a doctor called to the scene stated 'had entered the mouth, fracturing the lower jaw on the right side, and passed through the roof of the mouth on the left hand side. Death must have been instantaneous.'[256]

The coroner's inquest returned a verdict of accidental death. Queensberry among others suspected suicide, and he was beside himself with rage and grief. He sent a particularly venomous letter to his father-in-law, which read:

Sir
Now that the first flush of this catastrophe and grief is passed, I write to tell you it is a JUDGEMENT on the whole LOT OF YOU. Montgomerys, The Snob Queers like Roseberry [sic] & certainly Christian hypocrite Gladstone the whole lot OF YOU. Set my son up against me indeed and make bad blood BETWEEN us, may it devil on your own heads that he has gone to his REST and the quarrel not made up between him and myself. It's a gruesome message: If you and his Mother did not set up this business with that cur and Jew friend [?] LIAR Rosebery as I always thought – At any rate she [Lady Queensberry] acquiesced in it, which is just as bad . . . . I smell a Tragedy behind all this and have already GOT WIND of a more STARTLING ONE . . . . I am on the right track to find out what happened. CHERCHEZ LA FEME, when these things happen. I have already heard something that quite accounts FOR IT ALL.
                                                              Queensberry[257]

This letter was libellous, but Alfred Montgomery was too shrewd to allow the accusations to see the light of day. Oscar Wilde was to prove less shrewd.

Having come to the conclusion that he had lost one son through a homosexual intrigue, Queensberry was determined that he would not lose another. Earlier in 1894 he had ordered Bosie to stop seeing Wilde in one of the less offensive of his letters. He had written:

. . . I come to the more painful part of this letter – your intimacy with this man Wilde. It must cease or I will disown you and stop all money supplies. I am not going to analyse this intimacy, and I make no charge, but to my mind to pose as a thing is as bad as to be it. With my own eyes I saw you both in the most loathesome and disgusting relationship as expressed by your manner and expression . . . . No wonder people are talking as they are. Now I hear on good authority, but this may be false, that his wife is petitioning to divorce him for sodomy and other crimes. Is this true, or do you not know of it? If I thought the actual thing was true, and it became public property, I should be quite justified in shooting him on sight . . . .[258]

To this Bosie replied on 2 April with a brief telegram with the message WHAT A FUNNY LITTLE MAN YOU ARE. Relations between father and son had reached breaking-point, and Bosie chose to carry a loaded revolver. In *De Profundis*, Wilde alleged this went off by accident in the Berkeley.

Wilde was now trapped by the aggressive hatreds of father and son. This did not prevent him writing the most delicious of his comedies, *The Importance of Being Earnest*, in the summer of 1894, but he had no illusions about the dangers Queensberry and his son posed to him. On the triumphant opening night of *The Importance* (14 February 1895) Wilde had to have police posted at the doors of the theatre to deny the marquess admission. He had threatened to make a scene, but had to be content with leaving a bouquet of rotten vegetables at the stage door.

Queensberry then switched tactic, and on 18 February went to Wilde's club, the Albemarle, and left a calling card with an illegible message with the porter, Sidney Wright. Wright read it, placed it in an envelope, and filed it away. Ten days later Wilde visited the club, was given the card, and reading it as 'To Oscar Wilde, ponce and Somdomite' [sic] decided that Queensberry was implacable. His first instinct was to run away to Paris. But when he went to his hotel, the manager impounded his luggage and refused to let it go until the bill was paid. Wilde had no money, and approached George Lewis for advice. Lewis had been engaged by Queensberry, and could not help. He later said[259] that had he been free to offer advice, he would have told Wilde to tear up the card and ignore Queensberry. Robert Ross also advised taking no action, but when Wilde insisted something had to be done, suggested consulting the solicitor Sir Travers Humphreys.

Consequently on 1 March Wilde and Bosie visited Humphreys, and at this point Wilde crossed the Rubicon which led him to disaster. Humphreys asked him as a matter of routine whether there was any truth in the allegations. Both Wilde and Bosie denied there was. Wilde later recalled, 'What is loathsome to me is the memory of interminable visits paid by me to the solicitor Humphreys, when in the ghastly glare of a bleak room I would sit with a serious face telling serious lies to a bald man till I really groaned and yawned ennui'.[260] Boredom was the least of Wilde's worries. By lying to his solicitor, Wilde had staked all on a dangerous gamble. The gamble was that Queensberry could not substantiate his suspicions, and that he was still only able to argue that Wilde was 'posing as a sodomite' – which was what Queensberry was to state the message on the card actually read. Having received solemn assurances that the allegations were false, Humphreys naturally argued that a libel action could be won, and recommended that proceedings be taken against the marquess. His advice was taken.

Wilde had now triggered his own destruction. George Lewis withdrew from the action and Queensberry engaged a new and formidable barrister – Edward Carson. Carson knew what Wilde and Douglas did not, that Queensberry's detectives had discovered the lodgings of Alfred Taylor, the organizer of the group of rent boys patronized by Wilde, and had a list of names and addresses of young male prostitutes. These were rounded up and browbeaten into giving evidence against Wilde. Although Wilde did not know this, he had foreknowledge of a most ominous kind. When Wilde asked the journalist Frank Harris to act as a character witness, which Harris agreed to do, he revealed that he knew Queensberry had got hold of incriminating letters from Wilde to Douglas which had been secured by blackmailers. Harris immediately told him the case was lost. Supported by Bernard Shaw, he argued that no jury would convict Queensberry if the court knew that blackmailers had thought it worth their while to obtain the letters. Wilde and his wife should flee to Paris, from where he could write to *The Times* to say he despaired of getting justice. Otherwise Queensberry would be acquitted, and Wilde would be ruined.

Wilde almost saw the force of the argument, but was persuaded by a near-hysterical Bosie to continue with the action. They still did not choose to escape when they saw Queensberry's plea of justification for his charge.[261] Later, in the prison cell, Wilde bitterly commented that, 'blindly I staggered as an ox to the shambles, I had made a gigantic psychological error. I had always thought that my giving up to you in small things meant nothing; that when a great moment arrived I could myself re-assert my will-power in its natural superiority. It was not so. At the great moment my will-power completely failed me.'[262] And so Wilde lost the last chance to save himself by following Bosie in his blind desire to attack his father.

The libel action went as Frank Harris had predicted. Carson had all the evidence he needed. In his plea of justification, entered on 30 March, Queensberry specifically cited thirteen counts of indecent behaviour, with twelve different boys, ten of whom were named, plus two citations of indecent literature, including *Dorian Gray*. And it was precisely at the moment that Carson moved to call his witnesses to prove incitement to sodomy that Sir Edward Clarke, Wilde's barrister, called a halt to the proceedings and announced that the case would be dropped. Carson only agreed to this proceeding after he had forced Clarke to accept that Queensberry was justified in calling Wilde a sodomite in the public interest. Clarke had to agree to this, while conceding nothing as to Wilde's guilt as such. With that Queensberry was acquitted, and the public gallery cheered. It was nearly noon on 5 April, and prostitutes who had felt Wilde's rent boys had been unfair competition danced on the pavements outside the Old Bailey.

Wilde's fate was now sealed. The government was determined that Wilde should be prosecuted. The names of Rosebery and Gladstone had been mentioned during the trial – Clarke had read out some of the letters, hoping to convince the jury that Queensberry was unbalanced; the effect was to reinforce the impression that the Establishment had something to hide. Maurice Schwabe, nephew by marriage of Frank Lockwood, solicitor-general, had been named in Queensberry's plea of jstification, Arthur Balfour, future Tory prime minister,

A nineties tabloid. The Illustrated Police News, *13 April 1895, on the first Wilde trial*

and Asquith, the home secretary and future Liberal prime minister, were both intimates of Wilde's circle, and above all there were the previous and current prime ministers to consider. Rosebery's friend Sir Edward Hamilton noted during the last of the criminal trials against Wilde in May that: 'A verdict of guilty would remove what appears to be a widespread impression that the judge and jury were got at, in order to shield others of a higher status in life' – a reference to Labouchere's allegations against Salisbury.[263] Moreover the current prime minister, Rosebery, had retired to his Newmarket home with acute insomnia which brought him to the verge of collapse. Lord Esher recorded at the time, 'the Newmarket [horse racing] scum say that . . . his insomnia was caused by terror of being in the Wilde scandal'.[264]

The Liberal government simply could not allow Wilde to escape. He was arrested at the Cadogan Hotel at 6.30. Public opinion, especially that of the press, was jubilant. Wilde's old adversary W.E. Henly expressed the general mood. 'Oscar at bay was, on the whole, a pleasing sight. The air is alive with rumours, of course; but I believe no new arrests will be made, and that morality will be satisfied if Oscar gets two years, as of course he will. Why he didn't stay at Monte Carlo, once he got there, God alone knows. Seeing that . . . he returned to face the music . . . I can only conjecture that . . . he was stark mad.'[263]

Henly was right about the outcome. Wilde was tried, and though the jury disagreed in the first trial, as in Dublin in 1884 the authorities were implacable and dragged him through a second. He was convicted and sent to prison for the maximum allowed under the Labouchere amendment, two years' hard labour. There were no other prosecutions, and the extent to which homosexuality existed in the upper classes remains obscure. Public opinion was on the whole satisfied, though the impression of 'corruption in high places' was reinforced. When Wilde was convicted on 25 May, the judge gave his opinion that the sentence was 'totally inadequate for a case such as this'. Wilde tried to speak, crying out, 'And I? May I say nothing, my Lord?' The judge waved him away impatiently. Society had heard much from Oscar Wilde. It wished to hear no more.

The Politics of Morality Reviewed

When the prison door slammed behind Oscar Wilde, its closing marked the end of an era. Any hope of a modest move towards a liberal attitude towards homosexuality disappeared. The limited degree of tolerance extended in the Boulton and Park case was markedly absent in the trials of Oscar Wilde. It was unfortunate for Wilde that he challenged respectable morality at a time when public sensitivity over moral issues had become almost morbidly acute. It was doubly unfortunate for him that he had chosen to proclaim a theory of aesthetics which was sharply at odds with the morality of his time. 'Art for art's sake' clearly challenged the idea of a moral culture underpinning respectable society. For that very reason, Wilde's conviction was welcomed with almost total unanimity across that society.

The *Daily Telegraph* may be taken as representing a widespread consensus. In its editorial of 27 May 1895, it commented:

> No sterner rebuke could have been inflicted on some of the artistic tendencies of the time than the condemnation on Saturday of OSCAR WILDE at the Central Criminal Court . . . there has lately shown itself in London a contemporary bias of thought, an affected manner of expression and style, and a few loudly vaunted ideas which have had a limited but evil influence on all the better tendencies of art and literature. Of these the prisoner of Saturday constituted himself a representative . . . . 'Art for Art's sake' – that is the original catch-word of half the folly which is talked of in our midst . . . the modern disciple proceeds to urge that art, being non-moral, has no ethical bearing whatever, and therefore may deal frankly with the immoral. Hence has come upon us the destestable invasion of the foul and the squalid and the ugly, in what is called Realism; . . . We shall never get rid of the products unless we understand the cause; we shall never wash our hands clean of these stains unless we recognise how the waters of art have been foulled at their very source . . . . And if such a reaction towards simpler ideas be called Philistinism, then let us all be Philistines, for fear of national contamination and decay'.[266]

THE SIX-MARK TEA-POT.

Æsthetic Bridegroom. "IT IS QUITE CONSUMMATE, IS IT NOT?"
Intense Bride. "IT IS, INDEED! OH, ALGERNON, LET US LIVE UP TO IT!"

*Before the deluge. George du Maurier satirizing
Wilde in* Punch, *30 October 1880*

The editorialist had accurately identified the conjunction of amorality and
art which underpinned the aesthetics of the decadent movement, coupling
this aesthetic with fears of national decay. It was this combination of factors
which made the trials of Oscar Wilde so resonant for late Victorian Britons.

   Yet there were no more major trials of Wilde's circle, and if there was suspicion
that there was moral corruption in high places, the suspicion was not tested in the
courts. W.E. Henly was right to believe that morality would be satisfied if Wilde
got two years. A prosecution of Bosie was considered, but rejected. Charles Gill,
the prosecutor in the Wilde and Taylor case, wrote to Hamilton Cuffe, director of
public prosecutions, on l9 April to say:

> I have considered the question as to whether a prosecution ought to be
> instituted against Lord Alfred Douglas . . . and have come to the conclusion
> that no proceedings should be taken . . . . Having regard to the fact that
> Douglas was an undergraduate at Oxford when Wilde made his acquaintance –
> the difference in their ages – and the strong influence that Wilde has obviously
> exercised over Douglas since that time, I think that Douglas, if guilty, may
> fairly be regarded as one of Wilde's victims . . . .[267]

Gill clearly did not know Bosie if he believed he could be corrupted by Wilde.
Nor did Wilde have victims. All his relations were with consenting adults. But in
the climate of 1895, this was beside the point.

The conviction of Oscar Wilde spelt the death knell of the Aesthetic movement and its alleged tendency towards decadence. Its leading journal, *The Yellow Book*, founded in 1894 and condemned by *The Times* on 20 February of that year as 'a combination of English rowdiness with French lubricity', managed to stagger on till 1897, but the spirit had gone out of it. Its most brilliant figure, the illustrator and associate of Wilde, Aubrey Beardsley, died in 1898. Wilde himself died in exile in 1900, a broken man. Looking back on the Aesthetic movement a dozen years later, the commentator Holbrook Jackson argued that until the trial of Wilde, the British public had not realized the existence of the movement, 'and the suddenness with which the decadent movement in English literature and art ceased, from that time, proves . . . the tremendous power of outraged public opinion in this country'.[268]

There were certainly few people in the mid-1890s prepared to defend Wilde openly. Bernard Shaw, remembering that Wilde had been one of the few people prepared to sign his petition defending the Chicago anarchists, tried to get up a petition to have Wilde's sentence cut. After he found only Stewart Headlam would sign, he gave up. Several young Frenchmen of letters tried to get Zola to sign an appeal to Queen Victoria, but he refused. Frank Harris approached George Meredith to sign a similar petition to Shaw's, but the famous novelist declined. According to Hesketh Pearson, Robert Yelverton Tyrrell, Regius Professor of Greek at Trinity College, Dublin, was the only man who would sign Harris' petition.[269] The moral climate of the mid-1890s was too forbidding for prominent men to risk association with Wilde, even at a distance. The reaction covered serious scientific literature. When Havelock Ellis, the leading British sexual researcher of the day, published his major study of homosexuality, *Sexual Inversion*, in 1898, it was prosecuted as an indecent work. The publisher, Bedborough, refused to defend the action, and the book was eventually published in Germany.

The reaction of the literary world speaks volumes about the repressive moral climate of the time. The literati had patronized Wilde with acclaim till the fall. Once he had been put on trial, his plays vanished from the West End, his books disappeared from bookshops, and in September 1895 he appeared in the bankruptcy court. The speed with which Wilde became a non-person among the literary set speaks volumes about the underlying endorsement of conventional morality by the educated middle classes of London at the end of the nineteenth century.

The corrosive moral climate of late Victorian Britain forced its most eloquent critic, George Bernard Shaw, to protest. Shaw savagely criticized the English for their hypocrisy, particularly in lapping up biographies which he believed presented wholly sanitized, respectable portraits of their sitters. He argued:

> The publication of the truth about anything or anybody is attended with considerable risk in English Society. We have agreed to keep up a national pretence that black spots in human nature are white; and we enforce the convention by treating any person who betrays his consciousness of them . . . as a prurient person and an enemy of public morals . . . . The censors will tolerate

no offence against hypocrisy because . . . an offence against hypocrisy is an offence against decency, and is punishable as such.[270]

His own career demonstrated the accuracy of this assessment.

Shaw initially aimed to become an Ibsenite playwright of serious social comment drama, and cultivated the Dutch impresario J.T. Grein for this purpose. Grein had set up the Independent Theatre, initially to premiere Ibsen's *Ghosts* in 1891. The following year Grein encouraged Shaw to finish his drama, *Widowers' Houses*, which was produced as a 'Didactic, Realistic Play' in November 1892. It was not a great success and a second play was rejected. For his third play, Shaw turned to his long-standing interest in prostitution, which as a socialist he saw as a metaphor for a society which turned every human activity into a saleable commodity. The result was *Mrs Warren's Profession*.

Since the heroine was a prostitute, Shaw anticipated trouble with the authorities, writing to Grein that he expected difficulty in getting a licence from the lord chamberlain. He also anticipated that the Independent Theatre would have difficulty in hiring a venue. He did not anticipate that the theatre itself would reject the play, but so it proved. When he read the play to Mrs Theodore Wright, whom he hoped would play Mrs Warren, 'She rose up, declared that not even in her own room could she speak the part to herself, much less in public to a younger woman . . . [and] rushed out of the room in disorder'. Grein's reaction was even stronger. He thought the play 'unfit for women's ears', and that since it might lead even strong men to 'insanity and suicide' could not sanction a private production.[271]

If this was the reaction from the leading champion of Ibsen in Britain, Shaw realized that his prospects as a writer of serious social realism were nil. *Mrs Warren's Profession* did not achieve even private performance till 1902. It was not publicly performed till 1905, in America, and was promptly prosecuted. Prudery clearly operated on both sides of the Atlantic. There was no public performance in Britain until 1925, in which year Shaw had become Nobel Laureate for literature. He had however achieved his reputation by sparkling critical comedy, not Ibsenite blue-book plays on current social problems.

Shaw was not the only author to experience censorship in the 1890s. Although the decade saw a flowering of dramatic talent unseen since the Restoration, serious works fell foul of the censor. Wilde's *Salome* failed to get a licence (but the script was published; censorship was inconsistent) as did Fagan's *The Earth*, Granville Barker's *Waste* and Maeterlinck's *Monna Vanna*. Serious fiction writers were also experiencing difficulties, notably Thomas Hardy, the greatest living novelist. *Tess of the d'Urbervilles* ruffled feathers by making a seduced woman the heroine without the moral condemnation needed to satisfy Victorian opinion. *Jude the Obscure* earned Hardy such a storm of criticism for its sympathies with its working-class characters that he never wrote another novel.

Literature and drama are significant indicators of the moral climate. The audience was educated and relatively liberal. It had welcomed Wilde with enthusiasm, and dabbled with the Aesthetic movement, the social realism of Ibsen, and poets and painters considered deeply suspect by mainstream opinion.

That the literary world would not defend Wilde, and could not sustain *The Yellow Book*, or the work of serious writers such as Shaw and Hardy, is a telling comment on Lawrence Stone's belief in the permissive trend of the age. He contends that the middle classes were becoming more permissive from the 1870s onward, and that this trend to permissiveness spread to the social élite in the 1890s. If this were so, the trend would surely manifest itself in literature and the arts. The evidence does not support the case.

There is even less evidence of growing permissiveness in daily life, where the activities of the vigilance lobby gained in strength in the 1890s, particularly where prostitution was concerned. The moral purity crusade of the 1880s had led to a sustained attempt to repress prostitution which grew in strength in the nineties and lasted till the First World War. The relative toleration of prostitution by the authorities apparent in mid-century ceased. In the ten years before the Criminal Law Amendment Act legalized summary prosecution of brothels, there was an annual average of eighty-six prosecutions of bawdy houses in England and Wales. Between 1885 and 1914 this average jumped to over 1,200.[272] This marked a massive attack on the brothel, as the most visible aspect of prostitution. The police crackdown was not necessarily dependent on the change in the law – a crackdown had begun in Glasgow as early as 1870. In Manchester Ellice Hopkins had inspired religious leaders to form a Vigilance Committee led by manufacturer Frank Crossley, as early as 1882. When the police made the mistake of admitting they knew of 402 brothels, Crossley's committee set out to close them. Ten years later the police admitted knowing of only three. This was certainly an underestimate, but Manchester became a shining example of what could be done.

For the country as a whole, it was the combination of the change in the law in 1885 and the formation of the National Vigilance Association which provided the impetus for change. In Sheffield, Leeds and Liverpool the police enthusiastically enforced the law. The Sheffield police claimed that the number of brothels known to them fell from 300 to 7. Leeds boasted an active Vigilance Committee which in 1912 was said to have 'created . . . a public opinion behind the city council; the police took action in regard to the houses of ill fame, and the convictions went up leaps and bounds'.[273] In Liverpool, the agitation overturned the lax Tory council. Vigilance agitators swept to power in 1890 and forced 818 prosecutions in 1891. The chief constable, William Nott Bower, complained that 'irrational and irritating fanatics' were pushing the problem into respectable areas, notably in Cheshire and Bootle, but the agitation continued undiminished.

Vigilance patrols, which took to pasting the names of brothel customers on walls, took off, particularly in Celtic areas. This had already happened in Glasgow in the 1860s, and caught on in Cardiff, Belfast and Dublin in the 1880s. By 1892 respectable Mecklenberg Street in Dublin had been cleared – though the prostitutes reappeared in less fashionable districts.

London proved a more difficult nut to crack. As early as 1883, however, parish priests had begun to take a lead against prostitution, led by the Revd H.W. Webb Peploe, vicar of St Paul's, Onslow Square. He formed a Central Vigilance Society, later taken over by the NVA. In the East End, one Frederick Charrington led a crusade, aided by the NVA, which in 1886 obtained a High Court ruling that private persons could take out summonses against brothels without having to go through the parish authorities. Aided by this, Charrington and helpers from the Tower Hamlets mission stormed through Whitechapel, Stepney and Shadwell in the autumn of 1887, closing brothels. One of the unfortunate side effects of this may have been to aid Jack the Ripper. The police commissioner pointed out to Charrington that he had forced the women to 'exercise their calling in the streets' where they were horrifically butchered.[274] Charrington was not deterred. As the Ripper terror abated, he redoubled his efforts.

Other vigilance campaigns followed suit. In 1887 parish vicars in the West End set up a branch of the NVA and for the next three decades the Charing Cross Vigilance and Rescue Committee was an active force in the heart of the capital. South of the river the work did not start till 1894, when F.B. Meyer took over Christ Church, Westminster Bridge Road, and began an active campaign which in five years claimed to have closed 200 brothels. By 1905, the *Vigilance Record* could ask, 'Is London becoming morally better?' – and decide that it was.[275]

The attack on brothels was impressive testimony to the strength of the moral purity lobby, but it is more questionable how far its impact on prostitution actually went. Prostitutes could take evasive action. They could, and did, service their clients out of doors. At the height of one crackdown, in 1905, the number of females charged with having intercourse in the open rose sharply to 944.[276] They could resort to self-contained flats, which were not covered by the 1885 act. Or they could take a bully or pimp and live with him as man and wife. The last resort came to loom large in the demonology of the vigilance societies, particularly when London's chief magistrate, Sir John Bridge, blamed them for the growth of the phenomenon. In 1894 he commented that prostitutes were now dependent on pimps. 'Formerly they were only this in the rarest possible cases, but it was not so now for the vigilance societies had made this sort of crime more common than any other in London'.[277]

These developments led a combination of the London parishes and the NVA to press for legislation against living off immoral earnings. They succeeded in 1898 when the Tory government passed a Vagrancy Law Amendment Act tackling the issue.

The 1898 act was a triumph for the NVA, underlining its influence with government under the able leadership of its organizer, William Coote. Coote had long since overtaken his patron, W.T. Stead, as an influence in the moral purity lobby. Josephine Butler feared Coote, and in 1891 wrote to a colleague, 'Coote is most unsound . . . (at least) Bunting . . . is over him in the Vigilance Association . . . Coote loves coercion.'[278] Butler's belief that Percy Bunting could restrain Coote was unjustified. Bunting could not have remained chair of the executive committee had he opposed Coote, for Coote represented the hard-line puritanism of the rank and file. The National Vigilance Association had chosen the ideal man by employing Coote, and respect for his policies and organizing ability was universal. Bishop Creighton set up a Public Morality Council at the end of the century to unite religious denominations in London against vice, but he fell ill and it began to founder. Coote was called in to reorganize the council as deputy chair, and by 1901 the organization was on a solid foundation with over a thousand members.

It is clear that the events of the 1880s had marginalized Josephine Butler and her followers. The concern for the rights of the individual against a powerful state, and for the reclamation of prostitutes as valued human beings, had been swept away by a harsh repressive puritanism. The aim of saving prostitutes from police repression had been lost and replaced by a crusade against prostitution in which the women themselves were subjected to harsh police harassment. The moral purity lobby, particularly the Salvation Army, did make efforts to reclaim women; but on the whole, the emphasis of vigilance was on repression.

As the century came to a close, Coote and those he served had good grounds for satisfaction. Vigilance flourished and, with the 1898 Vagrancy Act on the statute books, was demonstrably influential at the highest levels of government. Coote aspired to extend his triumphs on the domestic scene to an international sphere. Accordingly he decided to tour the Continent, to obtain support for a conference to organize an international effort. His initiative was a complete success, and in 1899 the First International Congress for the Suppression of the White Slave Traffic took place. Coote was then at the centre of an extremely powerful international crusade.

After three decades of agitation, the British purity movement had emerged as a formidable political lobby which neither police, magistrates nor politicians could ignore. Locally, vigilance committees had enormous influence with police and magistrates, and could exert considerable political clout in local elections. Nationally, no government, whether Liberal or Conservative, could ignore the purity lobby, as the passage of the 1898 Vagrancy Act underlined. More legislation would emerge in the Edwardian era. Nor was the influence of the purity movement confined to conventional political lobbying. It had changed the moral climate within which politicians operated. The private lives of politicians had become legitimate subjects for investigation, and woe betide any politician who could not exhibit an unblemished personal life. In 1886 Gladstone was warned by his private secretary, Sir Edward Hamilton, and Lord Rosebery, his foreign secretary, against his long-established practice of walking the streets of London reclaiming prostitutes because of 'misconstructions which evil minds will put on all this'. After the events of 1885, Gladstone had no choice but to concur. He commented that, 'there was among some people a baseness and lack of charity which enabled them to believe the worst. Because of this he would cease to visit clearing houses, brothels or places of assignation . . . and he would promise never again to speak to women in the streets at night.'[279] Even Gladstone was not above suspicion. He had, however, read the signs correctly, and survived. Dilke and Parnell did not.

By the 1890s, then, respectability had powerfully tightened its grip on Victorian society. The view of that decade as the 'naughty nineties' completely misreads the importance of whatever elements of frivolity existed at the end of the century. The mood of the country was dominated by that mixture of anxiety and orthodoxy summed up by the phrase '*fin de siècle*'. And in that atmosphere, the vigilance lobby found very little difficulty in securing a powerful hold over the politics of morality.

There is, therefore, little reason to believe that Lawrence Stone is correct in seeing the late Victorian period as one of growing moral permissiveness. The picture is one of growing moral repression as a powerful vigilance lobby demanded ever stricter adherence to the existing moral codes. The growth of repressiveness was not simply due to vigilance activity, however. The widely reported series of scandals discussed in this book were not exclusively the product of vigilance agitation. This was a period of growing moral stringency, removing areas of moral laxity from public life. Jeffrey Weeks is right to see this as a period of repression, with social purity obtaining its first legislative successes in the 1880s. And his comment that it is from this period that the first critiques of 'Victorianism' stem is also perceptive.

Yet while the seeds of an anti-Victorian critique were laid in the last decades of Victoria's reign, they went almost unnoticed at the time. By the late 1890s vigilance was wholly dominant over the politics of morality in Britain. Josephine Butler and her libertarian supporters, with their humanitarian concern for prostitutes as sisters to be cherished, were wholly marginalized by the harshness of the attack on brothels and street walkers. Shaw and other sexual radicals were a tiny minority crying in the wilderness. Parnell was dead. Dilke was marginalized. Wilde was in exile, a broken man, and forgotten save as a bogey figure. Coote and his supporters were in command of the field.

They could hardly have imagined that in less than a century their victory would be reversed and they would be the ones marginalized. Coote, Stead, Hugh Price Hughes and their supporters are today largely forgotten, while Butler, Dilke, Parnell and Wilde have long since been rehabilitated as figures of stature. The sexual radicals, following Shaw and Havelock Ellis, came to dominate the politics of morality in twentieth-century Britain. Part of their triumph stemmed from their ability to stigmatize the whole Victorian period as one of hypocrisy and evasion, stereotyping middle-class Victorian males at least as deeply corrupt.

It is a stereotype which has proved of lasting influence. Ronald Pearsall has spoken for many in detecting a marked contrast beween the reality of Victorian behaviour and the image of a society which 'wanted to appear to posterity as good, noble, pure in word, heart, and deed; and that they have succeded so well is due not only to the energy with which they tackled this project, but to our own laziness in preferring the easy stereotype to the reality'.[280] This view is too simple. Part of the reason why the stereotype has proved so enduring is the reality of the respectable purity offensive from the 1870s to the 1890s. There is certainly abundant evidence that many Victorians, especially men, fell short of the ideal, prompting the charge of hypocrisy. But there is also abundant evidence than many did live lives informed by 'respectable values'. These demanded adherence to those values with increasing militancy from the 1870s onward. Thatcher and Ensor both have a point.

The debate between the idealizers of 'Victorian values' and their critics is ultimately fruitless. Both sides can produce evidence to support their view. It is the dialectic between the values espoused by Victorian respectables, and the behaviour derived from those values, which is important. And it is clear that in the late Victorian period, the balance shifted in favour of respectability and the puritans who enforced it. Their victory was never complete, and it is certainly possible to find evidence of people, especially in the aristocracy, who defied respectability. But this evidence does not change the overall picture. The late Victorian period saw a massive shift in the politics of morality in Britain towards puritanism and anti-permissiveness. It would be many years before those who felt like Bernard Shaw saw the balance shift back towards their position.

Notes

1. Ensor, *England 1870–1914*, p. 170.
2. Made in his speech to the Central Criminal Court, 4 November 1885 and published as a pamphlet by the Moral Reform Union, 1885. Reference is on p. 2.
3. Parliamentary Debates (Hansard), 3rd Series, Vol. 147, col. 853, 31 July 1857. Gladstone was surveying the state of British morality in the debate on the Divorce and Matrimonial Causes Bill, which made divorce possible through a divorce court. Gladstone opposed this, believing it would make a bad moral situation worse.
4. Parliamentary Papers 1881, House of Commons Paper No. 448 in Vol. 9, ordered to be printed 25 August 1881, evidence of Howard Vincent.
5. Stone, *The Family*, p. 680.
6. Weeks, *Sex, Politics and Society*, 1989, p. 23.
7. Parliamentary Papers 1881.
8. Pearson, *The Age of Consent*, p. 23.
9. Hudson, *Munby, Man of Two Worlds*, p. 28, diary entry for 20 March 1859.
10. Acton, *Prostitution*, Fitzroy edn, p. 221.
11. Acton, op. cit., pp. 222–3.
12. Blyth, *Skittles*, p. 75.
13. *The Times*, 3 July 1862, p. 12, col. 3.
14. Blyth, op. cit., p. 92. There is some debate as to whether Anonyma was Catherine Walters. See J.O. Field, *More Uncensored Recollections*, 1926, pp. 259–60.
15. Acton, *Prostitution*, p. 214.
16. Pearsall, *The Worm in the Bud*, note p. 288.
17. Walkowitz, *Prostitution*, pp. 21–2.
18. In *London Labour and the London Poor*, Stationers Hall Court, December 1861, republished Frank Cass, 1967, pp. 210–72.
19. *London Labour*, p. 223.
20. Finnegan, *Poverty and Prostitution*, p. 23.
21. Neild, *Prostitution in the Victorian Age*, no page numbers.
22. Acton, *Prostitution*, p. 101.
23. Acton, *Prostitution*, p. 32.
24. Acton, *Functions*, p. 33 – see table.
25. Acton, op cit., p. 36.
26. Acton, op cit., p. 32.
27. Walkowitz, op cit., p. 3.
28. Woodward, *Age of Reform*, p. 285.
29. Acton, op cit., p. 125.
30. Scott, *A State Iniquity*, p. 13.
31. McHugh, *Prostitution*, p. 35.
32. McHugh, *Prostitution*, p. 37.
33. Scott, *A State Iniquity*, p. 11.
34. Hansard, 2 March 1866, col. 816.
35. Hansard, 7 May 1883, col. 65.
36. Ereira, *The People's England*, p. 86.
37. Ereira, *The People's England*, p. 79.
38. 32 and 33 Victoria Cap 96.
39. Answer to Q 12,903.
40. *Daily News*, 1 January 1870. Reprinted in Butler, *Personal Reminiscences*, pp. 17–19.
41. Butler, *Personal Reminiscences*, p. 20.
42. Scott, *A State Iniquity*, p. 124.
43. Account of election in Scott, *A State Iniquity*, Ch. XIII; Butler, *Personal Reminiscences*, pp. 42–53.
44. Midgeley, *Women against Slavery*, Ch. 7.
45. Letter to Anne Humbert 1875, in Butler, *Personal Reminiscences*, pp. 319–20.
46. McHugh, *Prostitution*, p. 60.
47. McHugh, *Prostitution*, p. 61.
48. Royal Commission upon the Administration and Operation of the Contagious Diseases Acts, London 1871, minutes of evidence, 18 March 1871, p. 442.
49. Report of the Royal Commission . . . of 1871, p. 17, para 60, Parliamentary Papers, Health, Vol. 5.

50. Butler, *Personal Reminiscences*, pp. 85–98.
51. Letter to LNA branches, May 1872. Quoted McHugh, *Prostitution*, p. 85.
52. Royal Commission of 1871, p. 439, answer to Q 12,878.
53. Royal Commission of 1871, p. 17, para 59.
54. Debate on the Bastardy Laws Amendment Bill, Hansard, 19 June 1872, col. 1972.
55. Hansard, 19 June 1872, col. 1973.
56. Hansard, 2 April 1873, col. 480.
57. Hansard, 12 August 1875, cols 866–7.
58. McHugh, *Prostitution*, p. 103.
59. McHugh, *Prostitution*, p. 108.
60. McHugh, *Prostitution*, p. 205.
61. McHugh, *Prostitution*, p. 208.
62. *The Shield*, 12 August 1882, pp. 155–6.
63. Scott, *A State Iniquity*, p. 122. Scott credits the Political Committee with capturing the NLF for repeal.
64. McHugh, *Prostitution*, p. 205.
65. Quoted Davenport-Hines, p. 129.
66. Walkowitz, *Prostitution*, p. 90.
67. Figures on the size of the Commons from Wood, *Nineteenth Century Britain*, p. 436.
68. Walkowitz, *Prostitution*, p. 99.
69. Hansard, 31 July 1857, cols 852–3.
70. Butler, *Personal Reminiscences*, p. 168.
71. Butler, *Personal Reminiscences*, p. 257.
72. Account of developments in France from Butler, *Personal Reminiscences*, pp. 345–9.
73. Dyer, *European Slave Trade*, p. 7.
74. Terrot, *Maiden Tribute*, p. 25.
75. Terrot, *Maiden Tribute*, p. 26.
76. Terrot, *Maiden Tribute*, p. 45, cites (from the French) Pastor T. Borel, *The White Slavery of Europe*, 1875.
77. Dyer, *European Slave Trade*, pp. 8–9.
78. Pearson, *Age of Consent*, p. 41.
79. Dyer, *European Slave Trade*, p. 17.
80. Dyer, *European Slave Trade*, p. 22.
81. Dyer, *European Slave Trade*, p. 35.
82. Butler, *Personal Reminiscences*, p. 375.
83. Terrot, *Maiden Tribute*, p. 115.
84. Terrot, *Maiden Tribute*, p. 116.
85. Terrot, *Maiden Tribute*, p. 67.
86. Terrot, *Maiden Tribute*, p. 117; Pearson, *Age of Consent*, p. 82.
87. Hansard, 30 May 1881, col. 1605.
88. Hansard, 30 May 1881, cols 1608–9.
89. Hansard, 18 June 1883, col. 774.
90. Hansard, 3 April 1884, col. 1453.
91. Hansard, 3 April 1884, col. 1454.
92. Hansard, 24 July 1884, col. 1219.
93. Hansard, 13 April 1885, cols 1439–40.
94. Hansard, 13 April 1885, col. 1441.
95. Hansard, 22 May 1885, col. 1182. Debate closed at the end of the sentence quoted, with the bald comment: 'It being ten minutes before seven of the clock, the debate stood adjourned till to-morrow.' There was no tomorrow.
96. *Pall Mall Gazette*, 23 May 1885.
97. *Pall Mall Gazette*, 28 May 1885, p. 2.
98. Figures from Weeks, op cit., p. 20.
99. Hansard, 21 May 1885, col. 1024.
100. Stead, *Armstrong Case*, p. 6.
101. Pearson, *Age of Consent*, p. 111.
102. Hansard, 21 May 1885, cols 1022–3.
103 Pearson, *Age of Consent*, p. 113.
104. Stead, *Armstrong Case*, p. 5.
105. Robertson Scott, *Life and Death of a Newspaper*, p. 114.
106. Terrot, *Maiden Tribute*, p. 139.
107. File STED 1/8 Churchill College Archive Centre, Cambridge.
108. Robertson Scott, *Life and Death*, p. 114.
109. Terrot, *Maiden Tribute*, p. 147.
110. *Pall Mall Gazette*, 29 October 1885, p. 11.
111. *Pall Mall Gazette*, 29 October 1885, p. 12. Footnote 111 is cited four times in text.
112. Petrie, *Singular Iniquity*, pp. 245–6.
113. McHugh, *Prostitution*, p. 71.
114. Stead, *Armstrong Case*, p. 9.
115. *Pall Mall Gazette*, 6 July 1885, p. 1.
116. Michael Holroyd, *Bernard Shaw*, Vol. 1, p. 290.
117. Hansard, 7 July 1885, col. 1827.
118. Hansard, 7 July 1885, col. 1828.
119. Hansard, 9 July 1885, col. 198.
120. Hansard, 9 July 1885, col. 205.
121. Hansard, 9 July 1885, col. 207.
122. Hansard, 9 July 1885, col. 211.
123. See entries in British Library catalogue under *Pall Mall Gazette*. Publications at Paris, Leipzig and Lisbon.
124. Hansard, 30 July 1885, col. 578.
125. Hansard, 30 July 1885, col. 586.
126. Hansard, 30 July 1885, cols 588–9.
127. Terrot, *Maiden Tribute*, p. 178.
128. *Pall Mall Gazette*, 6 July 1885.
129. Letter from William Morris to Stead, 12 August 1885, File STED 1/8, Churchill College Archive Centre, Cambridge.
130. *Pall Mall Gazette*, 20 July 1885.
131. *Pall Mall Gazette*, 24 August 1885.
132. *Pall Mall Gazette*, 22 August 1885.
133. McHugh, *Prostitution*, p. 263.

134. 27th Annual Report of the Rescue Society, 1880, quoted Gordham, 'Maiden Tribute', p. 15.
135. Journal of the VADPR, 15 July 1881.
136. Pearson, *Age of Consent*, p. 176.
137. Hansard, 11 August 1885, col. 1739. The other MP was Hopwood.
138. Mews, 'The General and the Bishops', p. 214.
139. Pearson, *Age of Consent*, p. 181.
140. *Lloyd's Weekly London News*, 16 August 1885, p. 7 col. 4.
141. *Lloyd's Weekly London News*, 23 August 1885, p. 7 col. 3. This footnote is cited twice in the text.
142. Terrot, *Maiden Tribute*, p. 190.
143. *Methodist Times*, ed. Hugh Price Hughes, 10 September 1885.
144. Terrot, *Maiden Tribute*, p. 191.
145. Terrot, *Maiden Tribute*, p. 192.
146. Stead, *The Armstrong Case*, p. 16.
147. *The Times*, 28 September 1885, p. 13 col. 6.
148. Pearson, *Age of Consent*, p. 207.
149. *The Times*, 31 October 1885, p. 3 cols 3–5.
150. *The Times*, 3 November 1885, p. 3 col. 1.
151. Pearson, *Age of Consent*, pp. 209–10.
152. *The Times*, 5 November 1885, p. 3 col. 6.
153. *The Times*, 5 November 1885, p. 4 col. 2.
154. *The Times*, 9 November 1885, p. 3 col. 6.
155. *The Times*, 9 November 1885, p. 4 col. 4.
156. *The Times*, 9 November 1885, p. 4 col. 5.
157. Coote, *A Romance of Philanthropy*. Millicent Garrett Fawcett wrote a preface to the pamphlet.
158. Coote, *A Romance* , p. 24.
159. Letter of 11 November 1885. File STED 1/26, Churchill College Archive, Cambridge.
160. *Sentinel* report, February 1886, p. 19.
161. *Sentinel* report, February 1886, pp. 20–21.
162. Letter to Percy Bunting, 7 September 1885, quoted in Bristow, *Vice and Vigilance*, p. 113.
163. Whyte, *Life of Stead*, Vol. I, p. 189.
164. Whyte, *Life of Stead*, p. 198.
165. Whyte, *Life of Stead*, pp. 304–6.
166. *Sentinel*, April 1886.
167. Jenkins, *Sir Charles Dilke*, p. 106.
168. Jenkins, *Sir Charles Dilke*, p. 94.
169. British Library, Add. MSS 43906.
170. Jenkins, *Sir Charles Dilke*, p. 198.
171. Diary entry, 23 July 1885, Add. MSS 43927.
172. Horstman, *Victorian Divorce*, pp. 133–4.
173. Details of the case taken from *The Times* report, 13 February 1886, p. 12.
174. Jenkins asserts that Dilke's advisors could not find Fanny. He relies on Garvin's biography of Chamberlain.
175. British Library, Add. MSS 43927.
176. Gwynn and Tuckwell, *Sir Charles Dilke*, Vol. II, p. 173.
177. Gwynn and Tuckwell, *Sir Charles Dilke*, Vol. II, p. 174.
178. *The Times*, 13 February 1886, emphasis in the original.
179. *Pall Mall Gazette*, 13 February 1886, p. 1.
180. Dilke diary, British Library, Add. MSS 43927.
181. Jenkins, *Sir Charles Dilke*, p. 244.
182. *Methodist Times*, 10 September 1885.
183. File STED 1/9, Churchill College Archive, Cambridge.
184. *Sentinel*, April 1886, p. 47. Dilke re-entered Parliament on 3 March.
185. British Library, Add. MSS 43888.
186. Jenkins, *Sir Charles Dilke*, p. 248.
187. Jenkins, *Sir Charles Dilke*, p. 250.
188. All information on the second trial is from Jenkins, Ch. 13.
189. Jenkins, *Sir Charles Dilke*, pp. 309–10.
190. Jenkins, *Sir Charles Dilke*, pp. 314–15.
191. Jenkins, *Sir Charles Dilke*, p. 317.
192. Jenkins, *Sir Charles Dilke*, p. 319.
193. Jenkins, *Sir Charles Dilke*, p. 321.
194. Ensor, *England 1870–1914*, p. 169.
195. Dilke diary, op cit., 23 July 1885.
196. Moody and Martin, *Irish History*, Ch. 17.
197. Lyons, *Parnell*, p. 420.
198. Lyons, *Parnell*, p. 218; Harrison, *Parnell Vindicated*, p. 305.
199. Kee, *The Laurel*, p. 452.
200. Lyons, *Parnell*, p. 219. From the diary of Scawen Blunt, 1909.
201. Kee, *The Laurel*, p. 257.
202. Kee, *The Laurel*, p. 265. Lyons has 17 October, p. 129.
203. Kee, *The Laurel*, p. 275.
204. Lyons, *Parnell*, p. 152; O'Shea, *Parnell*, Vol. I, pp. 187–91.
205. Information on the trial from *The Times*, reports 17 and 18 November 1890.
206. *The Times*, 17 November 1890, col. 3.
207. *The Times*, 17 November 1890, col. 4 (cited in text 3 times).
208. *The Times*, 17 November 1890, col. 5 (cited in text 3 times).
209. *The Times*, 17 November 1890, p. 3 col. 6.

210. Kee, *The Laurel*, pp. 535–6.
211. Kee, p. 544 quotes Morley, *Recollections*, 1917 pp. 251–4.
212. Lyons, *Parnell*, pp. 462–3.
213. Harrison, *Parnell Vindicated*, pp. 136–51.
214. *The Times*, 17 November 1890, p. 4 col. 1.
215. *The Times*, 18 November 1890, quoted twice in text.
216. Lyons, *Parnell*, p. 489.
217. Kee, *The Laurel*, p. 549.
218. *Pall Mall Gazette*, 18 November 1890.
219. *Methodist Times*, 20 November 1890.
220. Kee, *The Laurel*, p. 556.
221. Glaser, *Parnell's Fall*, p. 125.
222. Lyons, *Parnell*, p. 490, quoted three times in text.
223. Lyons, *Parnell*, p. 491.
224. Lyons, *Parnell*, p. 492.
225. *Daily News*, 25 November 1890.
226. Lyons, *Parnell*, p. 514.
227. Lyons, *Parnell*, p. 544.
228. *Methodist Times*, 11 December 1890.
229. 4th Annual Report of the West London Mission, 1891, pp. 2–3.
230. 48 and 49 VIC, Cap 69, clause 11.
231. Smith, 'Labouchere's Amendment', p. 165, cited in text twice.
232. *Truth*, 16 April 1885.
233. *Truth*, 12 November 1885.
234. Hansard, 6 August 1885, col. 1397, cited in text twice.
235. Hyde, *Other Love*, p. 135.
236. Smith, 'Labouchere's Amendment', p. 166.
237. Smith, 'Labouchere's Amendment', p. 167. Smith claims that the papers of the relevant law officers, Sir Henry James and Sir William Harcourt, formerly in the Liberal government, and Sir Richard Webster and Sir Richard Cross, responsible officers for the Conservatives, contain no specific references to the clause.
238. Hyde, *The Other Love*, p. 121.
239. 'Yokel's Preceptor', quoted *Other Love*, p. 121. Davenport-Hines, p. 107, dates this as 1855.
240. Entry in *Oxford English Dictionary*, 2nd edn, Clarendon Press, 1989.
241. Croft-Cook, *Feasting with Panthers*, p. 51.
242. Weeks, *Inverts, Perverts and Mary-Anns*, p. 199. See also Hyde, *Other Love*, pp. 94–8.
243. *The Times*, 16 May 1871, p. 9.
244. Hyde, *Other Love*, p. 98.
245. Hyde, *Other Love*, p. 122.
246. Hyde, *Other Love*, p. 133.
247. Hyde, *Other Love*, p. 133.
248. Pine, *Oscar Wilde*, p. 23.
249. Pine, *Oscar Wilde*, p. 29.
250. Hyde, *Trials of Oscar Wilde*, p. 53.
251. Hyde, *Oscar Wilde*, p. 121.
252. Hyde, *Oscar Wilde*, pp. 117–18.
253. Wilde, *De Profundis*, pp. 39–40.
254. Wilde, *De Profundis*, pp. 117–18.
255. Roberts, *The Mad, Bad Line*, p. 160.
256. Roberts, *The Mad, Bad Line*, p. 183.
257. Ellman, *Oscar Wilde*, p. 402, errors in the original.
258. Letter of 1 April 1894. Ellman, *Oscar Wilde*, p. 394.
259. Ellman, *Oscar Wilde*, p. 412.
260. Wilde, *De Profundis*, p. 118.
261. According to Bosie in *The Autobiography of Lord Alfred Douglas*, p. 90, they saw this at least a week before the trial opened.
262. Wilde, *De Profundis*, p. 22.
263. Davenport-Hines, p. 137.
264. Davenport-Hines, pp. 137–8.
265. Pine, *Oscar Wilde*, pp. 106–7.
266. Goodman, *The Oscar Wilde File*, pp. 133–4.
267. Goodman, *The Oscar Wilde File*, p. 95.
268. Read, *England 1868–1914*, p. 276.
269. Pearson, *Life of Oscar Wilde*, pp. 318–19.
270. Holroyd, *Bernard Shaw*, Vol. I, p. 206.
271. Holroyd, *Bernard Shaw*, p. 296.
272. Bristow, *Vice and Vigilance*, p. 154.
273. Bristow, *Vice and Vigilance*, p. 161.
274. Bristow, *Vice and Vigilance*, p. 167.
275. Bristow, *Vice and Vigilance*, p. 168.
276. Bristow, *Vice and Vigilance*, p. 169.
277. Bristow, *Vice and Vigilance*, p. 170.
278. Bristow, *Vice and Vigilance*, p. 117.
279. Doig, *Westminster Babylon*, p. 29.
280. Pearsall, *The Worm in the Bud*, p. 19.

Bibliography

CONTEMPORARY SOURCES

Pall Mall Gazette, 1880–95, particularly 1885–6, British Library, Colindale
The Times, 1880–95, Keele and Birmingham Universities
Stead Papers, Churchill College, Cambridge
Josephine Butler Papers and related material, Fawcett Library, London Guildhall
  University
Dilke Papers, British Library, especially Additional MSS 43906, 43927
Lloyd's Weekly London News, 1885
Methodist Times, 1885–90
Parliamentary Debates (*Hansard*) Third Series
Royal Commission Reports, as noted in text
Select Committee Reports, as noted in text, especially Lords Committee of
  1881–2
The *Sentinel*, ed. Alfred Dyer, 1885–6, Josephine Butler Papers, Fawcett Library
Journal of the Vigilance Association for Personal Rights, 1881–6

SECONDARY SOURCES

Place of publication London, England, unless otherwise indicated.

Acton, William, *Prostitution: Considered in its Moral, Social and Sanitary Aspects,
  in London and other Large Cities: with Proposals for the Mitigation and
  Prevention of its Attendant Evils*, 1856, edited Peter Fryer, 1968 (Fitzroy edn),
  MacGibbon and Kee; 1870 edition, reprinted Frank Cass, 1972
Aronson, Theo, *Prince Eddy and the Homosexual Underworld*, John Murray, 1994
Aubyn, Giles St, *Edward VII*, Collins, 1979
Blyth, Henry, *Skittles, the Last Victorian Courtesan*, Rupert Hart-Davis, 1970
Bristow, Edward J., *Vice and Vigilance*, Gill and Macmillan, Dublin, 1977
Butler, Josephine Elizabeth, *Personal Reminiscences of a Great Crusade*, Horace
  Marshall, 1896
Collier, J., *The General Next to God, the Story of William Booth and the Salvation
  Army*, Collins, 1965
Cominos, Peter T., 'Late Victorian Sexual Respectability and the Social System',
  International Review of Social History, No. 8, 1963

Coote, W.A., *A Romance of Philanthropy*, National Vigilance Association, 1916

Croft-Cooke, Rupert, *Feasting with Panthers*, W.H. Allen, 1967

Davenport-Hines, Richard, *Sex, Death and Punishment*, Collins, 1990

Doig, Alan, *Westminster Babylon*, Allison and Busby, 1990

Douglas, Lord Alfred, *The Autobiography of Lord Alfred Douglas*, Martin Secker, 1929

Douglas, Francis A., 11th Marquis of Queensberry, with Percy Colson, *Oscar Wilde and the Black Douglas*, Hutchinson, 1949

Dyer, Alfred, *The European Slave Trade in English Girls, A Narrative of Facts*, Dyer Brothers, Amen Corner, Paternoster Row, 1880

Ellman, Richard, *Oscar Wilde*, Hamish Hamilton, 1987

Ensor, R.C.K., *England 1870–1914*, Oxford History of England, Oxford, Clarendon Press, 1936/1990

Ereira, Alan, *The People's England*, Routledge and Kegan Paul, 1981

Finnegan, Frances, *Poverty and Prostitution, a Study of Victorian Prostitution in York*, Cambridge University Press, Cambridge, 1979

Fryer, Peter, *Mrs Grundy: Studies in English Prudery*, Denis Dobson, 1963

Glaser, John F., 'English Nonconformity and the Decline of Liberalism', *American Historical Review* LXIII (1957–8)

Glaser, John F., 'Parnell's Fall and the Nonconformist Conscience'

Goodman, Jonathan, *The Oscar Wilde File*, Allison and Busby, 1989

Gordham, Deborah, 'The "Maiden Tribute of Modern Babylon",' in *Victorian Studies* 21 (1978)

Gwynn, S. and Tuckwell, G.M., *Life of Sir Charles Dilke*, 2 vols, 1917

Harrison, Brian, 'Josephine Butler', in J.F.C. Harrison, B. Taylor and I. Armstrong (eds), *Eminently Victorian*, 1974

Harrison, Brian, 'State Intervention and Moral Reform in Nineteenth Century England', in P. Hollis (ed.), *Pressure from Without in Early Victorian England*, Edward Arnold, 1974

Harrison, Henry, *Parnell Vindicated*, Constable, 1931

Hemyng, Bracebridge, 'Prostitution in London', in Henry Mayhew (ed.), *London Labour and the London Poor*, Vol IV, Stationer's Hall Court, London, December 1861, Reprinted Frank Cass, London, 1967

Hibbert, Christopher, *Edward VII*, Allen Lane, 1976

Holroyd, Michael, *Bernard Shaw Vol 1: The Search for Love*, Penguin, 1990

Horstman, Allen, *Victorian Divorce*, Croom Helm, 1985

Hudson, Derek, *Munby, Man of Two Worlds*, John Murray, 1972

Hyam, Ronald, *Empire and Sexuality*, Manchester University Press, 1990

Hyde, H. Montgomery, *The Other Love*, Heinemann, 1970

Hyde, H. Montgomery, *Oscar Wilde*, Eyre Methuen, 1976

Hyde, H. Montgomery, *The Trials of Oscar Wilde*, Penguin, 1962, Dover edn, New York, 1983

Jenkins, Roy, *Sir Charles Dilke*, Collins, 1958

Kee, Robert, *The Laurel and the Ivy*, Hamish Hamilton, 1993

Kent, John, 'Hugh Price Hughes and the Nonconformist Conscience', in G.V. Bennett and J.D. Walsh (eds), *Essays in Modern Church History*, 1966

Lee, Alan J., *The Origins of the Popular Press 1855–1914* (esp. Ch. 4, 'The Old Journalism and the New'), Croom Helm, 1976

Lees-Milne, James, *The Enigmatic Edwardian*, Sidgwick and Jackson, 1986

Logan, William, *The Great Social Evil*, Hodder and Stoughton, 1871

Lyons, F.S.L., *Charles Stewart Parnell*, Collins, 1977

Lyons, F.S.L., *The Fall of Parnell*, Routledge and Kegan Paul, 1966

McGlashan, W.J., *England on her Defence, a Reply to 'The Maiden Tribute of Modern Babylon'*, 1885

McHugh, Paul, *Prostitution and Victorian Social Reform*, Croom Helm, 1980

Marcus, Steven, *The Other Victorians*, Corgi/Bantam, 1969

Mews, Stuart, 'The General and the Bishops', in T.R. Gourvish and Alan O'Day (eds), *Later Victorian Britain, 1867–1900*, Macmillan, 1988

Midgley, Clare, *Women against Slavery*, Routledge, 1992

Millett, Kate, *Sexual Politics*, Virago, 1977

Moody, T.W. and Martin, F.X. (eds), *The Course of Irish History* (esp Chs 17–19), Dublin, Mercier Press, 1984

Mort, Frank, *Dangerous Sexualities*, Routledge and Kegan Paul, 1987

Neild, Kenneth, *Prostitution in the Victorian Age*, ed. K. Neild, Gregg International Publishers, 1973; Reprints of key contemporary articles

Norton, Rictor, *Mother Clap's Molly House: The Gay Sub-culture in England 1700–1830*, Gay Men's Press, 1992

O'Shea, Katherine, *Charles Stewart Parnell*, Cassell, 1914

Pearsall, Ronald, *The Worm in the Bud*, Weidenfeld and Nicolson, 1969

Pearson, Hesketh, *The Life of Oscar Wilde*, MacDonald and Jones, 1975

Pearson, Michael, *The Age of Consent*, David and Charles, 1972

Perkin, H.J., 'The Origins of the Popular Press', *History Today* (July 1957), 425

Petrie, Glen, *A Singular Iniquity, the Campaigns of Josephine Butler*, Macmillan, 1971

Pine, Richard, *Oscar Wilde*, Gill and Macmillan, Dublin, 1983

Playfair, Giles, *Six Studies in Hypocrisy*, Secker and Warburg, 1969

Read, Donald, *England 1868–1914*, Longman, 1979

Report from the Royal Commission on the Contagious Diseases Acts 1871, British Parliamentary Papers, Irish University Press, Shannon, Ireland, Health, Infectious Diseases, Vol. 5

Roberts, Brian, *The Mad, Bad Line*, Hamish Hamilton, 1981

Robertson Scott, J.W., *The Life and Death of a Newspaper*, Methuen, 1952

Scott, Benjamin, *A State Iniquity; Its Rise, Extension and Overthrow*, 1890/94, Kegan Paul, Trench, Trubner and Co, reprinted 1968, Augustus M. Kelley, New York, USA

Showalter, Elaine, *Sexual Anarchy: Gender and Culture at the Fin de Siècle*, Indiana, Bloomsbury, 1991

Smith, F.B., 'Labouchere's Amendment to the Criminal Law Amendment Act', *Historical Studies* 17 (1976)

Smith, F. Barry, 'Sexuality in Britain 1800–1900', in Martha Vincinus (ed.), *A Widening Sphere*, Bloomington and London, Indiana University Press, 1977

Stanley, Liz, *The Diaries of Hannah Cullwick, Victorian Maidservant*, ed. and introduced Liz Stanley, Virago, 1984

Stead, W.T., *The Armstrong Case: Mr Stead's Defence in Full*, printed and published W.T. Stead, 1885

Stead, W.T., *Speech of W.T. Stead at the Central Criminal Court, November 4th 1885*, Moral Reform Union, 1885

Stone, Lawrence, *The Family, Sex and Marriage in England 1500–1800*, Weidenfeld and Nicolson, 1977

Terrot, Charles, *The Maiden Tribute*, Frederick Muller, 1979

Thane, Pat, *Late Victorian Women in Later Victorian Britain 1867–1900*, ed. T.R. Gourvish and Alan O'Day, Macmillan, 1990

Thompson, Dorothy, *Queen Victoria: Gender and Power*, Virago, 1990

Thompson, F.M.L., *The Rise of Respectable Society*, Fontana, 1988

Tingsten, Herbert, *Victoria and the Victorians*, George Allen and Unwin, 1972

Trudgill, Eric, *Madonnas and Magdalens*, Heinemann, 1976

Walkowitz, Judith R., *City of Dreadful Delight*, Virago, 1992

Walkowitz, Judith R., 'The Making of an Outcast Group', in Martha Vincinus, (ed.), *A Widening Sphere*, Bloomington and London, Indiana University Press, 1977

Walkowitz, Judith R., *Prostitution and Victorian Society*, Cambridge, Cambridge University Press, 1980

'Walter', *My Secret Life*, ed. Gordon Grinley, Panther, 1972

Weeks, Jeffrey, 'Inverts, Perverts and Mary Anns' in M.B. Dubermann, Martha Vincinus, and George Chauncy (eds), *Hidden From History*, Penguin, 1991

Weeks, Jeffrey, *Sex, Politics and Society*, Longman, 1981 and 1991 editions

Weintraub, Sidney, *Disraeli*, Hamish Hamilton, 1993

Weintraub, Stanley, *Victoria*, Unwin Hyman, 1987

Whyte, Frederick, *Life of W.T. Stead*, vol. 1, Jonathan Cape, 1925

Wilde, Oscar, *De Profundis*, Methuen, 1949

Wilson, Angus, *The Naughty Nineties*, Eyre Methuen, 1976

Wood, Anthony, *Nineteenth Century Britain*, Longman, 1982

Woodward, L., *The Age of Reform*, 2nd edn, Oxford, Oxford University Press, 1962

Index